THE COOK'S ENCYCLOPEDIA OF
PASTA

THE COOK'S ENCYCLOPEDIA OF
PASTA

JENI WRIGHT

HH
HERMES
HOUSE

DEDICATION

I would like to dedicate this book to my very dear friend Elisa, who has inspired and delighted me with her wonderful Italian cooking, especially her home-made pasta.

This edition published by Hermes House in 2002

Published in the USA by Hermes House
Anness Publishing Inc. 27 West 20th Street,
New York NY 10011

Hermes House is an imprint of Anness Publishing Inc.

Publisher: Joanna Lorenz
Executive Editor: Linda Fraser
Copy Editor: Jenni Fleetwood
Indexer: Dawn Butcher
Production Controller: Don Campaniello
Designer: Patrick McLeavey
Photography: William Lingwood (recipes) and Janine Hosegood (techniques and cut-outs)
Food for Photography: Lucy McKelvie and Kate Jay (recipes) and Annabel Ford (techniques)

Also published as *The Pasta Bible*

Printed and bound in China

10 9 8 7 6 5 4 3 2 1

CONTENTS

Introduction

Pasta is one of the most popular foods in the world today. Available in an amazing range of shapes and flavors, it is incredibly versatile, and can be served in countless different ways. Students love it for the energy it gives them at low cost, chefs delight in introducing light and healthy sauces for modern palates, families favor casseroles that can be cooked in advance and that will stretch to serve extra guests. Simple or sophisticated, quick and easy to cook, it is the perfect choice for everyday and spur-of-the-moment meals.

Introduction

The origin of pasta

There is a great deal of controversy surrounding the origin of pasta. Who invented it? Was it the Chinese, the Italians or the Arabs? There is absolutely no doubt that Marco Polo brought noodles back to Italy from China in 1295, but most food historians agree that a kind of pasta was well-known in Italy long before this time. Wall paintings in an Etruscan tomb show utensils—a pastry board, rolling pin and wheel—that are remarkably similar to those used today for making pasta. There is also evidence that the Romans made an unleavened dough of flour and water, which they cut into pasta-like strips, fried and ate with a sauce. Apicius, the famous Roman gastronome of the 1st century A.D., described baked dishes in which a pasta-like dough was layered with other ingredients. A kind of Roman lasagne?

Wherever or whenever pasta was first "invented," it seems to have been the Sicilians who were the first to boil it in water. They learned irrigation and cultivation from the Arabs who conquered the island in the 9th century, and by the 12th century there is evidence they were eating a long thin type of pasta like spaghetti. Meanwhile, the Calabrians had mastered the art of twisting pasta strips to make tubes that resembled modern-day macaroni.

In a 13th-century Italian cookbook published just before Marco Polo's return from China, there are recipes for making different pasta shapes, including ravioli, vermicelli and tortelli. So one way or another, pasta did exist in Italy before Marco Polo, and the pasta museum in Rome has many writings, paintings and etchings to substantiate this.

By the time of the Renaissance, pasta featured frequently on Italian menus. The rich Florentines teamed it with costly sugar and spices, but the less well-off had to content themselves with eating pasta plain or with humble ingredients such as garlic, vegetables and cheese.

In those early days, pasta was simple, fresh and handmade, a far cry from the many different commercially produced dried shapes and flavors that we know today. The credit for inventing these must go to the Neapolitans.

The fertile soil in the region around Naples was found to be ideal for growing durum wheat, which makes the best flour for commercial pasta, and the unique combination of sun and wind in this part of southern Italy was just right for drying out the shapes. Once the Neapolitans discovered this, the pasta-making industry burgeoned around the city of Naples, and by the late 18th century the consumption of pasta in Italy had really taken off. Maccheroni, spaghetti and tagliatelle were among the first shapes to be produced commercially, made with flour and water only.

At this time pasta was generally regarded as food for the poor, and tended to be served with tomato sauces. Tomatoes loved the growing conditions in the south as much as the durum wheat, and once the Italians fell in love with the tomato there was no going back.

The egg-enriched pasta that northern Italians favored was not produced commercially at this time. Pasta all'uovo was

There is no doubt that Marco Polo brought back noodles to Italy from China in the late 13th century. However, an Italian cookbook, which was published just before his return, includes recipes for making pasta. His departure from Venice is depicted in this early 14th-century painting, Romance of Alexander.

Workers in the fields at Pitti Palace, Florence, in the late 19th century tending the hard durum wheat, which Italians call grano duro. This type of wheat produces the ideal pasta flour.

freshly made, often with a meat filling or sauce, and was served to the rich. It was not until the 20th century that improvements in industrial equipment made the manufacture of egg pasta a viable commercial proposition.

Pasta today

Wherever Italians went, they took their pasta with them. Those that emigrated to America and Great Britain adapted pasta shapes and sauces to suit local tastes and ingredients, a tradition that happily continues to this day.

Pasta is becoming more and more popular as a healthy, quick-cooking and versatile food, and Italian manufacturers have quickly responded to the demand, constantly developing new flavors and using the latest technology to create original shapes.

Commercially produced dried pasta has always been highly regarded in Italy. It is in no way inferior to fresh homemade pasta, but is simply a different form of this fabulous food. Italian cooks always keep a few packages of dried pasta in their pantries and use it on a daily basis—even in the north of Italy, where the tradition of always making fresh pasta at home endured for a lot longer than it did in the south of the country.

The right kind of wheat

The ideal variety of wheat for the flour used in commercial pasta making is durum (Triticum durum), which Italians call *grano duro*. This hard summer wheat produces a flour that is high in gluten. Dough made from durum wheat flour is pliable and easy to knead and shape. The majority of durum

wheat for the Italian pasta-making industry is grown in Italy or imported from North America. The flour from durum wheat, called *semola* in Italian, makes a high quality pasta that holds its shape well. Cooked properly until *al dente*; it should be just tender, with a pleasant nutty bite. When you are buying pasta in packages or boxes, always check that it is made from 100 percent durum wheat. The Italian phrase to look for is *pasta di semola di grano duro*. This type of pasta may be more expensive than one made with a mixture of durum wheat and soft wheat, but you will get a much better result. Inexpensive pasta made with soft wheat flour tends to stick together during cooking and its texture is often soft and flabby. Generally speaking, the Italian brands are the best. Ask the staff at your local market which brands they recommend, and spend as much as you can afford. There is a big difference in texture and taste between the higher priced Italian brands and the cheaper types of pasta, and you will quickly find that it pays to buy the best.

The northern preference for egg pasta

In southern Italy the majority of pasta is made with durum wheat and water only, and literally hundreds—if not thousands—of different shapes are manufactured. In northern Italy, the preference is for pasta with added egg, pasta all'uovo. The tradition for using this type of pasta began in Emilia, where filled and stuffed pasta shapes originated. Home cooks found that adding a little egg to the dough strengthened it and helped to keep the filling in during cooking. As Italian housewives began

Above: Healthy ingredients, such as olive oil, tomatoes, garlic and bell peppers, combine wonderfully well with pasta and are used over and over again by Italian cooks. This may be one of the reasons that the incidence of heart disease in Italy is one of the lowest in the world.

Below: The various sizes and shapes of holes in these commercial pasta dies allow for the production of a wide range of long and short pasta shapes.

Above right: In modern pasta factories sophisticated machines are used to weigh and pack the finished product.

to make less and less fresh pasta at home and started to buying it at stores, small factories started making dried egg pasta to meet the demand. Now it is fast becoming a huge industry, although there are fewer fancy shapes made with egg than there are with plain pasta. This is because egg pasta is more difficult to work with. It is not used for making long thin shapes like spaghetti because they would break too easily. Commercially manufactured pasta all'uovo may contain as many as 7 eggs to 2 1/4 pounds flour, so it has a richer taste than plain pasta and absorbs more water.

If you buy Italian egg pasta, the package should state that it is 100 percent durum wheat and egg *(semola di grano duro e uova)*. Pasta all'uovo complements the cream and butter sauces that are popular in the north. The tomato and olive oil sauces of the south have always been traditionally served with plain pasta, although pasta all'uovo is now catching on in the south, too.

The Nutritional Value of Pasta

Rich in protein, vitamins and minerals, pasta is a complex carbohydrate food. It provides as much energy as a pure protein like steak, but with little or no fat. Of the eight amino acids essential to make up a complete protein, pasta contains six, so it only needs a small amount of cheese, meat, fish, pulses or eggs—the traditional ingredients for serving with pasta— to make it complete. If you are using pasta all'uovo, you need even less additional protein.

The key to healthy eating lies in eating pasta as the Italians do, with only a small amount of extra ingredients. In Italy, it is traditional for pasta to be served as a first course, before the main course of fish or meat. Eaten with a small spoonful of sauce and a light sprinkling of grated cheese, nothing could be more well-balanced and nutritionally sound.

The incidence of heart disease in Italy is one of the lowest in the world, and doctors, nutritionists and scientists agree that the Italian diet plays a large and important role in this. In Italian cooking, healthy ingredients, such as extra virgin olive oil, fresh and canned tomatoes, garlic, onions, olives, red bell peppers and fresh parsley are used all the time, plus lots of fresh fish, vegetables and salad leaves, fruit, pulses and lemon juice. Most of these ingredients combine wonderfully well with pasta, and they are used over and over again in the recipes in this book.

Pasta is a completely natural food that contains no additives. Pasta with egg contains the most nutrients, while whole-wheat pasta has the highest percentage of vitamins and fiber. Always check the label when buying colored pasta, because some varieties include artificial coloring.

Pasta is inexpensive, quick and easy to cook, and incredibly versatile. It is the perfect convenience food: in the time it takes to boil the water and cook the pasta, most sauces are ready to serve. Pasta all'uovo is especially nutritious and good for children who don't like eggs in a more recognizable form. Another plus, which athletes appreciate, is that as a high-energy food, pasta is easy to digest and yet immensely satisfying.

It makes sense, therefore, to include pasta in our diets as often as possible, if not every day. Since everybody loves it, this should be very easy to do. People watching their weight may be surprised to know that a 3-ounce portion of cooked pasta yields only about 100 calories and can therefore be eaten as part of a calorie-controlled diet, as long as it is only lightly sauced.

Pasta as an everyday meal

In Italy, pasta is generally eaten as a first course (*primo piatto* or just *primo*) as part of the main meal of the day. This may be at lunchtime or in the evening, depending on family circumstances and whether the meal is served during the week or on the weekend. The meal usually begins with antipasto, which is followed by a *primo piatto* of either soup, pasta, rice or gnocchi. Pasta used to be served as a lunchtime first course when lunch was traditionally the main meal of the day, but now that more and more Italian women are working outside the home, these customs are changing and there are fewer hard-and-fast rules about lunch and dinner. After the *primo piatto*, the second course, *secondo piatto*, is served. This is either fish or meat followed by vegetables or salad, then cheese, fresh fruit and coffee. Desserts are normally reserved for special occasions.

When pasta is served as a first course, the usual amount is $2^1/2$–$3^1/2$ ounces uncooked weight per person. Sauce is added sparingly, tossed with the freshly drained hot pasta in the kitchen, and the mixture is then brought to the table in one large bowl. By the time the pasta

Colored pasta looks and tastes very good, but always check the label before buying, because some varieties include artificial coloring..

reaches the dining room it has mingled with the sauce and taken on some of its flavor. In some homes the bowl is passed around the table and everyone helps themselves, while in others one person does the serving. When you are serving pasta directly from the bowl, it looks most attractive if you retain a small ladleful of the sauce to put on top of the pasta after tossing, then sprinkle with cheese or herbs at the last moment.

If it suits your lifestyle best to serve pasta as a main course for lunch or supper, simply increase the weight of uncooked pasta to 4–6 ounces per person and make more sauce. For convenience, you may prefer to serve pasta in shallow soup plates or bowls or on dinner plates. Warm these beforehand and serve and eat the pasta as soon as possible so that it can be enjoyed at its best. If you accompany your main course with a fresh green salad and follow with some fresh fruit, you will have a tasty, nutritious and supremely satisfying meal. *Buon Appetito!*

Although traditionally served from one large bowl that is passed around the table, you may prefer to serve pasta in shallow individual soup plates or bowls.

Dried Pasta

The many hundreds of different types of dried pasta are divided into categories. Long, short and flat shapes are the most common, but there are also stuffed shapes, shapes suitable for stuffing and tiny shapes for use in soup. Among these, you will find some less well-known regional shapes and the more unusual and decorative designer shapes.

Only buy dried pasta that is made using 100 percent durum wheat. If you decant pasta shapes into storage jars, use up any remaining pasta before adding more from a new package. Older pasta may take longer to cook than that from a fresher package, and different brands of the same shape may not necessarily require the same cooking time.

LONG PASTA / PASTA LUNGA

Dried long pasta in the form of spaghetti is probably the best-known pasta of all time, and was certainly one of the first types to be exported from Italy. Spaghetti is still very widely used, but nowadays there are many other varieties of long pasta that look and taste just as good. There are no hard-and-fast rules when matching pasta to sauce, so experiment with alternative varieties to add interest to your cooking, always remembering that long pasta is best served with either a thin, rich sauce or one that is smooth and thick. If too thin and watery, the sauce will simply run off the long strands; if too chunky or heavy, the sauce will fall to the bottom of the bowl and you will be left with a bowl full of chunks and no pasta to eat it with. Rich sauces made with olive oil, butter, cream, eggs, finely grated cheese and chopped fresh herbs are good with long pasta. When ingredients such as vegetables, fish and meat are added to a smooth thick sauce, they should be very finely chopped.

Long pasta comes in different lengths, but 12 inches is about the average. In specialty food stores, you may see dried pasta that is much longer than this, but think twice before buying it because extra-long pasta can be tricky to cook and eat and often not worth the bother. The width of long pasta varies too; the strands can be flat, hollow, round or square, while other types have the pasta strands coiled up into nests.

Most long shapes are available in plain durum wheat only. The shapes made with egg (all'uovo) are very delicate, and are either packed in nests or compressed as waves. Fine long pasta, such as spaghetti, is far too delicate to be made with egg, but a short version from Emilia-Romagna, called capricciosa all'uovo, is available.

Bavette

Bucatini

Capelli d'angelo a nidi

Capelli d'angelo

Capellini

Bavette

This type of long pasta is known all over Italy, but is very common in the South. The noodles are narrow and flat, like tagliatelle, only slimmer. Indeed, some southern Italians use the name bavette to describe tagliatelle. Bavettine is a narrower version. Both types can be plain or all'uovo (with egg).

Capellini a nidi

Bucatini

This looks like spaghetti but is slightly chunkier. The strands are hollow (*buco* means hole), like hard, inflexible drinking straws. This type of pasta is best known in the Roman dish, *Bucatini all'Amatriciana*, which has a tomato, bacon and pepper sauce, and in Sicily it is traditionally served with a sauce of fresh sardines. Bucatoni is a fatter version, while perciatelli is bucatini by another name.

Capelli d'angelo

The name means angel's hair, which is an evocative description for this extremely fine pasta. It is used in broths and soups, and is popular with children. You may find it packed in nests, labeled capelli d'angelo a nidi. These nests are easy to handle and cook—one nest per person is the usual serving, so you can use as many nests as you need. Capellini and capel Venere are similar to capelli d'angelo.

Chitarra

Also known as spaghetti alla chitarra, this type of pasta is cut on a special wooden frame strung with wires like guitar strings (*chitarra* is Italian for guitar). It is therefore square-shaped rather than round, but can be used as an alternative to spaghetti.

Fusilli

Spaghetti spirals that look like long opened-out corkscrews. You may see these labeled fusilli lunghi or fusilli col buco, to distinguish them from the more widely known short fusilli and eliche. Fusilli is often used with tomato sauces.

Lasagnette

This flat pasta resembles tagliatelle, but the noodles are slightly wider. There are several types, most of which have frilly edges. Reginette is similar. You can use lasagnette in place of any ribbon pasta.

Linguine

In Italian, the name means little tongues and accurately describes a very thin spaghetti-like pasta that has flattened edges. You may also see linguinette and lingue di passera (sparrows' tongues), both of which are even narrower. Whole-wheat linguine is also available. All are good with the simple olive oil-based sauces and smooth tomato sauces of southern Italy.

Maccheroni

A very familiar form of pasta. We know a short version of it as macaroni, but in Italy the long thick tubes are widely used for all kinds of sauces—in some regions the word maccheroni is even used as a generic term for pasta and maccheroncini, is simply the name given to very thin, long pasta. Maccheroni comes in different lengths and thicknesses, with straight or angled ends, in plain, egg and whole-wheat varieties. There is even a square-shaped chitarra version, which comes from Abruzzi. There they call it maccheroni alla chitarra, but it also goes by the name of tonnarelli. Maccheroni is useful because it goes with so many different sauces.

Spaghetti alla chitarra

Fusilli lunghi

Lasagnette reginette

Lasagnette tripolini

Linguinette

Linguine

Maccheroncini

Maccheroni

Spaghetti

This familiar type of pasta takes its name from the word *spago*, which means string. Spaghetti means little strings; spaghettini is a thinner variety, and spaghettoni is thicker. Spaghetti originally came from Naples, but today it is made in other parts of Italy too, and the length and width vary from one region to another.

Numerous different brands, flavors and colors are available, including whole-wheat (integrali), spinach (spinaci) and chile (peperoncini) so the choice is yours, but avoid the inexpensive brands. Long Italian spaghetti tends to be very good; it is graded by number according to the thickness. Good-quality spaghetti made in Italy is still one of the best forms of pasta, despite the ever-increasing range of other shapes. It goes well with many different kinds of sauces.

Tagliatelle

The most common form of ribbon noodles, tagliatelle derives its name from the Italian verb *tagliare* meaning to cut. The noodles are usually about $1/3$–$1/2$ inch wide, but there are fine versions called tagliatellina, tagliarini and tagliolini, and an even finer type called tagliolini fini. Traditional tagliatelle comes from Bologna. It is made both with and without egg and with spinach (verdi), but new flavors and colors are constantly coming into the market.

All types of tagliatelle are sold coiled in nests, which conveniently unravel during cooking when given a good stir. Paglia e fieno, which literally means straw and hay, is a mixture consisting of half plain egg and half spinach egg pasta, packed together in separate bundles of each color. The noodles are usually quite thin, either tagliarini or tagliolini. Both tagliatelle and paglia e fieno are very popular because they go well with most sauces, although strictly speaking, tagliatelle should not be served with a fish sauce. Meat sauce is the classic, as in *Tagliatelle alla Bolognese*.

The Roman version of tagliatelle is called fettuccine. These long, flat noodles are virtually the same as tagliatelle, but slightly thinner.

Spaghetti

Spaghetti integrali

Spaghetti con spinaci

Spaghettoni

Spaghettini

Spaghettini con peperoncini

Tagliatelle / tagliatelle verdi

Vermicelli

Ziti

Mezza zita

Vermicelli

This sounds appealing, but the name means little worms, which is rather unfortunate. It describes a very fine form of spaghetti—the original Neapolitan name for spaghetti was vermicelli, and southern Italians still sometimes refer to spaghetti as vermicelli, which can be confusing. This type of pasta comes in plain and egg (all'uovo) varieties and is very versatile, going well with most light sauces, but especially the light, fresh tomato and seafood sauces for which Naples is famous. There is an even finer version called vermicellini, and a similar noodle called fidelini.

Ziti

This pasta takes its name from the word *zita*, meaning fiancée. In the old days it was traditional in southern Italy to serve ziti at wedding feasts and on other special occasions. Ziti is very long, thick and hollow—like maccheroni—and the custom is to break it into the length desired when you cook it. Because of their size, the tubes go well with robust and chunky sauces; they are also sometimes broken into short lengths and baked in a *timballo*, which is a cup-shaped mold. The pasta is used to line the mold, which is then filled with a savory mixture such as mushrooms, ham or chicken livers combined with a sauce and topped with cheese. Zitoni are fatter than ziti; mezza zita are thinner.

Tagliolini all'uovo

Paglia e fieno

Tagliarini all'uovo

SOME REGIONAL TYPES OF LONG DRIED PASTA

Fettuccine comes from Lazio, and these noodles are used in classic Roman pasta dishes, such as *Fettuccine all'Alfredo*. They are flat ribbons, like tagliatelle but narrower (about 1/4 inch wide), and always sold coiled into loose nests. The three most common types are plain durum wheat, with egg (all'uovo), and with spinach (verdi), and you can use them interchangeably with tagliatelle. Fettuccelle is similar, but is straight rather than coiled. Fettuccelle integrali is the whole-wheat variety.

Frappe is a type of pasta from Emilia-Romagna. The 1–11/2-inch wide noodles are flat, with wavy edges, about halfway in size between tagliatelle and lasagne. Made with egg and very delicate, the noodles are packed by a special machine that presses them into waves.

Pappardelle are broad ribbon noodles (3/4–1 inch wide), with wavy edges. They come from Tuscany, where they are still made fresh with egg every day, but dried versions are now becoming more widely available, many of them with only one wavy edge or straight edges. They are good with heavy meat and game sauces. Nastroni are similar straight-sided noodles that are sold coiled into nests.

Trenette are noodles from Liguria, where they are tradition-ally served with pesto sauce. The Genoese dish, *Trenette alla Genovese*, combines trenette with pesto, potatoes and beans. The noodles are about 1/8 inch wide, and are made with egg. They resemble bavette and linguine, which can be substituted for them if trenette proves difficult to find.

Fettuccine al nero

Pappardelle

Trenette

Fettuccelle

Frappe

Nastroni

SHORT PASTA / *PASTA CORTA*

There are literally hundreds of different short pasta shapes, and new ones are constantly arriving in stores. Some people prefer short pasta simply because it is easier to cook and eat than long pasta. It also goes well with many different sauces, and in most cases you can choose any shape you desire, regardless of whether your sauce is a smooth tomato-, cream- or olive oil-based type, or is chunky with large pieces of fish, meat or vegetables. Exceptions are regional dishes that are traditionally cooked with a specific shape, such as *Penne all'Arrabbiata* from Lazio.

Short pasta is divided into two main groups. Pasta secca is factory-made, using durum wheat flour and water. This is by far the largest group, and you will find that most packages of dried pasta list only these two ingredients on the label. Pasta all'uovo is made with the addition of eggs. It is naturally a brighter yellow than pasta secca and has more nutritional value. Popular in the north of Italy, especially in Emilia-Romagna, pasta all'uovo has different properties than plain pasta and goes especially well with the rich creamy and meaty sauces associated with that part of Italy. It has an advantage over plain durum wheat pasta in that it cooks slightly more quickly and is less likely to become overcooked and soggy. Although it is more expensive than plain pasta, egg pasta is becoming more popular and therefore more widely available, so look for it in an increasing number of shapes.

New flavors and colors in short pasta shapes are on the increase too. For many years, tomato (pomodoro) and spinach (verde) were all that was available, but today there seems to be no end to the number of different color and flavor combinations, ranging from garlic, chiles and herbs to beet, salmon, mushroom, squid ink and even chocolate. Often three colors (red, white and green) are packed together and labeled tricolore. Whole-wheat pasta, called pasta integrale is made from durum wheat and other cereals. It is higher in fiber than plain durum wheat pasta and takes longer to cook. It has a chewy texture and nutty flavor.

Benfatti

Benfatti

The word *benfatti* means well made and originally described the little scraps of pasta left over from making other shapes, such as tagliatelle. Traditionally these were used in soups so they would not be wasted, but they proved so popular that they are now made and marketed as a shape in their own right. Benfatti are available plain and with egg, and are good in salads as well as soups.

Chifferini rigatini

Chifferini

Also called chifferi, chifferoni and chifferotti, these are small curved tubes like short maccheroni that has been bent. Some versions are ridged (rigatini). The holes in the middle fill with sauce, making them an excellent shape for all types of pasta sauces and soups.

Conchigliette rigate

Conchiglie

As the name suggests, these shapes resemble small conch shells. Sometimes they are ridged, in which case they are called conchiglie rigate. They are one of the most useful small shapes because they are concave and trap virtually any sauce. For this reason they are extremely popular and are widely available in many different colors

Conchiglie rigate

Conchiglioni rigati

and flavors. Sizes vary too, from tiny conchigliette for soups to conchiglione, which are jumbo shells for stuffing.

Eliche

The name comes from the Italian word for screws or propellers, which is exactly what these shapes look like. They are often mislabeled as fusilli, which are similar, but when you see the two side by side there is a marked difference. Eliche are short lengths of pasta, each twisted into a spiral, like the thread of a screw. They are available in different thicknesses, colors and flavors, including whole-wheat and tricolore, and are good with most sauces, but especially those that are tomato-based. You may only be able to buy them labeled as fusilli—the two are interchangeable and their names often depend on which part of Italy they come from.

Eliche all'uovo

Eliche tricolori

Farfalle

Fusilli

Maccheroni

Farfalle verde

Fusilli con spinaci

Maccheroncelli

Farfalle salmonseppia

Fusilli all'uovo

Farfalle tricolore

Farfalle

The word means butterflies, but these shapes are sometimes also described as bow-ties—the Italian word for bow-tie is *cravatta a farfalla*. They are very pretty, with crinkled edges, and are sometimes ridged. Due to their popularity, they are available in a wide variety of colors and flavors, plain, with egg and tricolore (plain, tomato and spinach flavors, which are sold together in mixed packages). Farfalle can be served with any sauce, but they are particularly good with cream and tomato sauces. Children love them. In Modena, farfalle are known as strichetti.

Fusilli

These spirals of thin pasta look like tight coils or springs and are formed by winding fresh dough around a thin rod. The spiral opens out, rather than remaining solid as it does in the case of eliche, for which fusilli

are often mistaken. Check when buying, because most packages of fusilli are in fact eliche. Genuine fusilli is likely to be plain, neither made with egg nor colored. The shapes go well with thin sauces.

Lumache rigate

Lumachoni rigati

Gomiti rigati

Tubetti

Lumache

Snail shells were the inspiration for this attractively shaped pasta. Unlike conchiglie, they are not shaped like conch shells, but resemble a larger version of pipe, because they are fashioned out of hollow pasta. Lumache are excellent for trapping sauces. The most common type available is lumache rigate (ridged), and there is also a large version called lumaconi. Gomiti is a similar conch shell shape.

Maccheroni

When cooks in the south of Italy speak of maccheroni, they usually mean long pasta, but in the north of the country they prefer it short. It is the short type that is generally exported as macaroni (sometimes labeled "elbow macaroni," although some brands are straighter than others). This used to be the most common short pasta shape outside Italy, but other more interesting shapes now rival it in popularity. Being hollow, it is a good shape for most sauces and baked dishes, so will always remain popular. Both plain and egg maccheroni are available, and there are also many different sizes, including a thin, quick-cooking variety. Tubetti is the name given to a miniature version that is often used in soups.

Penne lisce

Penne rigate

Penne rigate con spinaci

Penne mezzanine

Mezze penne tricolori

Pennoni

Penne

Like maccheroni, penne are hollow tubes, but their ends are cut diagonally so they are pointed like quills (penne means feather or quill pen). In the popularity stakes, they seem to have taken over from maccheroni, possibly because of their more interesting shape. They go well with virtually every sauce and are particularly good with chunky sauces, as their sturdiness means they hold the weight well. Penne lisce are smooth; penne rigate are ridged. Other less common varieties include the small and thin pennette and even thinner pennini and penne mezzanine, the short and stubby mezze penne or "half penne," and the large pennoni. Penne made with egg and flavored penne are very common.

Pipe rigate

Pipe

These shapes look like a cross between conchiglie and lumache. They are curved and hollow (the name means pipes) and more often than not ridged (pipe rigate). As short pasta shapes go, they are quite small. They are excellent for catching sauce and make an interesting change from other more common hollow varieties. Plain and whole-wheat types are available, and there is also a smaller version called pipette.

Rigatoni

Mezzi rigatoni

Elicoidali

Elicoidali con basilico

Rigatoni

From the maccheroni family, these are ridged, hollow, chunky-looking shapes. They are very popular because they are sturdy enough to hold chunky sauces, and they come in many flavors. There is a short version called mezzi rigatoni and a straight, stubby version called millerighe. The texture of rigatoni always seems slightly chewier than that of other short pasta. Similar in shape but slightly narrower are elicoidali, which have curved ridges (their name means helixes). Elicoidali can be plain or flavored with ingredients such as basil.

Rotelle

Rotelle tricolore

Rotelle

These are cartwheel shapes. There is a ridged variety, rotelle rigate, and sometimes this shape goes by other names, such as ruote, ruote di carro and trulli. Although not a classic Italian shape, the spokes of the wheels are very good for holding chunky sauces. Children like them, and most supermarkets sell them in different colors and flavors. The plain Italian brands taste very good.

SOME REGIONAL TYPES OF SHORT DRIED PASTA

Garganelli come from Emilia-Romagna. They are tubular egg pasta shapes that resemble penne, but look more like scrolls than quills because you can clearly see how they have been rolled. This is done on a special tool, called *il pettine*, that looks like a large comb.

Gnocchi sardi are from Sardinia. They are named after the gnocchi potato dumplings, but are smaller, like little razor shells. Gnocchetti sardi are smaller still, and are mostly used in soups. Malloreddus is another Sardinian name for gnocchi. These shapes are often flavored with saffron and served with traditional meat and vegetable sauces. They are quite chewy in texture.

Orecchiette, or little ears, are from Puglia in the south-east of Italy. Always made with durum wheat, they have a chewy texture and are served with the traditional sauces of the region, especially those made with broccoli.

Pizzoccheri are buckwheat noodles from Valtellina in Lombardy, not far from the border with Switzerland. They are thin and flat and usually sold in nests (a nidi) like fettuccine, but they are about half the length. Pizzoccheri are also sometimes cut to make short noodles. Their flavor is nutty, and they go well with the robust flavors of northern Italian cuisine, most famously with cabbage, potatoes and cheese in the baked dish of the same name.

Strozzapreti, which literally translated means priest stranglers, come from Modena. They are said to derive their name from the story of a priest who liked them so much he ate too many—and nearly choked to death. In fact, strozzapreti consist of two pieces of pasta twisted or "strangled" together. Other similar twisted shapes are caserecce, fileia and gemelli. The Genoese trofie, although not twisted, are similar, and can be substituted for strozzapreti.

Trofie are from the Ligurian port of Genoa, where it is traditional to serve them with pesto sauce. They are rolls of solid pasta with pointed ends, quite small and dainty. At one time you could only get homemade trofie, but now they are available dried at Italian specialty stores, in which case the shapes are sometimes open along one side rather than solid. They are well worth buying if you want to make an authentic *Genoese Trofie al Pesto*.

Above from the top: Garganelli all'uovo, garganelli paglia e fieno, girondole di Puglia, gnocchi sardi integrali and gnocchetti sardi

Gnocchetti sardi

Pizzocheri a nidi

Strozzapreti

Orecchiette

Short-cut pizzocheri

Trofie

FLAT PASTA

Although there are many kinds of long flat ribbon pasta, such as fettuccine and tagliatelle, there is really only one broad, flat pasta used for baking in the oven (al forno), and that is lasagne. Thin sheets of lasagne are designed to be baked between layers of sauce in the oven, or cooked in boiling water until *al dente*, rolled around a filling to make cannelloni, then baked. All types of lasagne are designed to be used in this way, and are never served with a separate sauce.

Plain lasagne

Made from durum wheat and water, this type of lasagne comes flat-packed in boxes. There are three different colors— yellow (plain), green (verdi), which is made with spinach, and brown or wholewheat (integrali). The shape varies according to the manufacturer, from narrow or broad rectangles to squares. Most sheets are completely flat, but some are wavy all over. Others have crimped or curly edges, which help to trap the sauce and look attractive too. Get to know the different brands and their sizes and choose the ones that fit your baking dish, to avoid having to cut them to fit. This makes light work of assembling the layers before baking. Check the cooking instructions on the box because regular plain lasagne needs to be pre-cooked before being layered or rolled. The usual method is to plunge about four sheets at a time into a large pan of salted boiling water, boil for about 8 minutes until *al dente*, then carefully remove each sheet with a large slotted spoon and/or tongs and lay it flat on a damp cloth to drain. The sheets need to be drained in a single layer or they will stick to each other. This method is fairly time-consuming and messy, but once it has been completed and the lasagne has been assembled, the cooking time is usually only about 30 minutes.

Lasagnette are long, narrow strips of flat pasta, which are crimped on one or two sides. They are used in the same way as lasagne, layered with sauces, then topped with grated cheese and baked. Festonelle are small squares of lasagnette, which are also used in baked dishes.

Lasagne verdi

Lasagnette

Lasagnette

Festonelle

Pantacce

Lasagne

Lasagne

Lasagne verdi

Lasagne verdi all'uovo

Pantacce are tiny diagonal pieces cut from lasagnette. They are similar to the hand-cut quadrucci and can be used in baked dishes, but are more often added to soups.

Lasagne all'uovo

This type of lasagne is made with durum wheat and water like plain lasagne, but with the addition of egg. This makes it a brighter yellow than plain lasagne, and richer in flavor and nutrients. It is available as plain

egg (lasagne all'uovo) and egg and spinach (lasagne verdi all'uovo). Like the plain lasagne, it comes in different shapes and sizes with a variety of different edgings.

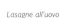

Lasagne

Lasagne all'uovo

Easy-cook Lasagne

Although a relatively recent innovation, easy-cook lasagne is fast becoming the number one favorite. Sometimes labeled "no pre-cooking required," it does not need to be boiled first, but is layered in the baking dish straight from the package, so

saving lots of time and mess. As with the plain and egg lasagne, it comes in all sorts of different shapes, sizes and colors, with straight or fancy edges. It is easiest to use if it is the right shape to fit neatly into your baking dish, although it can be broken to

fit. Baking time is slightly longer than with the pre-boiled varieties, so allow at least 40 minutes. Make sure that the sauce you use is runnier than usual because this type of lasagne absorbs liquid during baking and needs extra sauce to stay moist.

Tortellini all'uovo

Tortellini verdi

Ravioli all'uovo

Agnolotti all'uovo

DRIED STUFFED PASTA

The most common dried stuffed pasta shapes are tortellini (little pies), a specialty of Bologna said to be modeled on the shape of Venus's navel. They are made from rounds or circles, of pasta, so they look like little plump rings, another name for them is anolini. Some Italian specialty stores also sell dried cappelletti (little hats), which resemble tortellini but are made from squares of pasta and have little peaks. Cappelletti are more likely to be sold fresh than dried. The same goes for ravioli and agnolotti, although you will find them frozen at most supermarkets. Tortellini are popular dried because they are tradition-ally used *in brodo*—simmered in a clear beef or chicken stock until they swell and plump up to make a satisfying soup. Most

Italian cooks keep a package or two of tortellini in the pantry for just this purpose, and *Tortellini in Brodo* is often served for an evening meal when the main meal of the day has been at lunchtime. You can also be sure that *Tortellini in Brodo* will be served as a pick-me-up if ever a member of the family is unwell. They are also traditionally served on New Year's Eve in Bologna, perhaps as an antidote to the excesses of Christmas.

Dried tortellini are generally available with a choice of fillings—with meat (*alla carne*) or cheese (*ai formaggi*). The pasta is made with egg and may be plain and yellow in color, green if flavored with spinach, or red if flavored with tomato. All types of tortellini need to be cooked for at least 15 minutes to allow time for the pasta to swell and the ingredients in the filling to plump up and develop their flavor. Meat fillings are a mixture of pork sausage and beef with bread crumbs, Parmesan cheese and spices. Cheese fillings usually consist of a minimum of 35 percent cheese mixed with bread crumbs and spices.

Dried tortellini are a useful pantry item as they will keep for up to 12 months (but always check the use-by date on the package). For a soup, only a handful or two of the filled shapes are needed and the package can be resealed. Tortellini are also good boiled, then drained and tossed in melted butter and herbs or a cream, tomato or meat sauce, and served with grated Parmesan. Children like their shape, and they provide a good way of persuad-ing them to eat meat and cheese. A 9-ounce package will serve four people.

DRIED PASTA FOR STUFFING

Large pasta shapes are made commercially for stuffing and baking in the oven. Fillings vary, from meat and poultry to spinach, mushrooms and cheese, and the pasta can be baked in either a béchamel or a tomato sauce. Keep the filling moist and the sauce runny to ensure that the finished dish will not be dry. Dried shapes make an interest-ing change from lasagne, especially for children's meals, and they are attractive as a first course for a dinner party. They do not need to be boiled before being stuffed.

Cannelloni

Cannelloni

These large pasta tubes (their name means large reeds) are about 4 inches long. Plain, spinach and whole-wheat versions are available. In Italy, cannelloni is traditionally made from fresh sheets of lasagne rolled around a filling, but the ready-made dried tubes are convenient and less time-consuming to use. They are easy to stuff, using either a teaspoon or a piping bag.

Conchiglie

Conchiglie

Sometimes also called conchiglioni, these jumbo conch shells are available in plain, spinach and tomato flavors, both smooth and ridged. There are often two sizes—medium and large—both of which are suitable for stuffing, although you will probably find the larger ones less difficult.

Lumaconi

Lumaconi

These are like conchiglie, but are elbow-shaped—like large snail shells—with an opening at either end. The ones most commonly available are plain and ridged, but you may find different colors in specialty stores. You may also come across similar shapes called chioccioloni, gorzet-toni, manicotti and tuffolini.

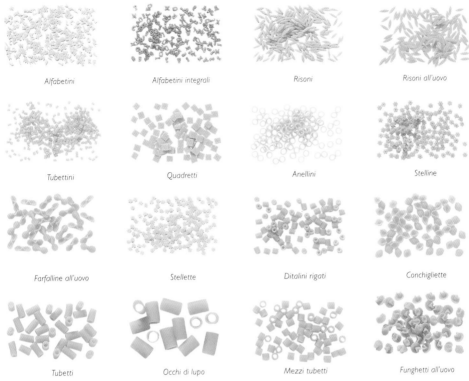

Alfabetini	*Alfabetini integrali*	*Risoni*	*Risoni all'uovo*
Tubettini	*Quadretti*	*Anellini*	*Stelline*
Farfalline all'uovo	*Stellette*	*Ditalini rigati*	*Conchigliette*
Tubetti	*Occhi di lupo*	*Mezzi tubetti*	*Funghetti all'uovo*

DRIED PASTA FOR SOUP / *PASTINA*

Teeny-weeny pasta shapes are called pastina in Italian, and there are literally hundreds of different ones to choose from. They are mostly made from plain durum wheat, although you may find them with egg and even flavored with carrot or spinach. In Italy, they are always served in broths and clear soups, and are regarded almost as nursery food because they are so often served for children's meals (many Italian babies are weaned on them) or as a pick-me-up for adults who are not feeling well. If you stay in an Italian hospital, you are likely to be served *Pastina in Brodo*.

Shapes of pastina vary enormously, and seem to get more and more fanciful as the market demands.

The smallest and most plain pasta per minestre (pasta for soups) are like tiny grains. Some look like rice and are in fact called risi or risoni, while others are more like barley and are called orzi. Fregola, from Sardinia, look like couscous, and have a

similar nutty texture and flavor. Semi di melone are like melon seeds, as their name suggests, while acini de pepe or peperini are named after peppercorns, which they resemble in shape and size if not in color. Coralline, grattini and occhi are three more very popular tiny shapes.

The next size up are the ones that are most popular with children. These include alfabeti and alfabetini (alphabet shapes), stelline and stellette (stars), rotellini (tiny wagon wheels) and anellini, which can be tiny rings, sometimes with ridges that make them look very pretty, or larger hoops. Ditali are similar to anellini but slightly thicker, while tubettini are thicker still.

Another category of pasta per minestre consists of slightly larger shapes, more like miniature versions of familiar types of short pasta. Their names end in "ine," "ette" or "etti," denoting that they are the diminutive forms. These include conchigliette (little shells), farfalline and farfallette (little bows), funghetti (little mushrooms), lumachine

Peperini

(little snails), quadretti and quadrettini (little squares), orecchiettini (little ears), renette (like baby penne) and tubetti (little tubes). The size of these varies: the smaller ones are for use in clear broths, while the larger ones are more often used in thicker soups, such as minestrone.

Designer Pasta

Relative newcomers to the market are the pasta shapes that bear little or no resemblance to the traditional or regional Italian varieties. Many of these are made outside Italy in any case, while the ones made in Italy are often for export only. It seems that the majority of Italians are happy enough with the pasta they know and love.

Supermarkets and food halls, gourmet stores and specialty stores are the best places to find these new shapes. Quality varies enormously, and some of them are nothing more than a gimmick, with very disappointing textures and flavors. Others are more successful, especially the ones made by long-established Italian firms. They are a nice change from the more common shapes and are often an interesting conversation piece, especially when you are entertaining. As a general rule, flavored pasta is best served with very simple sauces based on olive oil or butter, otherwise the flavors of the pasta and sauce tend to cancel each other out.

LONG SHAPES AND NOODLES

Spaghetti and tagliatelle are often flavored and colored. These shapes are either dramatically long or coiled in nests (a nidi), and you can even buy a type of pasta called spagliatelle, which is like a cross between the two. You can choose from a single flavor in one package, or up to five different flavors combined, and they can be either plain durum wheat pasta or made with the addition of egg and labeled "all'uovo". Spinach, tomato, mushroom, beet, saffron and smoked salmon are all popular flavors, but there are also other stronger flavors, such as chile and garlic (singly and together) and black squid ink (nero di seppia). One of the most fanciful

Tagliatelle flavored with red and green chiles

Egg and smoked salmon-flavored tagliatelle

Three-color tagliatelle

Porcini-flavored tagliatelle

Tagliatelle flavored with squid ink and bottarga (mullet roe)

Porcini-flavored bavette

Multicolored arlecchino

Garlic- and chile-flavored spaghetti

Porcini-flavored tagliatelle

Poppy seed tagliatelle

Five-color spagliatelle

Basil-flavored strangozzi

combinations comes from Venice. Called arlecchino (harlequin), it is a mixture of black (squid ink), green (spinach and herbs), red (tomato and beet) and blue (blueberry and blue Curaçao liqueur). More common and perhaps most successful is tagliatelle speckled with herbs or seeds or, if it comes from Tuscany, flavored with wild mushrooms (porcini). A broad variety of tagliatelle called bavette from Puglia is also flavored with porcini. Strangozzi is an unusual thin noodle from Umbria. It comes plain and flavored with spinach, basil, spinach and basil, or tomato. It is sometimes sold twisted into a long, thick braid, which looks pretty in the package but is best broken into short lengths to cook.

SHORT SHAPES

The most inventive and unusual designer shapes fall into this category. Short pasta is the easiest pasta to eat and so it's the most popular. Manufacturers, ever on the lookout to make and sell more, quickly realised that new short shapes had the most appeal and so developed this sector of the market more than any other. Ever since the 19th century competition in the pasta industry has thrived on the "design" of different short shapes, with some more successful at holding sauces than others. Among these are the frilly ballerine, fiorelli, gigli del gargano, rocchetti and spaccatella, all of which trap sauces quite well but somehow create a strange sensation in the mouth. Shapes such as banane, creste

di gallo, radiatori and riccioli, are perhaps too gimmicky for their own good; so too are the mixed bags of highly colored pasta shapes, such as the seven-color orecchiette (little ears) and five-color chioccioloni (snails), which include chocolate-flavored pasta along with the more run-of-the-mill plain, tomato, squid ink and wild mushroom (porcini) varieties. These colored designer pasta shapes are often labeled *lavorazione artigianale* or *prodotto artigianale*, to indicate that they are made by artisans or local craftsmen, but they are too often disappointing, and they rarely match up to the more traditional shapes that have been tried and tested over very many years.

Five-color chioccioloni are made from plain pasta and pasta flavored with squid ink, chocolate, tomato and porcini

Spinach, plain and tomato conchiglie (hand-crafted shells designed for stuffing)

Spaccatella

Gigli del gargano

Seven-color orecchiette are made from plain pasta and pasta flavored with spinach, tomato, saffron, squid ink, beet and porcini

Rocchetti rigati

Fiorelli tricolori

Three-color pennoti rigati

Three-color cappelletti

Coralli rigati

Fresh Pasta

In Italy, there has long been a tradition for buying fresh pasta, and now the custom has caught on in other countries too. Italians buy from their local *pastificio* or baker, where the beautiful window displays are such a tempting feast for the eye, while we have to content ourselves with supermarkets. Yet here too, creative talent is running wild when it comes to making fresh pasta, and the choices of different shapes, flavors and fillings are continually increasing—by popular demand. It seems that everybody loves fresh pasta, and we simply can't get enough of it. Quality is excellent, especially with the loose kinds sold in some good markets. Pre-packaged brands, although labeled fresh, are obviously not as "just-made" and silky-textured as the pasta made on a daily basis, but they are quite good nevertheless. Flavors vary, but the most common are spinach, tomato, chestnut, mushroom, beet juice, saffron, herbs, garlic, chiles and squid ink.

Buy freshly made pasta on the day you need it, or you defeat the purpose of buying it; otherwise keep it in its wrapping and use within 1–2 days of purchase (or according to the storage time given on the package). If you buy fresh pasta loose, ask the storekeeper for advice on storage. Fresh pasta is made with egg, which shortens its storage time, but on the plus side this increases its nutritional value and flavor, and gives the plain varieties a lovely sunshine-yellow color.

Fresh pasta takes much less time to cook than dried pasta, but the cooking technique is generally the same for each type. Most plain shapes will be *al dente* in 2–4 minutes, while stuffed shapes take 5–7 minutes, but always ask for advice in the store where it is made (or check the label).

The same rules apply for matching sauces to shapes as with dried pasta—long shapes are best with smooth sauces, while chunky sauces go better with short shapes.

LONG AND FLAT SHAPES

These were the first forms of fresh pasta to be available commercially, and were generally made in the local Italian markets by the proprietor or his wife. The choice used to be between plain egg tagliatelle and fettuccine, possibly flavored with spinach, but now there are many more exciting varieties. Pre-packaged long fresh pasta comes in standard shapes and sizes, but Italian markets sometimes have weekend specials when they offer different flavors and colors according to the seasonal availability of ingredients. This is often the case when a market supplies a local restaurant with fresh pasta. If a special order is made for a restaurant, the market may make extra to sell to individual customers. These occasional treats are well worth looking for, as are regional specialties. If the owners of your local Italian market are from Lazio you may find fresh homemade fettuccine on sale. Ligurians are more likely to make trenette, whereas pappardelle indicates that the owners of the shop probably have family ties with Tuscany or Bologna.

Fettuccine

These long, flat ribbon noodles are the narrow Roman version of tagliatelle, and are traditionally made about ¼ inch wide.

They are readily available, made with egg and flavored with spinach. You may also see similar noodles called fettuccelle. The two are interchangeable, and are at their best served very simply with butter and cream.

Fettuccine all'uovo

Fettuccine al nero

Chile-flavored fettuccine

Fettuccine verde

Spaghetti all'uovo

Spinach-flavored lasagne

Tomato-flavored lasagne

Lasagne all'uovo

Egg and spinach-flavored
capelli d'angelo

Egg and spinach-
flavored linguine

Pappardelle

Spaghetti

This pasta is widely available, in various widths. A narrow version, spaghettini, is popular, and can be found at some markets. Serve fresh spaghetti or spaghettini Neapolitan style with sauces based on olive oil and tomatoes. Both spaghetti and spaghettini are also good with fish and shellfish, as long as the pieces are cut small. Capelli d'angelo, plain or flavored with spinach, is also available.

Lasagne

Sheets of lasagne can be found plain, with egg, and flavored with spinach or tomato. Depending on the manufacturer,

they may be rectangles, squares or strips with plain or frilly edges. Lasagne al forno (baked lasagne) made with fresh sheets of pasta tastes much better than that made with dried pasta, so the fresh sheets are well worth buying.

Linguine

These look like strands of flattened spaghetti and are very narrow and thin. They are made with egg (all'uovo), and go well with a simple dressing of olive oil and flavorings, such as finely chopped garlic, chiles or freshly ground black pepper. Linguine is also good with fish and shellfish sauces.

Pappardelle

Flat egg noodles, these vary in width from 3/4–1 inch wide. Traditional pappardelle have wavy edges, but you may see them with plain edges—the main thing is that they are wider than any of the other ribbon noodles. They originated in Tuscany, but are also popular in the city of Bologna in Emilia-Romagna. In both of these regions, pasta is often served with a rich meat or game sauce, and pappardelle are the perfect choice because the noodles are wide and strong enough to support the chunkiest mixtures. Pappardelle are available plain and flavored, sometimes with sun-dried tomatoes or porcini.

Squid ink tagliolini

Tagliolini all'uovo

Salmon-flavored tagliolini

Spinach-flavored tagliolini

Tagliatelle all'uovo

Spinach-flavored tagliatelle

Tagliatelle

This is probably the best-known form of fresh pasta. The noodles are long and straight, about $^1/2$ inch wide. They are available everywhere, in a wide variety of flavors and colors. After plain egg tagliatelle, spinach is the most popular, but it is often flecked and flavored with fresh herbs, garlic, porcini, sun-dried tomatoes, pepper, chiles and other spices, or beautifully colored with saffron or tomato. When made with squid ink, it is black and dramatic. Tagliatelle comes from Bologna, where it is always served with Bolognese sauce, but it goes well with any meat sauce. Tagliarini and tagliolini are very thin versions of tagliatelle, about $^1/8$ inch wide, sold either as plain egg (all'uovo) or as paglia e fieno—half white and half green. Mixed packages are versatile and attractive because you can cook the different colors together or keep them separate, depending on the visual effect required. They go well with tomato and cream sauces.

SHORT SHAPES

Supermarkets and other large stores sell fresh short shapes, but the range is limited. Italian markets sometimes sell a few simple homemade shapes but because many short shapes need special machines for cutting and shaping there is seldom a wide range at small stores, and making them by hand would be too time-consuming to be commercially viable. Short shapes tend to stick together, so in supermarkets they are kept in plastic containers in the refrigerated section; these packages are useful in that they can be stored in the freezer. In some small shops excess moisture is removed by briefly fan-drying the shapes right after they are made. These are then described as semi-dried and must be sold within 24–48 hours. Shapes vary widely, depending on whether they come from large manufacturers or individual stores. Conchiglie, fusilli and penne are easy to find, while other shapes, such as garganelli and ballerine, are less widely available.

Conchiglie

These shell shapes come in different sizes and colors, and conchiglie tricolore (red, white and green) are popular. They are one of the best shapes for trapping chunky sauces. If they are ridged, so much the better. Conchiglie are also good in salads because they hold dressings well.

Fusilli

Resembling the threads of screws, these should correctly be called eliche, but they are almost always labeled fusilli. Plain, spinach and tomato flavors, either sold separately or combined, are easy to obtain. Squid ink fusilli are made in some stores. The versatile shape of this type of pasta means that it goes well with most sauces and is also good in salads.

Garganelli

Sold at some specialty markets, these are made from a very special type of egg pasta from Emilia-Romagna and look like ridged scrolls. Garganelli need to be made

Ballerine

Penne rigate

Eliche all'uovo

Conchiglie

Semi-dried garganelli

with a special tool, called *il pettine* in Italian. Squares of fresh dough are rolled around a rod and against the *pettine*, which has teeth like a comb. The teeth produce the characteristic fine ridges on the outside of the pasta. Plain and spinach flavors are available, either sold separately or combined. In Emilia-Romagna, garganelli are traditionally served with a rich meat sauce, but you can use them in any recipe that calls for short maccheroni or penne. They are especially good with rich, creamy sauces.

Penne

Sometimes called quills, these come in a variety of sizes and colors, both smooth and ribbed, just like their dried counter-part. In Rome, fresh penne is served with the chile-hot arrabbiata sauce, but it goes well with just about any sauce.

STUFFED SHAPES

Until recent years, the only stuffed fresh pasta shapes available were the classic ones traditionally associated with specific regions of Italy. Ravioli was the best known shape, followed by tortellini. These regional specialties are still popular, but nowadays the traditional shapes and fillings are often varied, whether they are being made by a large-scale manufacturer or a single cook working at a local market. Individual interpretations on the basic shapes, a wide variety of fresh seasonal ingredients for the fillings, plus eye-catching color combinations for both the pasta and the fillings make variations on the theme seemingly endless. New ideas are being developed all of the time, some more successful than others, so experiment with different kinds of stuffed shapes to find the ones you like the best. Listed here are the most popular and widely available shapes, following the regional tradition.

Agnolotti

These filled pasta shapes come from northern Italy and are a specialty of Piedmont in particular. Traditionally they were shaped like plump little half moons and stuffed with meat, but this is no longer the case: nowadays you will see round and square shapes with vegetable fillings labeled as agnolotti. Square agnolotti with a pleat in the center are called *dal plin* (with a pleat). One characteristic that all agnolotti should share is a crinkled edge, made by cutting the dough around the filling with a fluted pasta wheel.

Cappelletti

These take their name from the Italian word for "little hats." In Emilia-Romagna, small squares of dough are filled and folded to make triangular shapes, then two of the ends are wrapped around and the

Semi-dried agnolotti all'uovo

Semi-dried cappelletti all'uovo

Cappelletti all'uovo stuffed with mushroom filling

Semi-dried tomato-flavored cappelletti stuffed with sun-dried tomato filling

bottom edge turned up to make a party hat shape with a brim. In some central regions of Italy, however, cappelletti are made with either plain or fluted rounds of dough instead of squares. The dough for cappelletti can be plain or egg (all'uovo), or flavored with tomato or spinach. Cappelletti are traditionally filled with ground meat and cheese and are eaten in northern and central regions of Italy at Christmas and New Year, especially in clear broth – *Cappelletti in brodo*. You can use them in this way or serve them as a pasta course with a little melted butter and freshly grated Parmesan cheese or, alternatively, toss the cappelletti in a tomato or cream sauce.

*Semi-dried raviolini (mini ravioli)
all'uovo with a simple ground meat filling*

*Oval ravioli, which are sometimes called
rotondi, stuffed with artichoke filling*

Ravioli all'uovo with ground chicken filling

Large rectangular ravioli stuffed with Roquefort cheese

Handmade plain and spinach-flavored ravioli

*Plain ravioli stuffed with asparagus filling (left), squid ink-flavored
ravioli stuffed with an herb filling and saffron-flavored ravioli
stuffed with smoked salmon and mascarpone cheese*

Large ravioli stuffed with ground chicken and asparagus

Pansotti

Sometimes spelled pansoti, these stuffed pasta shapes are Ligurian. The word means chubby, and they are triangular in shape with little potbellies of filling in the center. It is traditional to fill pansotti with chopped cooked spinach, chopped hard-boiled eggs and grated pecorino cheese, then serve them with a walnut sauce. Pansotti are made with small squares of pasta dough and may have straight or fluted edges.

Ravioli

These are usually square with fluted edges, but size and shape vary enormously. Along with tortellini, they are the most widely made of the fresh stuffed pasta shapes, and everyone seems to have their own favorite way of making them. Plain, spinach and tomato doughs are used for the pasta (although other flavors, such as squid ink and saffron, are becoming increasingly available), and the fillings can be anything from vegetables, such as spinach, artichoke and mushroom, to fish and shellfish, and ground veal and chicken. Very tiny ravioli are called raviolini, while the name for ravioli with a pumpkin filling is cappellacci. Tiny round ravioli are sometimes called madaglioni. Large round, oval and rectangular ravioli, stuffed with cheese or vegetable fillings, are occasionally available at Italian delicatessens and markets. Oval ravioli are sometimes called rotondi, while the large rectangular shapes may be called cannelloni rather than ravioli.

Plain and spinach-flavored tortelloni

*Sacchetti filled with a spinach and ricotta filling
and tied with thin strips of scallion*

*Tomato-flavored madaglioni all'uovo
stuffed with a shrimp and trout filling*

Cappelli all'uovo stuffed with minced salmon

*Tortellini stuffed with an artichoke
and truffle oil filling*

Sacchettini

*Candy-shaped caramelle all'uovo stuffed
with spinach and ricotta cheese*

*Spinach cannelloni stuffed with an herb
and cream cheese filling*

Tortellini

Very popular, these look more or less like cappelletti, but are made from rounds or circles of dough rather than squares, so they do not have peaks. They are usually slightly larger than cappelletti, while tortelloni and tortelli are larger still. Tortellini are a specialty from the city of Bologna in Emilia-Romagna, where the traditional filling is ground meats and prosciutto (Parma ham). At Christmas it is the local custom to eat *Tortellini in Brodo* as a first course soup before the main course of roast capon or turkey. Nowadays, tortellini are available everywhere and are eaten all year round. There are a wide variety of color combinations and fillings. Black squid

ink, garlic, herbs, green olive, spinach and sun-dried tomatoes are among the many ingredients used to flavor the dough, while for the fillings you can choose from such delicacies as white crab meat, pumpkin, ricotta, asparagus, cream cheese, caramelized onions, mushrooms, marinated tuna, eggplant, sweet red bell peppers, artichokes and even truffles. A mixture of four cheeses is a popular filling.

Other stuffed pasta shapes

Creative cooks have started a trend for making shapes that are not based on regional traditions, so check out your local Italian market or supermarket for the latest shapes to arrive—you will find

new ones appearing all the time. Two very popular pasta shapes are caramelle and sacchetti. Caramelle means "caramel," and this pasta shape takes its name from the familiar shape of caramels or toffees with their wrappings twisted at both ends. The filling is encased in the lozenge-shaped center and is often ricotta-cheese based, while the pasta itself is made with egg and may be plain, spinach-or tomato-flavored. Sacchetti are little purses or money bags with scrunched tops. The pasta may be plain or flavored and the fillings based on cheese or meat. Sacchettini are a tiny version, most often served in soups but also good with smooth, creamy sauces.

Equipment

Pasta demands little in the way of specialty equipment. You need to have a large saucepan for cooking the pasta and a colander for draining, while for making sauces you need only a sharp knife and a cutting board for chopping ingredients, a skillet or saucepan for cooking, and a large bowl plus spoons and forks for tossing and serving. There are a few items that will, however, make cooking and serving easier, and if you eat pasta frequently you will find them a wise investment. They are all available at good kitchenware stores and department stores.

GENERAL COOKING EQUIPMENT

You may already have some of these basic items in your kitchen.

Pasta cooking pot

Made of stainless steel, this pan has straight sides with two short handles and an inner perforated draining basket, which also has two short handles. Different sizes are available, so choose the one that suits your needs best. One that will comfortably hold at least 2½ quarts of water is adequate if you usually cook for 2–3 people, whereas a 4-quart pan is the one you will need if you often have to cook enough pasta for 6–8 servings. Pasta pots are quite expensive as pans go, but they are so practical that if you buy one you will wonder how you ever managed without it. The pasta is boiled in the inner basket, which is lifted out of the water once the pasta is *al dente*, making draining very easy and safe. This kind of pan is also quite versatile: You can use it with the draining basket for cooking or steaming vegetables or use the outer pan on its own for cooking stocks, soups, stews— and even preserves. When buying a pasta cooking pot, choose one that is not too heavy or you will find it difficult to manage once it is filled with water.

Skillet

A skillet was originally a cooking pot that stood on three or four legs in the hearth. In the United States, the term came to mean a frying pan. Nowadays, it is used on both sides of the Atlantic to describe a wide, deep pan—like a cross between a wok and a frying pan—with a long handle and a lid. This is the perfect pan for making

sauces. Look for one that is at least 9 inches in diameter (10–12 inches is ideal) and 2–3 inches deep. If you often cook for a crowd or for varying numbers of people, it is worth buying two of these pans, in different sizes. Choose the best quality you can afford. Some skillets have non-stick surfaces, which is fine as long as they are of good quality.

Left: This pasta pot comes complete with an inner perforated basket for draining the pasta.

Above: A wide, deep skillet or frying pan is the ideal pan for making sauces, while a large, deep saucepan will double as a pasta pot if you don't have a specially-made one.

Left: A large, deep-bowled ladle is extremely useful. It can be used for serving broths and soups as well as for spooning sauces over pasta.

A large perforated ladle (left) and a flatter scoop (right) are ideal for lifting short pasta shapes out of boiling water.

Right: This odd-looking tool is useful for measuring spaghetti—each hole holds a different amount of pasta.

Above: These simply designed tongs can be used for lifting long strands of pasta out of boiling water.

Left: A long-handled wooden fork is the best tool to use for stirring pasta to separate the strands during cooking.

Pasta measurer

Spaghetti is difficult to put on a scale, and measuring by the handful is not always accurate. This wooden gadget has four or five holes, each of which hold enough pasta for a given number of people.

Long-handled fork

This is useful for stirring pasta during cooking to help keep the strands or pieces from sticking together. A wooden fork is better for separating pasta than a solid wooden spoon. There are also wooden pasta rakes or hooks, which look like flat wooden spoons with prongs attached to one side. They do a good job because the pasta does not slip off when it is lifted, but sometimes the teeth come unglued in the boiling water.

Tongs

Nothing is more effective for picking strands of spaghetti and long noodles out of hot water than a good pair of tongs. Sturdy stainless steel tongs are the best, preferably with long handles for safety, but the most important thing is that they feel comfortable in your hand, so check this before buying. Some tongs have awkward mechanisms, springs and hinges—the simpler the design the better. Tongs can be used for lifting out individual strands to check for doneness and for serving individual portions of long pasta.

Scoop or draining spoon

A large perforated, slotted or mesh spoon is the perfect utensil for lifting short pasta shapes out of boiling water. Choose one that is large and deep, preferably made from stainless steel.

Ladle

For spooning sauce over pasta and for serving soups, a deep-bowled ladle is the most effective utensil. Sizes vary from small and pointed with a lip for easy pouring, to very large, functional-looking types. Stainless steel is the best material.

Parmesan knife

This is a short, quite stubby little knife with a shaped handle and blade. It is by no means an essential item, but is quite effective for scraping off shavings of Parmesan cheese from a block. It also looks good if you are serving Parmesan on a cheese board.

Below: The choice of Parmesan graters available includes a small, rotary grater with a storage space for a piece of Parmesan; a standard, stainless steel box grater; and the traditional small, hand-held Parmesan grater, which is ideal for using at the table.

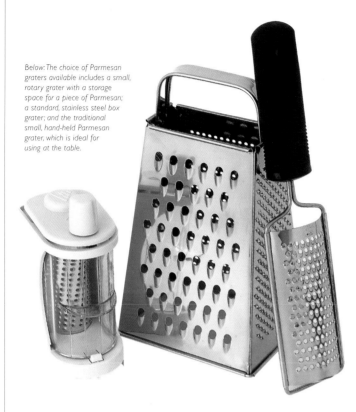

Equipment for Making Pasta at Home

You can make pasta at home with nothing more sophisticated than a scale, some measuring spoons, a work surface and an ordinary rolling pin, but there are a few items of special equipment that will make the job easier. They are all available at specialty kitchenware stores and good department stores.

Tapered rolling pin

The traditional pin used in Italy for rolling out pasta dough is very long—it measures almost 32 inches in length. It is about 1 1/2 inches wide in the center and tapers almost to a point at either end. This type of rolling pin is very easy to use and is well worth buying if you enjoy making pasta by hand and don't intend to buy a special machine. A conventional, straight rolling pin can be used instead, but try to get one that is quite slim—no more than 2 inches in diameter.

Mechanical pasta machine

The same type of hand-cranked pasta machine has been used in Italian kitchens for many, many years. It has stood the test of time well, because it is still manufactured and used today, with very little modification. Made of stainless steel, it has rollers to press out the dough as thinly as possible and cutters for creating different shapes. The standard cutters usually allow you to make tagliatelle and tagliarini, but you can get attachments and accessories for other shapes,

Parmesan graters

There is a huge choice of graters, ranging from the very simple hand grater to electrically operated machines. A simple stainless steel box grater will grate Parmesan and other hard cheeses, such as pecorino, but it can be cumbersome to use with its choice of different-size teeth. It is possible to buy a small grater especially for Parmesan. This consists of a single rectangular grating plate that is designed specifically for grating hard cheese finely, and has a small handle, which can be grasped firmly. The grater is small and unobtrusive, ideal for using at the table. Mechanical Parmesan mills

are also good, as are small, hand-cranked rotary graters, and there are special Parmesan graters available, which have a box and a lid so the cheese can be stored after grating. Electric Parmesan cheese graters are only worth buying if you frequently grate a lot of cheese; a less expensive alternative is to use a small electrical chopper, the kind used for chopping herbs.

including pappardelle, ravioli and cannelloni. The machine is clamped to the edge of a work surface or table and worked by turning the handle. If you make pasta frequently, it is an excellent buy because it is inexpensive, easy and fun to use, and makes excellent pasta in a very short time. It takes all of the hard work out of making pasta by hand, and you can even get an electric motor for it so you don't have to turn the handle.

Above: The traditional Italian pasta rolling pin is very long, slightly wider in the center and narrow at both ends.

Left: The traditional hand-cranked pasta machine with rollers to press out the dough and cutters for tagliatelle and tagliarini is still one of the best ways of making pasta.

Electric Pasta Machines

Tabletop electric pasta machines mix the dough, knead it and then extrude it through cutters, so all you have to do is put the ingredients in the machine and turn it on. You can make more shapes with this type of machine than the mechanical one, but you have less control over the dough because you don't actually handle it at all. Electric pasta machines are only sold in some specialty kitchenware stores. They are expensive to buy, but are a worthwhile investment if you frequently make a lot of pasta—they can make up to 2¼ pounds at a time—and have the space to house the machine in a convenient spot.

Left: A stainless steel pasta wheel makes light work of cutting ravioli.

Pasta wheel

This is a useful gadget for cutting noodles, such as lasagne and tagliatelle, when you don't have a pasta machine, and for cutting out small stuffed shapes. The wheel can be straight or fluted, and there are some types that will cut several lengths of noodle at a time. A sharp knife can be used instead, but a pasta wheel is easier and gives a neater finish. With a pasta wheel, the pasta edges are less likely to be dragged out of shape or torn.

Above: This special metal tray is used for making mini ravioli.

sheet of dough is placed on top. The ravioli squares are cut out by rolling a rolling pin over the serrated top. This is good for making very small ravioli, which are difficult and time-consuming to make individually. Sometimes the tray is sold as a set with its own small rolling pin, or as an accessory for a pasta machine.

equipment. For round ravioli, tortellini and anolini you can use a round cookie cutter if you have one. The most useful sizes are 2 inches and 3 inches.

Ravioli cutter

This is virtually the same as a fluted cookie cutter except that it has a wooden handle and can be square or round. If you want to make square ravioli and cappelletti, you can use a pasta wheel instead of this cutter, so it isn't a vital piece of

Ravioli tray

You can buy a special metal tray for making ravioli. A sheet of rolled-out dough is laid over the tray, then pressed into the indenta-tions. The filling is then spooned into the indenta-tions and another

A specially designed ravioli cutter (right), which can be round or square, isn't essential, because fluted and plain cookie cutters (left) do the same job.

How to Cook and Serve Pasta

It is very easy to cook pasta properly, but without care and attention it is equally easy to cook it badly. A few simple guidelines need to be observed if pasta is to be at its best.

Once you have mastered these, you will be able to cook pasta successfully every time, no matter whether it is dried, homemade or bought fresh.

Cooking Pasta in the Microwave

Because of the large amount of water needed to boil pasta, you will not save any time by cooking it in the microwave, but for short shapes and quantities under 8 ounces, you may find it more convenient than cooking the pasta on top of the stove. The results can be quite successful. Large and long shapes, such as lasagne sheets and spaghetti, need to be cooked in batches, so there doesn't seem to be much point. Where the microwave comes into its own is in reheating pasta sauces and for reheating previously baked pasta dishes, such as lasagne and cannelloni, especially individual portions of these. The microwave is also useful for thawing and reheating sauces and baked dishes that have been stored in the freezer.

How to microwave short pasta shapes

Put the pasta in a large heatproof bowl with salt to taste and pour over boiling water to cover by 1 inch. Carefully transfer the bowl to the microwave and cook on High (100 percent power) for 3–4 minutes for fresh pasta and 8–10 minutes for dried, then let stand for 5 minutes before draining.

1 Synchronize sauce and pasta

Before starting to cook either sauce or pasta, read through the recipe carefully. It is important to know which needs to be cooked for the longest time—sometimes it is the pasta and sometimes the sauce, so don't always assume one or the other. The sauce can often be made ahead of time and reheated, and it is quite unusual for the timing of a sauce to be crucial, but pasta is almost like a hot soufflé—it waits for no one. This is especially true if you are cooking fresh pasta, for which cooking time is often only a few minutes, so the sauce needs to be ready and waiting before the pasta hits the water.

3 Use a large quantity of water

The recommended amount is 4 quarts water for every 1 pound pasta. If you are cooking less pasta than this, use at least 2½ quarts water. If there is not enough water, the pasta shapes will stick together as they swell and the pan will become over-crowded. This will result in unpleasant, gummy-textured pasta.

WATCHPOINT

It is best not to cook more than 1 1/12 pound pasta at a time, even if you have a very large saucepan, because of the danger in handling such a large amount of water. If you are using the microwave to cook pasta it is best not to cook more than 8 ounces pasta at a time. Use a large heatproof bowl, don't overfill the bowl and transfer it carefully to and from the microwave using oven mitts.

2 Use a big pan

There needs to be plenty of room for the pasta to move around in the large amount of water it requires, so a big pan is essential. The best type of pan is a tall, lightweight, straight-sided, stainless steel pasta cooking pot with its own in-built draining pan. Both outer and inner pans have two handles each, which ensure easy and safe lifting and draining. If you cook pasta a lot, it is well worth investing in one of these special pans; otherwise use the largest saucepan you have for cooking the pasta plus a large stainless steel colander, preferably one with feet for stability for draining it.

4 Get the water boiling

Before adding the pasta, the water should be at a fast rolling boil. The quickest way to do this is to boil water in the kettle, then pour it into the pasta pan, which should be set over high heat. You may need as much as 2–3 kettlefuls, so keep the water in the pan simmering, covered by the lid, while you boil the kettle again.

5 **Add enough salt**
Pasta cooked without salt is more or less tasteless, and with insufficient salt it is hardly any better. The recommended amount is 1 1/2–2 tablespoons salt for every 1 pound pasta. There is no need to use sea or rock salt; regular salt is perfectly acceptable. Add the salt when the water is boiling and just before you are ready to add the pasta. The water will bubble furiously just as the salt is added, which is your cue to add the pasta.

6 **Add the pasta all at once**
Try to get all of the pasta into the boiling water at the same time so that it will cook evenly and be ready at the same time. The quickest and easiest way is literally to shake it out of the package or the bowl of the scale, covering the surface of the water as much as possible.

7 **Return the water quickly to a boil**
Once the pasta is submerged in the water, give it a brisk stir with a long-handled fork or spoon and then cover the pan tightly with the lid—this will help to bring the water back to a boil as quickly as possible. Once the water is boiling, lift off the lid, turn down the heat slightly and let the water simmer over medium to high heat for the required cooking time.

8 **Stir the pasta frequently during cooking**
To prevent the pasta strands or shapes from sticking together, stir them frequently during cooking so they are kept constantly on the move. Use a long-handled wooden fork or spoon so you can stir right down to the bottom of the pan.

9 **Drain carefully and thoroughly**
If you have a pasta pot with an inner drainer, lift the draining pan up and out of the water. Shake the draining pan vigorously and stir the pasta well so that any water trapped in pasta shapes can drain out as quickly as possible. It is a good idea to reserve a few ladlefuls of the pasta cooking water in case the pasta needs a little extra moistening when it is tossed with the sauce before serving.

Accurate Timing is Essential for Cooking Pasta
Start timing the pasta from the moment the water returns to a boil after adding the pasta. Always go by the time given on the package or, in the case of fresh homemade pasta, by the time given in the recipe. For the greatest accuracy, use a kitchen timer with a bell or buzzer because even half a minute of overcooking can ruin pasta, especially if it is freshly made. Dried egg pasta is more difficult to spoil, so if you are new to pasta cooking and nervous about getting it right, start with this type.

For fresh pasta
As a general guide, thin fresh noodles will take only 2–3 minutes, thicker fresh noodles and pasta shapes 3–4 minutes, and stuffed fresh pasta 5–7 minutes.

For dried pasta
The cooking time for dried pasta will vary from 8–20 minutes depending on the type and the manufacturer. Always check the cooking time provided on the label.

38

Cooking Fresh Pasta

1 For freshly made pasta that has been drying on a dish towel, gather the cloth up around the pasta in a loose cylindrical shape and hold it firmly at both ends.

2 Hold the towel over the water, then let go of the end nearest to the water so that the pasta drops in.

Cooking Long Dried Pasta

1 For spaghetti you need to coil the pasta into the water as it softens. Take a handful at a time and dip it in the boiling water so that it touches the bottom of the pan.

2 As the spaghetti strands soften, coil them around using a wooden spoon or fork until they are all submerged.

Cooking Stuffed Pasta

1 Stuffed shapes require more gentle handling or they may break open and release their filling into the water, so stir them gently during cooking.

2 The best method of draining stuffed shapes after cooking is to lift them carefully out of the water with a large pasta scoop or slotted spoon (left).

When is it cooked?

The Italian term *al dente* is used to describe pasta that is cooked to perfection. Literally translated this means "to the tooth," meaning that it should be firm to the bite, which is how Italians like their pasta, and therefore how it should be served. Dried pasta, which is made from durum wheat, is always served *al dente*, whereas fresh pasta is made from a softer wheat and so is never as firm as dried, but it should still have some resistance to it. Overcooked pasta is limp and unpalatable, even slimy, and an Italian cook would not serve it. To check that the pasta is ready, test pasta frequently toward the end of the recommended cooking time by lifting out a piece with tongs, a pasta scoop or a slotted spoon and biting into it. When you are satisfied that it is done to your liking, it is time to stop the cooking.

At-a-glance Amounts

Amounts of pasta given here are intended only as a guide to the number of people they will serve. If you are cooking fresh pasta, you may need a little more than if you are using dried, but the difference is really negligible. What is more significant is whether you are serving a light or substantial sauce with the pasta.

For an Italian-style first course (primo piatto) for 4–6 people, or a main course for 2–3 people:

2½ quarts water
1 tablespoon salt
9–12 ounces fresh or dried pasta

For a first course for 6–8 people, or a main course for 4–6 people:

4 quarts water
1½–2 tablespoons salt
11 ounces–1 pound fresh or dried pasta

Combining the Pasta and Sauce

Recipes vary in the way they combine sauce and pasta. The majority have you add the sauce to the pasta, but with some it is the other way around. There are no hard-and-fast rules. If you are going to add the sauce to the drained pasta, the most important thing is to have a warmed bowl ready. The larger the bowl the better, because this will allow room for the sauce and pasta to be tossed together easily so that every piece of pasta can be thoroughly coated in sauce.

1 After draining, immediately transfer the pasta to the warmed bowl, then pour the sauce over the pasta and quickly toss the two together.

2 If the pasta is not moist enough, add a little of the pasta cooking water. Some recipes call for extra butter or oil to be added at this stage, others have grated Parmesan or pecorino cheese tossed with the pasta and sauce.

3 Use two large spoons or forks for tossing, or a large spoon and a fork. Lift the pasta and swirl it around, making sure you have scooped it up from the bottom of the bowl. The idea is to coat every piece of pasta evenly in sauce, so keep tossing until you are satisfied that this is done.

4 Occasionally, recipes call for the pasta to be returned to the cooking pan, to be combined with oil or butter and seasonings and tossed over heat until coated. A sauce may be added at this stage too, but care should be taken not to cook the pasta too much in the first place or it may overcook when it is reheated.

Serving and Presentation

Most important of all is to have your family and friends waiting at the table for the pasta, not the other way around. With the exception of baked dishes, all pasta should be eaten as soon as it is cooked and tossed with the sauce, so invite everyone to sit down just before you are ready to drain the pasta.

In most cases, pasta and sauce are tossed together in a large serving bowl in the kitchen, and the bowl is then brought straight to the table. Each person is served straight from the bowl—or the bowl is passed around the table for everyone to help themselves.

To give the pasta a finishing touch, a little Parmesan or pecorino cheese can be grated on top, or a few chopped fresh herbs, such as parsley or basil, can be sprinkled on. The choice of garnish depends on the dish and the cook, but as a general rule, grated cheese is never served with fish and shellfish sauces. For guidance, follow the garnishing instructions in individual recipes.

Occasionally, the pasta and sauce are divided among individual plates or bowls before serving—as is the practice in restaurants. This is not the traditional custom in Italian homes, but it sometimes helps to get the pasta served quickly. It is an especially good idea when you are entertaining because each individual serving can have its own attractive garnish.

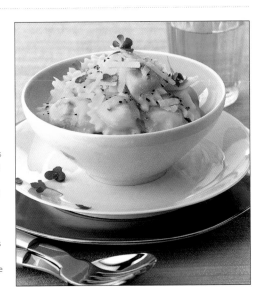

Matching Sauces to Recipes

Some regional dishes are always made with the same pasta shape. *Bucatini all'Amatriciana, Penne all'Arrabbiata* and *Fettuccine all'Alfredo* are all classic Roman recipes, for example, and it is rare to see them served with anything other than the named pasta. The same applies to *Tagliatelle alla Bolognese* from Emilia-Romagna and *Trenette con Pesto* from Genoa. These classics are few and far between, however, and with the ever-increasing number of different shapes on the market it may seem difficult to know which sauces and shapes go well together. Happily, there are no rigid rules, and common sense usually prevails. Heavy sauces with large chunks of meat are unlikely to go well with thin spaghettini or tagliolini, simply because the chunks will slide off, so these sauces and others like them are always served with wide noodles, such as pappardelle, maccheroni and tagliatelle, or with short tubular shapes, such as penne, fusilli, conchiglie and rigatoni.

In the south of Italy, olive oil is used for cooking rather than butter, so sauces tend to be made with olive oil and they are usually served with the dried plain durum wheat pasta such as spaghetti and vermicelli that is also popular in the south. These long, thin shapes are traditionally served with tomato and seafood sauces, most of which are made with olive oil, and with light vegetable sauces. Spaghetti and vermicelli are also ideal vehicles for minimalist sauces like *Aglio e Olio* (garlic and olive oil) from Rome. Grated cheese is not normally used in these sauces, nor is it sprinkled on them.

Classic dishes, such as Bucatini all'Amatriciana (left), Penne all'Arrabbiata (below) and Fettuccine all'Alfredo (above), are almost always served with the named pasta.

Grated cheese is often tossed with pasta and sauce at the last moment, as well as being sprinkled over individual servings at the table.

In the North, butter and cream are used in sauces, and not surprisingly these go well with the egg pasta that is made there, especially fresh homemade egg pasta, which absorbs butter and cream and makes the sauce cling to it. Butter and cream also go well with tomato sauces when these are served with short shapes, especially penne, rigatoni, farfalle and fusilli.

Eating Pasta

Opinions vary as to whether pasta should be eaten from a plate or a bowl. There are no rules, so you can serve it on either. Large, shallow soup plates seem the ideal compromise, and setting each warmed soup plate on a large, cold underplate makes for easy carrying from kitchen to table.

If the recipe recommends extra Parmesan or pecorino for serving, grate the cheese just before the meal and pass it in a bowl with a small spoon so that people can help themselves. Salt and pepper shakers should also be on the table for those who like to adjust the seasoning.

Pasta is traditionally eaten with a single fork. Spaghetti and other long shapes should not be difficult to manage if they have been well tossed with the sauce. The trick is to twirl only a small amount around the fork at a time.

Wines to Serve with Pasta

It is impossible to recommend a particular wine to go with every pasta dish, but there are a few guidelines you can follow. If you know where the dish comes from, choose a wine from the same region. If a red or a white wine is used in the cooking of the sauce, select a good-quality wine for cooking and serve the rest with the meal. Otherwise, look at the main ingredient of the sauce and choose a wine that is recommended for that. Many pasta sauces are strong-tasting, garlicky or spiced with chiles, and some are served with mature Parmesan or pecorino cheese; for these you will need to choose a robust, full-flavored wine.

Barbaresco
A great red wine from Piedmont. Full-bodied and complex in flavor. Good with poultry and meat sauces.

Barbera
A medium-bodied red from Piedmont, which varies from young and slightly sparkling to rich and concentrated in flavor. Good with meat lasagne.

Bardolino
This fresh-tasting, light and fruity red from Veneto is very good to serve with poultry sauces.

Barolo
A full-bodied red made in Piedmont from Nebbiolo grapes. Good with red meat and game sauces.

Castel del Monte
Full-bodied smooth red and rosé wines from Puglia. Good with poultry and meat.

Chianti
Famous, uncomplicated red from Tuscany. Look for Chianti Classico to serve with red meat, poultry and game sauces.

Cirò
Fresh, zingy white and full-bodied red from Calabria. Drink the white with fish and shellfish sauces, the red with red meat and game sauces.

Est! Est!! Est!!!
A clean-tasting, dry white from the Lazio region. It is good with fish and shellfish sauces.

Frascati
A crisp and fruity dry white from the town of Frascati, which is near Rome in the Lazio region. Good with the very spicy Amatriciana sauce.

Lambrusco
This effervescent red from Emilia-Romagna is good with pork and rich meat sauces.

Orvieto Secco
Dry white, from the town of the same name in Umbria. Serve with fish, shellfish and poultry sauces.

Pinot Grigio
A fresh, fruity dry white from Friuli-Venezia. It is good with any sauce or pasta dish.

Soave
Light, dry white from Veneto made from Garganega grapes. It is good with any sauce or pasta dish, and is reasonably priced.

Valpolicella
Fruity red, sometimes with a bitter aftertaste, from Veneto. The name means "valley of many cellars." It is good with red meat sauces.

Valtellina
This perfumed red from Lombardy is made from Nebbiolo grapes. Look for Grumello, Inferno, Sassella and Valgella. It is good with rich meat, poultry and game sauces.

Verdicchio
Crisp, dry white with character from Marche in central Italy. It comes in a carved bottle shaped like a Roman amphora. Good with all kinds of fish and shellfish sauces.

Vernaccia
Rich, nutty red from the island of Sardinia that goes well with fish and shellfish sauces.

How to Make Pasta

Homemade pasta has a wonderfully light, almost silky texture—quite different from the so-called fresh pasta that you buy pre-packaged at some stores. If you use egg in the mixture, which is recommended if you are making pasta at home, the dough is easy to make, either by hand or machine, and the initial process is not that different from making bread. Kneading, rolling and cutting require some patience and practice, but if you invest in an inexpensive mechanical pasta machine, this part of the process will become quick and easy—and fun, too.

Pasta all'Uovo

Pasta with Eggs

The best place to make, knead and roll out pasta dough is on a wooden kitchen table, the larger the better. The surface should be warm, so marble is not suitable.

INGREDIENTS

2³/4 cups flour

3 eggs

1 teaspoon salt

Ingredients for Pasta with Eggs

Only three inexpensive ingredients are used: eggs, flour and salt. However, ultimate success depends as much on their quality as on the technique used for making the dough. Olive oil is added to the mixture by some cooks, especially in Tuscany, but it is by no means essential. It gives the pasta a softer texture and a slightly different flavor, and some say it helps make the dough easier to work with, especially if you don't have a pasta machine. For a 3-egg batch of dough, use 1 tablespoon olive oil and add it with the eggs.

The best flour is called Farina Bianca 00 or Tipo 00, available at Italian specialty stores and markets. Imported from Italy, this is a very fine, soft white wheat flour. If you use ordinary flour, you will find the dough quite difficult to knead and roll, especially if you are doing this by hand. If you can't get 00 flour, use a strong bread flour.

Very fresh eggs are essential, and the deeper the yellow of the yolks the better the color of the pasta. Buy the eggs fresh and use them at room temperature. If they have been stored in the refrigerator, take them out for about 1 hour before using.

Salt is important for flavor.

1 Mound the flour on a clean work surface and make a large, deep well in the center with your hands. Keep the sides of the well quite high so that when the eggs are added they will not run out of the well.

2 Crack the eggs into the well, then add the salt. With a table knife or fork, combine the eggs and salt, then gradually start incorporating the flour from the sides of the well. Try not to break the sides of the well or the runny mixture will escape and quickly spread over the work surface.

3 As soon as the egg mixture is no longer liquid, dip your fingers in the flour and use them to work the ingredients together until they form a rough and sticky dough. Scrape up any dough that sticks to the work surface with a knife, then scrape this off the knife with your fingers. If the dough is too dry, add a few drops of cold water; if it is too moist, sprinkle a little flour over it.

5 Give the dough a quarter turn counterclockwise, then continue kneading, folding and turning for 5 minutes if you intend to use a pasta machine, or for 10 minutes if you will be rolling it out by hand. The dough should be very smooth and elastic. If you are going to roll it out and cut it by hand, thorough kneading is essential.

4 Press the dough into a rough ball and knead it as you would bread. Push it away from you with the heel of your hand, then fold the end of the dough back on itself so that it faces toward you and push it out again. Continue folding the dough back a little further each time and pushing it out until you have folded it back all the way toward you and all the dough has been kneaded.

6 Wrap the dough in plastic wrap and let it rest for 15–20 minutes at room temperature. It will then be ready to roll out.

COOK'S TIP

Don't skimp on the kneading time or the finished pasta will not be light and silky.

Making Pasta Dough in a Food Processor

If you have a food processor, you can save a little time and effort by using it for making pasta dough. It will not knead the dough adequately, however, so you may find it just as quick and easy to make it by hand, especially if you take into account the washing and drying of the bowl and blade. The ingredients are the same as when making pasta by hand.

1 Put the flour and salt in the bowl of a food processor fitted with the metal blade.

2 Add 1 whole egg and then pulse-blend until the ingredients are mixed.

3 Turn the food processor on at full speed and add the remaining whole eggs through the feeder tube. Keep the machine running for just long enough to let dough to be formed.

4 Turn the dough out onto a clean work surface. Knead as when making pasta by hand, then wrap in plastic wrap and let rest at room temperature for 15–20 minutes.

Making Pasta Shapes by Hand

Once you have made your pasta dough and let it rest, it is ready to be rolled out and cut into various shapes. If you don't have a pasta machine, the following steps show how to do it by hand. The technique is quite hard work, and the pasta may not be quite as thin as that made in a machine, but it is equally good nevertheless. If you enjoy making your own pasta and think you would like to make it regularly, it is well worth buying a mechanical pasta machine to save you both time and effort.

1 Unwrap the ball of dough and cut it in half. Roll and cut one half at a time, keeping the other half wrapped in plastic wrap as before.

2 Sprinkle a very large, clean work surface lightly with flour. Put the unwrapped dough on the surface, sprinkle it with a little flour and flatten it with the heel of your hand. Turn the dough over and repeat the process to form the dough into a 5-inch disk.

3 Using a lightly floured rolling pin, start to roll the dough out. Always roll the dough away from you, stretching it outward from the center and moving the dough around a quarter turn after each rolling. If the dough gets sticky, sprinkle the rolling pin, dough and work surface lightly with flour.

4 Continue rolling, turning and stretching the dough until it is a large oval, as thin as you can possibly get it. Ideally it should be about 1/8-inch thick. Try to get it even all over or the shapes will not cook in the same length of time. Don't worry if the edges are not neat; this is not important.

Cutting Ribbon Noodles

1 Before you begin, have ready plenty of clean dish towels lightly dusted with flour; you will need to spread the shapes out on them after cutting. Dust the sheet of pasta (called *la sfoglia* in Italian) lightly with flour. Starting from one long edge, roll up the sheet into a loose cylinder.

2 With a large sharp knife, cut cleanly across the pasta roll. Cut at $^1/_2$-inch intervals for tagliatelle, slightly narrower (about $^1/_4$-inch) for fettuccine, and as narrow as you can possibly get for tagliarini or capelli d'angelo. Take care not to drag the knife, or the edges of the ribbons will be ragged.

3 With floured fingers, unravel the rolls on the work surface, then toss the noodles lightly together on the floured dish towels, sprinkling them with more flour.

4 Repeat the rolling and cutting with the remaining pasta. Let the strips dry on the dish towels for at least 15 minutes before cooking, tossing them occasionally and sprinkling them with a little flour if they become sticky.

Cutting Pappardelle

Cutting Lasagne and Cannelloni

1 Using a fluted pasta wheel, cut the pasta sheet into long strips about $^3/_4$–1 inch wide. Try to keep the strips the same width or they will not cook evenly.

2 Spread the pappardelle strips out in a single layer on floured dish towels and sprinkle them with a little more flour. Let the pappardelle dry on the towels for at least 15 minutes before cooking.

1 With a large sharp knife, cut the pasta sheets into 5–6 x 3–4-inch rectangles or whatever size fits your baking dish best.

2 Spread the rectangles out in a single layer on floured dish towels, sprinkle them with more flour and let dry for at least 15 minutes before cooking. They can be used for both lasagne and cannelloni.

Cutting Quadrucci (for Soups)

1 Stack two pasta sheets on top of each other, with a light sprinkling of flour in between. With a large sharp knife, cut the pasta diagonally into $1^1/_2$-inch wide strips, then cut across the strips in the opposite direction to make $1^1/_2$-inch squares.

2 Spread the squares out on floured dish towels and sprinkle with more flour. Let dry for at least 15 minutes before cooking.

Cutting Maltagliati (for Soups)

1 Dust one pasta sheet lightly with flour. Starting from one long edge, roll the sheet up into a cylinder. Lightly flatten the cylinder, then, with a sharp knife, slice off the corners at one end, making two diagonal cuts to form two sides of a triangle. Cut straight across to complete the triangle. Repeat all the way along the cylinder, then unfold the maltagliati.

2 Spread out the maltagliati on floured dish towels. Sprinkle the shapes with a little more flour and let them dry for at least 15 minutes before cooking.

COOK'S TIP

Maltagliati means badly cut, so don't worry if the pasta is misshapen—it is meant to be. Quadrucci and maltagliati can also be cut from fresh lasagne rectangles, but this will take slightly longer.

Making Short Pasta Shapes

Most small pasta shapes are best left to the professionals, because they either take too long to make or require specialty equipment. There are a couple of shapes that are an exception: garganelli and farfalle. Garganelli are traditionally made with a special tool called *il pettine*, but you can improvise with an old-fashioned butter paddle and a round pencil.

Making Garganelli

1 Cut the pasta sheets into 2-inch squares. Lay the butter paddle ridges horizontally on the work surface, with the ridges facing toward you. Angle the square so that it is diamond-shaped and place it over the ridges. Put a pencil diagonally across the corner of the square that is closest to you.

2 Roll the pasta square up around the pencil, pressing down hard on the ends of the pencil as you go. The ridges of the butter paddle will imprint themselves on the pasta.

3 Stand the pencil upright on the work surface and tap the end so that the tube of pasta slides off.

4 Spread the garganelli out in a single layer on floured dish towels, sprinkle them with more flour and let them dry for at least 15 minutes before cooking.

Making Farfalle

1 With a fluted pasta wheel, cut the pasta sheets into rectangles measuring 1 1/4 x 1-inch. Pinch the long sides of each rectangle between your index finger and thumb and squeeze hard to make a bow-tie shape. If the pasta will not hold the shape, moisten your fingers with water and squeeze again.

2 Spread the farfalle out in a single layer on floured dish towels, sprinkle them with a little more flour and let dry for at least 15 minutes before cooking.

Making Pasta Shapes Using a Machine

Rolling the Dough

A machine makes light work of rolling pasta dough. It makes thinner, smoother pasta than you can make by hand, and the thickness is always even. Some shapes, such as lasagne, are cut by hand, but for cutting noodles, a machine is invaluable.

1 Clamp the machine securely to your work surface and insert the handle in the roller slot. Set the rollers at their widest setting and sprinkle them lightly with flour. Unwrap the ball of pasta and cut it into quarters. Work with one quarter at a time, wrapping the other three pieces of pasta dough in plastic wrap.

2 Flatten the quarter of dough with lightly floured hands and make it into a rough rectangle, just a little narrower in width than the rollers of the machine. Feed this through the rollers of the machine.

3 Fold the dough into thirds, then feed it lengthwise through the rollers. Repeat the folding and rolling five times.

4 Turn the roller setting one notch. Sprinkle the pasta lightly with flour and feed it through the rollers again, only this time unfolded.

5 Turn the roller setting another notch and repeat the rolling, then continue in this way without folding the dough until you get to the last setting, turning the roller setting another notch after each rolling and sprinkling it lightly with flour if it becomes sticky. The dough will get longer and thinner with every rolling until it reaches 35 inches–3 feet in length. Once the dough has been rolled, it is ready for cutting into the required shape.

COOK'S TIPS

• About halfway through the rolling process, you may find that the pasta strip becomes too unwieldy and difficult to handle because it is so long. In this case, cut the strip in half or into thirds and work with one piece at a time. Remember to return the notch on the roller to the setting where you left off when you start with the next piece of dough.

• You may find that the dough is thin enough on the penultimate setting, in which case you can stop there. This will definitely be the case if you are going to make tonnarelli or spaghetti alla chitarra.

• Keep sprinkling the pasta dough lightly with flour if it becomes sticky, and keep the rollers lightly floured to prevent the pasta from sticking to the machine.

• Any trimmings and leftover pieces of pasta dough can be re-rolled and more shapes can be cut from them.

• Once they are dry, noodles and pasta shapes can be stored in a paper bag for 3–4 days, or frozen in plastic bags for up to 1 month.

Cutting Lasagne and Cannelloni

1 Using a sharp knife, cut the rolled pasta strip into 5–6 × 3–4-inch rectangles, or whatever size fits your baking dish best.

2 Spread out the rectangles in a single layer on floured dish towels and sprinkle with flour.

Cutting Tagliatelle and Fettuccine

1 Insert the handle in the slot for the widest cutters and sprinkle these cutters lightly with flour. Cut the pasta strip to about 12 inches long if you haven't done so already, and sprinkle it lightly with flour. Feed the pasta through the widest cutters.

2 Continue turning the handle of the pasta machine slowly and steadily, guiding the strands with your other hand.

3 Toss the tagliatelle or fettuccine in flour and spread the noodles out on a floured dish towel. Let dry while rolling and cutting the remaining dough.

Cutting Tonnarelli and Spaghetti alla Chitarra

1 Stop rolling the pasta strip after the second to last or next to last setting, then insert the handle in the slot for the narrowest cutters and feed the pasta through the machine.

2 Proceed as for tagliatelle or fettuccine, turning the handle and guiding the long strands with your other hand. Toss the tonnarelli or spaghetti in flour and spread out on floured dish towels.

Making Ravioli

1 Using a large sharp knife, cut the rolled pasta strip into two 18–20-inch lengths, if this has not been done already.

2 Using a teaspoon, put 10–12 little mounds of your chosen filling along one side of one of the pasta strips, spacing them evenly.

3 Using a pastry brush, carefully brush a little water onto the pasta strip around each mound of filling.

4 Fold the plain side of the pasta strip over the filling.

5 Starting from the folded edge, press down gently with your fingertips around each mound, pushing the air out at the unfolded edge. Sprinkle lightly with flour.

6 With a fluted pasta wheel, cut along each long side, then in between each mound to make small square shapes.

7 Put the ravioli on floured dish towels, sprinkle lightly with more flour and let dry while repeating the process with the remaining dough. For a 3-egg dough, you should get 80–96 ravioli, more if you re-roll the trimmings.

COOK'S TIPS

•Ravioli made in this way are not perfectly square, but they look charmingly homemade. If you prefer a more precise finish, you should use a ravioli tray, which you can buy at specialty kitchenware store. The ravioli tray can be bought on its own or as an extra accessory to a pasta machine. Another alternative is to use a hand-held ravioli cutter or a round plain or fluted cookie cutter.
•Have ready 3 or 4 floured dish towels before you begin cutting the pasta shapes. Arrange the stuffed shapes on the towels, well-spaced and in one layer, because if you overlap them, they may stick together.
•Once they are dry, stuffed pasta shapes can be frozen for up to 1 month, layered between sheets of plastic wrap in plastic bags.

Fillings for Stuffed Pasta
These vary from one or two simple ingredients to special traditional recipes. The ingredients are combined and often bound with beaten egg, Seasoning is added to taste.
Simple ideas
•*spinach, Parmesan, ricotta and nutmeg*
•*crab, mascarpone, lemon, parsley and chiles*
•*taleggio cheese and fresh marjoram*
Regional specialities
•*ground pork and turkey with fresh herbs, ricotta and Parmesan*
•*fresh herbs, ricotta, Parmesan and garlic*
•*puréed cooked pumpkin, prosciutto, mozzarella and parsley*

1 Using a sharp knife, cut the rolled strip of pasta dough by hand into two 18–20-inch lengths, if this has not been done already.

2 Using a teaspoon, put 8–10 little mounds of your chosen filling along one side of one of the pasta strips, spacing them evenly.

3 Using a pastry brush, carefully brush a little water onto the pasta strip around each mound of filling.

4 Fold the plain side of the pasta strip over the filling.

5 Starting from the folded edge, press down gently with your fingertips around each mound, pushing the air out at the unfolded edge. Sprinkle lightly with flour.

6 Using only half of a 2-inch fluted round ravioli or cookie cutter, cut around each mound of filling to make a half-moon shape.

7 If desired, press the cut edges of the agnolotti with the tines of a fork to give a decorative effect.

8 Put the agnolotti on floured dish towels, sprinkle lightly with more flour and let dry while repeating the process with the remaining dough. For a 3-egg dough, you should get 64–80 agnolotti, more if you re-roll the trimmings.

COOK'S TIPS

• When cutting out the agnolotti, make sure that the folded edge is the straight edge.
• Don't re-roll the trimmings after cutting each pasta strip, but wait until you have done them all. If there is no filling left for the rolled pasta trimmings, you can use them to make noodles or small shapes for soup.

Making Tortellini / Tortelloni

1 Using a sharp knife, cut the rolled strip of pasta dough by hand into two 18–20-inch lengths, if this has not been done already.

2 To make tortellini: with 2-inch fluted ravioli or cookie cutter, cut out 8–10 disks from one of the pasta strips. For tortelloni use a 2¹/₂-inch cutter.

3 Using a teaspoon and a fingertip, put a little mound of your chosen filling in the center of each disk.

4 Brush a little water around the edge of each disk.

5 Fold the disk in half over the filling so that the top and bottom edges do not quite meet. Press to seal.

6 Wrap the half-moon shape around an index finger and pinch the ends together to seal.

Making Pansotti and Cappelletti / Cappellacci

Pansotti are made from 2-inch squares of pasta that are folded in half over the filling to make triangles. Moisten the edges of the triangles and press to seal in the filling.

Cappelletti and cappellacci are made in the same way as tortellini, using squares of pasta rather than disks. The edges are turned up so they look like little hats.

7 Put the tortellini or tortelloni on floured dish towels, sprinkle with flour and let dry while repeating the process with the remaining dough. For a 3-egg dough, you should get 64–80 tortellini, more if you re-roll the trimmings.

Making Flavored and Colored Pasta

There are many different ingredients you can use to change the flavor and color of pasta, whether you are making the dough by hand or machine, although you will find it easier to get a more even color with a machine. Some flavors are more trouble than they are worth, so it is best to restrict your choice to the tried and tested ones. The following flavorings are the most successful, and the amounts of ingredients given are for a 3-egg batch of pasta all'uovo (pasta dough with eggs).

Black pepper

Chile

Porcini

Tomato

Black pepper

Put 2 tablespoons black peppercorns or mixed peppercorns in a mortar and crush them coarsely with a pestle. Add to the eggs in the well before you start to incorporate the flour.

Chile

Add 1–2 teaspoons crushed dried red chiles to the eggs in the well before you start to incorporate the flour.

Porcini

Soak ¹/2 ounce porcini (dried wild mushrooms) in ³/4 cup warm water. Drain the porcini and squeeze to remove as much water as possible. Dry the mushrooms thoroughly on paper towels, then chop them finely and add them to the eggs in the well before you start to incorporate the flour. The dough will be stickier than usual, so you will need to add more flour during kneading, rolling and cutting. If desired, you can add the porcini soaking water to the water for boiling the pasta. This will intensify the mushroom flavor of the pasta.

Tomato

Add 2 tablespoons tomato paste to the eggs in the well before you start to incorporate the flour. The pasta dough will be stickier than usual, so you will need to add more flour during kneading, rolling and cutting.

Spinach

Wash 5 ounces fresh spinach leaves and place them in a large saucepan with only the water that clings to the leaves. Add a pinch of salt, then cover the pan and cook over medium heat for about 8 minutes or until the spinach is wilted and tender. Drain the spinach, let sit for a few minutes until cool enough to handle, then squeeze it hard in your hands to remove as much water as possible. Dry the spinach thoroughly on several sheets of paper towel, then finely chop it using a large sharp knife or a food processor and add it to the eggs in the well before you start to incorporate the flour. The pasta dough will be much stickier than usual, so you will need to add a little extra flour during kneading and when rolling and cutting the dough.

Squid ink

Add 8 grams of squid ink to the eggs in the well before you start to incorporate the flour. The dough will be stickier than usual, so you will need to add more flour during kneading, rolling and cutting.

Herb

Wash and dry three small handfuls of fresh herbs. Basil, flat leaf parsley, sage and thyme are all good choices, either singly or together. Finely chop the herbs and add them to the eggs in the well before you start to incorporate the flour. The dough may be a little more sticky than usual, in which case you may need to add a little extra flour during kneading and when rolling and cutting it.

Saffron

Sift 3 or 4 sachets of saffron powder with the flour before starting to make the pasta dough.

Spinach

Squid ink

Herb

Saffron

Making Striped Pasta

You can use different colors to make striped dough that can be cut into rectangles for lasagne and cannelloni. It is quite tricky, and the rolling out is best done with a pasta machine.

Plain or saffron yellow and spinach doughs look very good together, and another excellent combination is plain or saffron yellow dough contrasted with dough colored with tomato or squid ink. To make pasta tricolore (three-colored pasta), mix stripes of tomato dough, squid ink or spinach dough and plain dough. Some creative chefs make checked and plaid patterns with colored pasta, but this is very time-consuming for the home cook.

1 Roll out two different colored pieces of dough on a pasta machine, keeping them separate and taking them up to and including the second to last setting.

2 With a fluted pasta wheel, cut one strip of each color lengthwise into three or four narrower strips. Select three strips of one color and two of the other, setting the rest aside for the next batch of striped pasta.

3 The aim is to join the pasta strips together, using water as glue. Brush one long edge of one pasta strip with a little water, then join a pasta of a different color to it, placing it over the moistened edge and pressing it firmly to seal the join. Repeat this process, alternating the pasta colors until you have a length of pasta that resembles a scarf, with three stripes of one color and two stripes of the other.

4 Sprinkle the pasta liberally with flour, lift it very carefully and put it through the pasta machine, which should be set to the next to last setting.

COOK'S TIPS

• When cutting flavored tagliatelle or tagliarini on a pasta machine, sprinkle the cutters liberally with flour before putting the dough through. The noodles tend to stick together as they come through the machine, so you may need to separate them gently with floured hands before putting them on dish towels and tossing them in more flour.
• When cooking flavored pasta, start testing for doneness earlier than usual. The ingredients added for some flavors make the pasta more moist and soft than usual, and this means that it cooks a little more quickly.
• You can use striped pasta for making ravioli: keep the strips fairly narrow and make sure they are well sealed, otherwise the ravioli may split open during cooking.

5 Cut the dough into rectangles or squares for cannelloni or lasagne and spread these out in a single layer on floured dish towels. Sprinkle them with flour and let dry for at least 15 minutes before cooking.

Making Silhouette Pasta

Fresh herbs can be rolled between sheets of pasta for a very pretty decorative effect. The pasta needs to be very thin, so it is best to roll it out on a pasta machine. Use only soft, leafy herbs, such as flat-leaf parsley, chervil, green or purple basil or sage. Silhouette pasta can be boiled and served with melted butter and grated Parmesan, or cooked in a clear soup (*in brodo*).

1 Roll out a piece of dough on a pasta machine, taking it up to and including the last setting. Moisten one side of the strip of dough lightly with water. A mister or spray bottle is ideal for this.

Above: Fresh herbs, such as basil (top left), flat-leaf parsley (left) and sage (right), can be rolled between sheets of dough to make pretty silhouette pasta.

2 Arrange individual fresh herb leaves on the moistened half of the dough, placing them at regular intervals. Fold the dry half of the dough over the herbs and press the edges firmly to seal.

3 Sprinkle the pasta liberally with flour and put it through the machine, on the penultimate setting.

4 With a floured pasta wheel, cut around each herb leaf to make square ravioli shapes. Spread the shapes out in a single layer on floured dish towels. Sprinkle them with more flour and let dry for at least 15 minutes before cooking.

As an alternative to using a pasta wheel for cutting out rectangular shapes, use a small, fluted cookie cutter and stamp out round shapes.

The Pasta Pantry

Certain ingredients crop up time and time again in sauces for pasta. Some can be kept in the pantry, while fresh ones must either be bought just before use, or kept in the refrigerator. Fresh herbs and leaves, spices, oils, vinegars and other less well-known ingredients are used to add flavor. Canned and dried fish and shellfish are useful additions to your pantry, while fresh vegetables, such as eggplant, tomatoes and bell peppers, along with garlic and sun-dried vegetables, play an important part in many pasta dishes. Cheese and cream are used in sauces, in fillings and for baked pasta dishes.

FRESH HERBS AND LEAVES

These are used extensively for flavoring sauces for pasta, and for presentation and garnishing. Italian cooks keep pots of fresh herbs growing on the windowsill or in the garden, and think nothing of tossing in a handful of this or that herb to freshen up the flavor of their cooking. Herbs are added according to the individual cook's taste, and are seldom measured.

Marjoram

Basil

Basil
Basilico

The variety known as sweet basil is used in Italian cooking, and this is the one you are most likely to find in stores. It is used all over Italy, but most of all in Liguria, where it grows prolifically and is used in large quantities for pesto. Basil has a special affinity with tomatoes and is frequently used with them in sauces for pasta. It is best torn or shredded and added at the last moment. Fine chopping and long cooking spoil its pungent flavor.

Marjoram and Oregano
Maggiorana e Origano

These two herbs are closely related, but their flavors are quite different. Marjoram is sweet and delicate, while oregano, a wild variety of marjoram, is a pungent herb that should be used sparingly. They are both used in sauces for pasta, especially tomato-based ones, but marjoram is used more in Liguria and the north of Italy and oregano in the south, where it is perhaps best known for being sprinkled on pizza. Both marjoram and oregano are best chopped quite finely. They are sometimes used dried in the winter.

Mint
Mentuccia

Mint is not an herb usually associated with Italian cooking, but it is fre-

Mint

quently used in Roman dishes, in the cooking of central Italy, and even as far south as Calabria. Mentuccia is a particular kind of wild mint with small leaves grown in Rome, and there is also another variety called nepitella. You may come across the flavor of fresh mint in pasta soups, and very occasionally in sauces for pasta.

Parsley
Prezzemolo

Italians use the flat-leaf variety of parsley, which is also sold as Italian parsley. It looks very similar to cilantro, and has a stronger flavor than curly parsley. It is used frequently in sauces for pasta, in fairly large amounts, and is often roughly chopped and fried in olive oil with a *battuto* of onion and garlic at the beginning of sauce making. It is popular all over Italy and is only used fresh.

Oregano

Bay
Alloro/lauro
Both fresh and dried bay leaves are used all over Italy for flavoring soups and broths and long-cooking sauces, especially those made with meat, poultry and game. The leaves are removed before serving.

Bay leaves

Flat leaf parsley

Radicchio

Radicchio di Treviso

Radicchio di Verona

Radicchio

This ruby red and white salad leaf is a member of the chicory family. The most common variety, *radicchio di Verona*, is small and round with very tightly furled leaves, but there is another type called *radicchio di Treviso*, which is streaked creamy white and red with looser, long and tapering leaves. Both have a bitter flavor, which is much appreciated in small amounts in pasta sauces. Shredded leaves should be added at the last moment, to preserve their color.

Arugula

Arugula
Rucola

Peppery *rucola* loses its pungency when cooked, so it is added to pasta sauces at the last minute, or strewn liberally on top of pasta dishes just before serving. Bunches of large-leaved *rucola* from the greengrocer are best; the small packets sold at supermarkets are very expensive and seem to lack flavor. Use *rucola* as soon as possible after purchase because the leaves can quickly go limp and yellow, especially in warm weather.

Rosemary

Rosemary
Rosmarino

This most fragrant and pungent herb is very popular all over Italy. Rosemary is used sparingly in meat and tomato sauces, either very finely chopped or on the sprig, which is then removed from the sauce before serving. Dried rosemary is sometimes used in the winter months.

Sage
Salvia

Along with parsley, basil and rosemary, sage is one of Italy's favorite herbs. It is frequently used by Roman cooks who sizzle fresh sage in butter to create a classic sauce to serve with ravioli. Fresh sage leaves are also used with meat, sausage, poultry and game sauces, either finely shredded or chopped or as whole leaves, which are removed before serving. Fresh sage is preferred to dried, but dried sage is occasionally used in the winter, in sauces that are cooked for a long time.

Sage

Thyme
Timo

This aromatic and distinctively flavored herb is used both fresh and dried. It is a Mediterranean herb that goes well with tomato-based sauces and with meat and poultry, and it is also good mixed with rosemary and bay.

Thyme

SPICES AND SALT

Spicy, highly seasoned foods are not normally associated with Italian cooking, but the use of spices in cooking dates back to Roman—and even Etruscan—times, when spices were used freely, often to excess. Nowadays, spices tend to be used more sparingly and the range tends to be limited to a few favorites.

Dried chiles

Fresh chiles

Chile flakes

Chile
Peperoncino

Small red chiles are immensely popular in the south of Italy and Sardinia, and they are frequently used in sauces for pasta. Sometimes the sauce is a classic that depends on chiles for its essential flavor— the hot and spicy *Penne all'Arrabbiata* from Rome being perhaps the most famous. Most often, however, chiles are added more sparingly with the aim of livening up a sauce and intensifying its flavor rather than giving it a fiery punch.

Fresh chiles tend to be fried with a *soffritto* of olive oil, onion, garlic and parsley at the beginning of sauce making, whereas dried chiles are popped into the sauce when it is bubbling. Both fresh and dried chiles are often added whole to sauces in order to impart a subtle flavor. They are later lifted out and either discarded or chopped or crumbled, then returned to the sauce. The seeds may be included or left out, depending on the degree of heat required (the seeds contain most of the heat). Crushed dried red chiles or chile flakes (sold in little jars) are very handy when just a pinch or two of chile is required in a recipe.

Cinnamon
Cannella

Ground cinnamon is used in stuffings for pasta, both with meat and cheese. It gives a fragrant aroma and subtle sweetness and is always used sparingly.

Nutmeg
Noce moscata

Whole nutmeg is grated fresh when needed. It is used for flavoring *la beschiamella* (béchamel sauce) and is often used in combination with spinach and ricotta cheese. In Emilia-Romagna, it is traditionally used for flavoring meat sauces and stuffings for pasta.

Pepper
Pepe

Black peppercorns are ground fresh from a pepper mill as and when they are needed, both in cooking and at the table. Black pepper is used in just about every pasta sauce that is made, and it is also used to speckle and flavor homemade pasta. If coarsely crushed peppercorns are required, they are ground with a mortar and pestle.

Saffron
Zafferano

The most expensive spice in the world, saffron comes in two different forms. Threads of saffron, the actual dried stigmas of the crocus, are usually wrapped in cellophane and sold in sachets. They can be sprinkled into a sauce, but are more often soaked in warm water for 20–30 minutes, so that the water can be strained off and used for coloring and flavoring. Saffron powder is sold in sachets and can be sprinkled directly into sauces. It is less

Saffron

expensive than the threads and considered by many to be inferior, but it is more convenient to use. Saffron has a delicate but distinctive flavor, which is good with both cream and butter-based sauces as well as fish and shellfish. The spice is also used to color homemade pasta.

Salt
Sale

Coarse sea salt and rock salt are ground in a salt mill and used both as a seasoning in cooking and at the table. It is essential that salt is added to the water when boiling pasta to give it flavor, but for this you can use refined cooking salt rather than the more expensive sea or rock salt. Just about every pasta sauce will have salt as a seasoning, except perhaps those containing salty anchovies or bottarga (air-dried mullet or tuna roe).

Peppercorns (left) and sea salt

OILS AND VINEGARS

Oil and vinegar are essential pantry items for the Italian cook. Don't buy cheap brands; it's not worth it. Good olive oil and wine or balsamic vinegar will lift the flavor of a sauce or salad and enhance the other ingredients in it.

Olive oil
Olio d'oliva

Extra virgin olive oil is the best and most expensive of the olive oils. This is the oil that is secreted when the olives are crushed mechanically by cold presses.

No other processing or any heat is involved in the making of extra virgin olive oil. It should have an acidity level of one percent or less, but as this information is seldom on the label of the bottle, this is difficult to check.

Extra virgin is the oil to use for salads, since heating may spoil its natural olive flavor. It is also the one to use for sprinkling on warm food or for tossing with pasta in dishes, such as *Spaghetti Aglio e Olio*, that rely on olive oil for their predominant flavor.

Fruity, often peppery, Tuscan oil is reputed to be among the best of the extra virgin olive oils, although some cooks prefer oil from Umbria, or from Veneto or Liguria, which are more delicate. Oils from the South are stronger and more intensely flavored, and these may be more to your taste. Brands vary enormously, so experiment to find what suits you best.

For cooking and heating, virgin olive oil is the one to use. This is less expensive than extra virgin because it has a higher acidity

level (up to four percent), but it is cold pressed and not refined in any way so it still has a good, full flavor. Many pasta sauces start with the frying of flavoring ingredients, such as onion, garlic, celery, parsley, chiles and carrot. If these are fried in an oil with a good flavor, the sauce will have a strong base (*soffritto*), the flavor of which will then permeate through the other ingredients during cooking.

Vinegar
Aceto

Occasionally a splash of red or white wine vinegar may be added to a pasta sauce, but wine vinegar is more often used in salad dressings. Flavorwise, red and white vinegars are interchangeable, but the color of the salad ingredients may dictate whether you use red or white.

Balsamic vinegar (aceto balsamico) from Modena in Emilia-Romagna is a different thing altogether. It is a dark, syrupy vinegar that is aged in wooden casks for many years. The best and most authentic *aceto balsamico* will have been aged in casks or barrels of different woods for 40–50 years. Labeled *tradizionale di Modena*, this vinegar is only used a drop at a time, usually at the moment of serving, on fish or meat, salads and even fresh strawberries. For flavoring a pasta sauce or salad, use the much less expensive balsamic vinegar that has been aged between five and ten

Virgin olive oil (left), extra virgin olive oil (center) and balsamic vinegar (right)

years. Its flavor does not compare with the genuine article, but it is musky and slightly sweet, and very good.

FLAVORINGS

Some special ingredients are used in different regions of Italy, and you may need to buy them for a particular sauce.

Salted capers

Capers
Capperi

Capers bottled in brine

Capers are the fruit of a flowering shrub that grows in the Mediterranean. They are sold in various ways. The best are the large, salted capers sold in small jars at Italian markets. Check before buying that the salt is white and has not discolored at all. Yellow salt is a sign that the capers are past their best and may have a rancid taste. Before use, salted capers need to be soaked in several changes of water for 10–15 minutes, then drained, rinsed in fresh water and dried, but after this initial preparation they taste very fresh and good. They can be chopped and used to add piquancy to sauces—you will often find them in recipes from the south of Italy and Sicily and Sardinia.

It is also possible to buy tiny capers sold in small bottles of brine or vinegar. These have a strong flavor and should be rinsed well before use. Despite this, they almost always taste sharp and vinegary, so chop them very finely and use them sparingly.

Olives

Olive

Both black and green olives are used in making sauces and salads, although black olives are more highly favored. The best type for pasta sauces are the small, shiny, very black *gaeta* olives from Liguria. Buy the plain ones for cooking, not those with additional flavorings, such as herbs, garlic, chiles and other spices, which are intended for antipasto. Olives are best added to a sauce toward the end of cooking. They need no cooking, only heating through, and if added too early they can impart a bitter flavor. When using olives in a pasta sauce or salad, pit them first, because the pits are awkward to manage when you are eating pasta.

Olives

Pancetta

Pancetta

This is cured belly of pork, the Italian equivalent of bacon, which has a spicy, sweet flavor and aroma. Unsmoked pancetta is sold in a roll at Italian deli-catessens, and is called pancetta arrotolata or pancetta coppata. A machine is used to slice it very thinly to order and it can be eaten as it is for an antipasto, or cut into strips or diced for use in cooking. Pancetta affumicata is smoked and comes in strips, which look like bacon complete

*Smoked (left) and
unsmoked pancetta*

with rind. There is a version called pancetta stesa, which is long and flat. Smoked pancetta is cut into strips or dice and used as the base for ragù and many other pasta sauces, the most famous of which is carbonara. Some supermarkets sell packages of diced pancetta. The quality and flavor are generally good, so these are well worth buying for convenience. If you are unable to get pancetta, bacon can be used instead, and you can buy smoked or unsmoked, whichever flavor you prefer.

Pine nuts

Pinoli

Best known for their inclusion in pesto, these small, creamy white nuts have an unusual waxy texture and resinous flavor. They look and taste good sprinkled on pasta salads, and they add a welcome crunchy bite. To enhance their flavor, they are often toasted before use. Only buy the amount of pine nuts you need because they do not keep well and quickly go rancid. They are sold shelled in small packages at many super-markets.

Pine nuts

FISH AND SHELLFISH

Pasta sauces made with fish or shellfish are quick and delicious. Fresh seafood is often the main ingredient, but there are a few other staples that are used over and over again.

Anchovies

Acciughe

The best anchovies are the salted ones that are packed in large cans. You see them on the counters of Italian markets, where they are sold loose by the pound. They must be rinsed, skinned and filleted before use, but

are plumper and more flavorsome than the fillets sold in jars and cans, so repay the effort. Anchovies are used in sauces for pasta all over Italy, but particularly in the hot South and in Sicily and Sardinia where strong and salty flavors are so popular. When chopped and heated gently with a little olive oil, they melt down to a creamy paste that is packed with flavor, so you only

Anchovies in brine (left) and salt

need to use a small amount at a time. If you can't get salted anchovies, try to locate anchovy fillets that are bottled in olive oil. These taste better than the ones canned in vegetable oil.

Bottarga

Bottarga

This is the salted and air-dried roe of mullet or tuna. The best is the mullet, bottarga di muggine. It is a great delicacy in Sardinia, Sicily and the Veneto, where they like it grated over pasta or very thinly sliced as an antipasto with lemon juice and olive oil. You can buy bottarga quite easily at Italian markets, where it is kept in vacuum packs in the refrigerator. Mullet bottarga is delicate, moist and golden, like a pale, thin version of smoked cod's roe, and bears little resem-blance to tuna bottarga, which comes in a thick, dark block. For grating over pasta you

Tuna bottarga

Grated bottarga

Mullet bottarga

Canned tuna

tender texture and sweet flavor, which make them ideal for pasta sauces. Don't be tempted to buy the large ones. Some fishmongers sell frozen small clams, which are a good substitute for fresh; otherwise, you should buy the bottled shelled clams in natural juice that are sold at Italian markets Check labels carefully and don't buy the ones in vinegar or brine—these are intended for antipasto; their sharp flavor will spoil a pasta sauce. You can also buy bottled clams in their shells. These are packed in oil and, although intended primarily for antipasto, they also make an attractive garnish for a clam sauce.

Squid ink
Nero di seppia
If you want to color homemade pasta black, you can buy handy little sachets of squid ink at fishmongers and Italian markets and delicatessens. There is usually about 4 grams of ink in each sachet, and the sachets are sold in pairs. Two sachets are enough to color a 3-egg batch of pasta all'uovo.

Tuna
Tonno
For pasta sauces, use only best-quality canned tuna in olive oil, not the kind packed in vegetable oil, water or brine. Some large supermarkets sell it; otherwise you will have to go to an Italian market. The flesh of good-quality tuna is moist and meaty; inferior brands are watery and tasteless. The cost of a good can of tuna is generally less than that of fresh fish, poultry or meat, so no matter how much you spend on it, pasta with a tuna sauce will still be an inexpensive meal.

VEGETABLES
Tomatoes are not the only vegetable to be used in sauces for pasta. Many others play an important part, either as a main ingredient or in a more minor role. Dried vegetables, such as porcini mushrooms, peppers and tomatoes, are used almost as often as fresh; valued for the intense flavour they impart to sauces and soups.

Dried grilled eggplant

Eggplant
Melanzane
Fresh eggplant is used as a main ingredient in many pasta sauces, especially in southern Italy, Sicily and Sardinia. Dried eggplant is not used as a substitute for fresh, but is added to fresh vegetables for its characteristic earthy flavor and meaty texture. Sold in cellophane packages, they are thin slices of eggplant that have been dried in the sun, and are a good pantry item, in that you can use as few or as many as you like. They need to be rehydrated in boiling water with a splash of white wine vinegar for 2 minutes before use, then drained and dried. They can then be snipped into strips and either added immediately to a simmering pasta sauce or fried first in olive oil.

need only a small amount and it can be kept in the refrigerator for a long time (check the use-by date). You can also buy grated bottarga in small jars, but this product has a dry texture, and the flavor does not compare with that of freshly grated bottarga.

Clams
Vongole
In Italy, small fresh clams are frequently used in pasta sauces on the coast and in Sicily and Sardinia, but they are not always easy to get in other parts of the country or further afield. Names vary from one region and one country to another, but the name is not important; it is the size that counts. Small *vongole* cook quickly and have a

Fresh clams (left) and canned clams

Garlic
Aglio

Crushed, sliced and chopped garlic is used in many pasta sauces, but especially in those from the south of Italy, and whole garlic cloves are sometimes fried in olive oil at the beginning of cooking, then removed to leave behind a subtly flavored base for a sauce. One famous Roman pasta dish, *Spaghetti Aglio e Olio*, holds garlic in such high esteem that the sauce contains only two ingredients—garlic and olive oil—and in Rome they maintain it is the best cure for a hangover. The best Italian garlic is pink or purple tinged, with plump juicy cloves. In spring and early summer you can buy it fresh at some greengrocers and Italian markets

Garlic

This is the newly picked garlic that is sweet, moist and mild. As it dries out it becomes more pungent, so you need to adjust quantities accordingly. Buy garlic little and often so it neither sprouts green shoots nor becomes papery and dry.

Porcini mushrooms
Funghi porcini

Dried porcini (*boletus edulis*) are invaluable for the intense, musky aroma and flavor they impart to pasta sauces and soups. Italians use them all year round, not as a substitute for fresh porcini, but as a valued ingredient in its own right. A few dried porcini added to ordinary fresh mushrooms, for example, will give them the flavor of wild mushrooms. Don't buy cheap porcini, but look for packets containing large pale-colored pieces. Although they will seem expensive, a little goes a long way, and 15–25g/¹/₂–1oz is the most you will need in a recipe that serves

Dried porcini mushrooms

4–6 people. Before use, dried porcini must be reconstituted in warm water for 15–20 minutes. Drain, rinse and squeeze dry, then slice or chop as required. Don't throw the soaking liquid away. Strain it to remove any grit and use it in soups and stocks, or add it to the water when cooking pasta to impart a mushroomy flavor—this is especially effective with fresh pasta.

Peppers
Peperoni

Sun-dried red peppers are sold in cellophane packets. They resemble sun-dried tomatoes, but their flavor is more peppery

Bottled roasted peppers

and piquant. They are used in the same way as tomatoes, to add a firm meaty bite to sauces and soups, especially those made with vegetables. Before use they should be rinsed under the cold tap, then dried and cut into thin strips or chopped.

Roasted peppers can be bought loose or in jars, packed in olive oil or brine. Although you can easily roast fresh peppers yourself when you need them, it is handy to keep a jar of commercially roasted peppers in the refrigerator. Just one piece of roasted pepper, sliced or chopped, will add a wonderful smoky flavor to pasta sauces, salads and soups. The best ones come from Italian markets where the peppers are grilled by hand and sold loose in extra virgin olive oil.

Dried peppers

Tomatoes
Pomodori

In summer, when fresh Italian plum tomatoes are ripe and full of flavor, it is wonderful to use these for sauce making, but at other times of the year you will get a much better flavor and color by using preserved tomatoes.

There are plenty of excellent tomato products to choose from, most of which come from southern Italy, where the hot sun ripens the tomatoes on the vine to an incomparable flavor.

Canned peeled plum tomatoes (pomodori pelati) come whole and chopped. Don't buy cheap brands; instead, opt for the top-quality Italian brands,

Chopped canned plum tomatoes

Filetti di pomodoro (plum tomatoes in water and salt)

naturale in water and salt. They are about the nearest thing you can get to bottling tomatoes yourself at home, which Italians do in summer to preserve surplus tomatoes for winter use. Crushed tomatoes come in many guises, and are a real boon for sauce making because they take all the hard work out of peeling, seeding and chopping. They are plum tomatoes that have been mechanically peeled and crushed, then sieved to remove the seeds. You can choose from passata, which is quite smooth, to polpa and sugocasa, which are quite chunky.

Bottles and jars of these products are good in that they allow you to see what you are buying. Cartons of very smooth passata take up less room and are lighter to carry; they are very popular with Italian cooks for making almost instant sauces.

Sun-dried tomatoes (pomodori secchi) are sold in two different forms—as dry pieces and in oil. Both types are piquant in flavor, but the dry pieces have a chewier texture than those in oil. Dried tomatoes are sold in cellophane packages and can be snipped directly into a long-cooking pasta sauce to intensify its tomato flavor, but generally they are best if softened in hot water for 2–3 hours before use. Sun-dried tomatoes in oil are sold in jars and can also be bought loose at some markets. For the best flavor, buy the ones in olive oil. They are soft and juicy and can be used as they are, either sliced or chopped, in sauces and salads.

Sun-dried tomato paste is a thick mixture of sun-dried tomatoes and olive oil. It can be used on its own as a quick sauce for pasta or added by the spoonful to tomato sauces to color and enrich them.

Although thick in texture, the flavor of sun-dried tomato paste is sweet and mild compared with tomato paste, and the color is paler.

especially those that identify the tomatoes as San Marzano on the label. If you ask at your local Italian market, they will give you good advice. Plain chopped tomatoes are a good buy because they save you from having to chop them yourself, but they are slightly more expensive. If they are labeled polpa di pomodoro, they are likely to be very finely chopped or even crushed. Flavorings, such as garlic and herbs, should be added fresh, so don't buy chopped canned tomatoes containing these.

Filetti di pomodoro are sold in jars at good Italian markets and specialty food stores. These are plum tomatoes that have been halved or quartered and bottled *al*

Sun-dried tomatoes bottled in oil (top), and dry pieces

Tomato paste or concentrate (concentrato di pomodoro) is a very strong, thick paste made commercially from tomatoes, salt and citric acid. You can buy it in tubes, jars or cans, and its strength varies according to the manufacturer.

Clockwise from left, sugocasa, polpa and passata

Get to know the brand you like because some are quite bitter and sharp, and can overwhelm other flavors in a sauce. Only use tomato paste in small amounts or it may make a dish too acidic. A way to counteract acidity is to add a pinch or two or a lump of sugar.

Sun-dried tomato paste (left) and tomato paste

Cheese and Cream

Italy's magnificent cheeses are famous all over the world, both as table cheeses and for their use in cooking. Many of them are used in sauces for pasta, in fillings for stuffed pasta and in baked dishes.

Fontina

Fontina

A mountain cheese from the Val d'Aosta in the northwest of Italy, fontina is used in baked pasta dishes, such as lasagne. It has superb melting qualities and a wonderful nutty, slightly sweet flavor. Some large supermarkets sell it; otherwise you can get it at specialty and cheese stores.

Gorgonzola

This blue-veined cheese comes from Lombardy. Although it is a table cheese, it melts quickly and well, so it is good in sauces and stuffed pasta, and its sharp flavor tastes very good combined with cream and leafy greens, such as spinach, sorrel and

Gorgonzola

herbs. Gorgonzola piccante is the very strong version, while dolcelatte is milder and sweeter, almost buttery.

Mascarpone

This is a full-fat cream cheese with a smooth silky texture, often used in pasta

Mascarpone

sauces instead of cream. It melts without curdling and has a slightly tangy flavor. It is widely available in tubs in at Italian markets and supermarkets.

Mozzarella

A soft white cheese, which is used in both salads and cooking, mozzarella melts quickly in hot sauces to serve with pasta, but must not be overcooked or it may become stringy. The whey should be drained off and discarded before the cheese is used. By

Mozzarella

tradition mozzarella should be made with buffalo's milk, but today it is often made with cow's or sheep's milk. Buy only the type that is swimming in whey in little bags—blocks of mozzarella are rubbery and tasteless. Mozzarella di bufala has the best texture and the most flavor, but it is more expensive than cow's or sheep's milk mozzarella and not so easy to find.

Parmesan

Grated Parmesan is most often used for sprinkling on pasta at the table, although it is also tossed with pasta after draining or added to sauces at the end of cooking. Genuine Parmigiano Reggiano has its name stamped on the rind and comes only from the area between Parma, Modena, Reggio-Emilia, Bologna and Mantua. It must be aged

for a minimum of 2 years, which is one of the reasons why it is so costly. Grana Padano is a similar, less expensive, cheese, which is used in the same way as Parmigiano Reggiano. Both are excellent melting cheeses, but Reggiano has a milder,

Pecorino (left) and Parmigiano Reggiano

less salty flavor and its texture is more flaky. Never buy these cheeses pre-grated. Buy them in a block and grate when you need, or shave into curls with a vegetable peeler.

Pecorino

This salty, hard sheep's milk cheese is called Pecorino Romano if it comes from Lazio, and Pecorino Sardo if it is Sardinian. It is used for grating in the same way as Parmesan, but because its flavor is sharper, it is used with the strong-tasting and spicy sauces associated with southern Italian and Sardinian cooking.

Ricotta salata (right) and ricotta

Enhancing Commercial Sauces

There are lots of bottled sauces for serving with pasta, ranging from chopped tomato sugocasa to classics, such as vongole, arrabbiata and alfredo , as well as unusual combinations of ingredients created by individual manufacturers. Generally speaking, it is best to stick to the Italian brands that are sold at supermarkets because these are the ones that Italians keep in their own pantries for times when they want to serve pasta at a moment's notice. You can use these sauces just as they are, but they will taste more homemade if you enliven them by adding something fresh.

Pesto
Both classic basil pesto and red pesto—made using sun-dried tomatoes—are available in jars and are useful pantry standbys. Grate a little fresh Parmesan cheese over the pasta before tossing with the pesto, and add a spoonful or two of extra virgin olive oil for a more fruity flavor. For a richer pesto sauce, add a spoonful or two of mascarpone cheese or cream (*below left*). Just before serving, sprinkle the pasta with more freshly grated Parmesan or with toasted pine nuts or shredded basil leaves.

Sugocasa/Chopped tomatoes
Add a little sun-dried tomato paste and/or a splash of red or white wine when heating up sugocasa, and season well with salt and ground black pepper. If you like a creamy tomato sauce, add up to $2/3$ cup *panna da cucina*, heavy cream or crème fraîche. For a spicy kick, add a sprinkling of crushed dried red chiles. Finish the sauce with a small handful of shredded fresh basil or rocket, or use 1–2 tablespoons chopped fresh marjoram or oregano.

Arrabbiata
Strew a generous handful of finely shredded arugula leaves on top of the tossed pasta and sauce just before serving.

Alfredo
Stir a few spoonfuls of fresh cream into the sauce while it is heating up, then top with thin shavings of Parmesan cheese once the sauce and pasta have been tossed together.

Vongole
Add a splash of wine, some chopped fresh parsley and garlic. You can add all of these ingredients or just one or two of them. A few pitted and sliced black olives also look and taste good with a vongole sauce.

Ricotta
Fresh ricotta is a very soft white cheese, sold loose by the pound at Italian markets. It has superb melting qualities and is used in fillings for stuffed and baked pasta dishes, and for tossing with fresh raw vegetables, such as tomatoes, spinach and arugula, for uncooked sauces. Ricotta is low in fat and has a bland flavor, so it goes well with flavorful ingredients, such as herbs and garlic. Fresh ricotta does not keep well, so check before buying and only buy it if it is snowy white in color. If not, it is better to buy the ricotta sold in tubs—these are widely available at supermarkets. Ricotta salata is a hard, salted version of ricotta, cut from the block at Italian markets. It too is very white and low in fat. Ricotta salata is used for grating or crumbling over soups and pasta, especially in the south of Italy. You will find it saltier than Parmesan, Grana Padano or pecorino, so will need less.

Cream
Panna da cucina
For creamy pasta sauces, Italians use a type of cream called panna da cucina (cream for cooking). It is sold in little tubs, often joined together in pairs. Each tub contains a scant $1/2$ cup, which is enough to make a

Panna da cucina

pasta sauce to serve 4 people. Panna da cucina is a long-life product, so it is well worth buying to keep in the pantry for making impromptu sauces. It is available in Italian markets.

Pasta Recipes

Pasta proves its enormous versatility in this section. There are 150 recipes, plus many variations, and since there are very few hard-and-fast rules with sauces for pasta you can personalize them to your heart's content—and make even more. The recipes in the Broths and Soups chapter range from clear light liquids supporting delicate pieces of pasta to chunky soups that are meals in themselves. Tomato Sauces can be smooth and subtle, fiery or hearty, while Cream Sauces are deliciously rich and luxurious, and unbelievably quick to make. The Fish and Shellfish recipes have fabulous flavors, and some of which are surprisingly spicy and strong. They make good first courses and after-work suppers, as do the recipes in Meat and Poultry, many of which you will recognize as traditional and regional favorites. In Vegetables and Vegetarian, some of the recipes are classic, but most are new. They're quick and easy, colorful and light, and they look and taste absolutely stunning. There's a choice of both family favorites and dinner party dishes in Baked Pasta, while in the Stuffed Pasta chapter you can have fun making your own dough. You'll be amazed how easy it is, and delighted with the results too. The chapter devoted to Fresh and Healthy recipes proves the point that pasta not only looks and tastes good, but it's nutritionally sound too, something that can also be said of pretty Pasta Salads, the final section of the book.

Broths
and
Soups

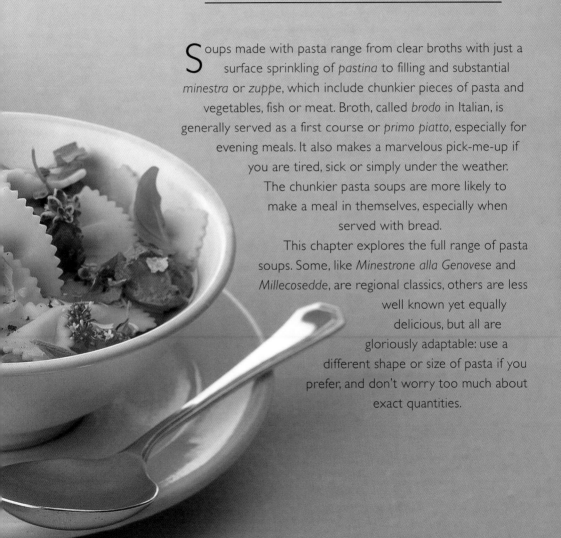

Soups made with pasta range from clear broths with just a surface sprinkling of *pastina* to filling and substantial *minestra* or *zuppe*, which include chunkier pieces of pasta and vegetables, fish or meat. Broth, called *brodo* in Italian, is generally served as a first course or *primo piatto*, especially for evening meals. It also makes a marvelous pick-me-up if you are tired, sick or simply under the weather. The chunkier pasta soups are more likely to make a meal in themselves, especially when served with bread.

This chapter explores the full range of pasta soups. Some, like *Minestrone alla Genovese* and *Millecosedde*, are regional classics, others are less well known yet equally delicious, but all are gloriously adaptable: use a different shape or size of pasta if you prefer, and don't worry too much about exact quantities.

Broths and Soups

Little Stuffed Hats in Broth

THIS SOUP IS SERVED in northern Italy on Santo Stefano (St Stephen's Day—December 26th) and on New Year's Day. It makes a welcome light change from all the special celebration food the day before. In Italy, the stock is traditionally made with the Christmas capon carcass.

INGREDIENTS

5 cups chicken stock
1 cup fresh or dried cappelletti
2 tablespoons dry white wine (optional)
about 1 tablespoon finely chopped fresh
    Italian parsley (optional)
salt and ground black pepper
about 2 tablespoons freshly grated
    Parmesan cheese, to serve
shredded Italian parsley, to garnish
Serves 4

1 Pour the chicken stock into a large pot and bring to a boil. Add a little salt and pepper to taste, then drop in the pasta.

2 Stir well and bring back to a boil. Lower the heat to a simmer and cook according to the instructions on the package, until the pasta is *al dente*. Stir frequently during cooking to make sure the pasta cooks evenly.

3 Swirl in the wine and parsley, if using, then taste for seasoning. Ladle into four warmed soup plates, then sprinkle with grated Parmesan and Italian parsley. Serve immediately.

COOK'S TIP

Cappelletti is just another name for tortellini, which come from Romagna. You can buy them or make your own.

Tiny Pasta in Broth

IN ITALY THIS SOUP is often served with bread for a light evening supper.

INGREDIENTS

5 cups beef stock
3/4 cup tiny soup pasta, e.g. funghetti
2 pieces bottled roasted red pepper,
    about 2 ounces
salt and ground black pepper
coarsely shaved Parmesan cheese, to serve
Serves 4

COOK'S TIP

Stock cubes are not really suitable for a recipe like this in which the flavor of the broth is so important. If you don't have time to make your own stock, use two 11-ounce cans condensed beef consommé, adding water as instructed on the labels.

1 Bring the beef stock to a boil in a large pot. Add salt and pepper to taste, then drop in the soup pasta. Stir well and bring the stock back to a boil.

2 Lower the heat to a simmer and cook until the pasta is *al dente*: 7–8 minutes or according to the package instructions. Stir frequently during cooking to prevent the pasta shapes from sticking together.

3 Drain the pieces of roasted pepper and dice them finely. Place them in the bottom of four warmed soup plates. Taste the soup for seasoning. Ladle into the soup plates and serve immediately, with shavings of Parmesan passed separately.

VARIATION

You can use other tiny soup pasta in place of the funghetti.

Genoese Minestrone

IN GENOA they often make minestrone like this, with pesto stirred
in toward the end of cooking. It is
packed full of vegetables and has a
good strong flavor, making it an
excellent vegetarian supper dish
when served with bread. There is
Parmesan cheese in the pesto, so
there is no need to serve extra
with the soup.

INGREDIENTS

1 onion

2 celery stalks

1 large carrot

3 tablespoons olive oil

5 ounces green beans, cut into
2-inch pieces

1 zucchini, thinly sliced

1 potato, cut into $^1/_2$-inch cubes

$^1/_4$ Savoy cabbage, shredded

1 small eggplant, cut into $^1/_2$-inch cubes

1 can (7 ounces) cannellini beans, drained
and rinsed

2 Italian plum tomatoes, chopped

5 cups vegetable stock

$3^1/_2$ ounces spaghetti or vermicelli

salt and ground black pepper

For the pesto

about 20 fresh basil leaves

1 garlic clove

2 teaspoons pine nuts

1 tablespoon freshly grated
Parmesan cheese

1 tablespoon freshly grated pecorino cheese

2 tablespoons olive oil

Serves 4–6

1 Chop the onion, celery and carrot
finely, either in a food processor or
by hand. Heat the oil in a large
saucepan, add the chopped mixture
and cook over low heat, stirring
frequently, for 5–7 minutes.

2 Mix in the green beans, zucchini,
potato and cabbage. Stir-fry over
medium heat for about 3 minutes. Add
the eggplant, cannellini beans and
tomatoes, and stir-fry for 2–3 minutes
more. Pour in the stock with salt and
pepper to taste. Bring to a boil. Stir well,
cover and lower the heat. Simmer for
40 minutes, stirring occasionally.

3 Meanwhile, process all the pesto
ingredients in a food processor
until the mixture forms a smooth
sauce, adding 1–3 tablespoons water
through the feeder tube if necessary.

4 Break the pasta into small pieces
and add it to the soup. Simmer,
stirring frequently, for 5 minutes. Add
the pesto sauce and stir it in well,
then simmer for 2–3 minutes more,
or until the pasta is *al dente*. Taste for
seasoning. Serve hot, in warmed soup
plates or bowls.

COOK'S TIP

*If you are in a hurry, use the pesto in jars
which can be found in most supermarkets—the traditional green basil pesto
rather than the red sun-dried tomato
pesto. You will need about 3 tablespoons.*

Minestrone Ricco

Rich Minestrone

THIS IS A SPECIAL minestrone made with chicken. Served with crusty Italian bread, it makes a hearty meal.

INGREDIENTS

1 tablespoon olive oil

2 chicken thighs

3 lean bacon strips, chopped

1 onion, finely chopped

a few fresh basil leaves, shredded

a few fresh rosemary leaves,
  finely chopped

1 tablespoon chopped fresh Italian parsley

2 potatoes, cut into $^1/_2$-inch cubes

1 large carrot, cut into $^1/_2$-inch cubes

2 small zucchinis, cut into $^1/_2$-inch cubes

1–2 celery stalks, cut into $^1/_2$-inch cubes

4 cups chicken stock

1$^3/_4$ cups frozen peas

scant 1 cup stellette or
  other tiny soup pasta

salt and ground black pepper

coarsely shaved Parmesan cheese, to serve

fresh basil leaves, to garnish

Serves 4–6

1 Heat the oil in a large frying pan, add the chicken thighs and fry for about 5 minutes on each side. Remove with a slotted spoon and set aside.

3 Return the chicken thighs to the pan, add the stock and bring to a boil. Cover and cook over low heat for 35–40 minutes, stirring the soup occasionally.

2 Lower the heat, add the bacon, onion and herbs to the pan and stir well. Cook gently, stirring constantly, for about 5 minutes. Add all the vegetables, except the frozen peas, and cook for 5–7 minutes more, stirring frequently.

4 Remove the chicken thighs with a slotted spoon and place them on a board. Stir the peas and pasta into the soup and bring back to a boil. Simmer, stirring frequently, until the pasta is *al dente*: 7–8 minutes or according to the instructions on the package.

5 Meanwhile, remove and discard the chicken skin, then remove the meat from the bones and cut it into $^1/_2$-inch pieces. Return the meat to the soup and heat through. Taste for seasoning. Serve hot in soup bowls; sprinkle over Parmesan shavings and garnish with one or two basil leaves.

COOK'S TIP

For extra flavor, add any Parmesan rind to the simmering soup.

Millecosedde

Pasta, Bean and Vegetable Soup

THIS IS A CALABRIAN speciality. The name comes from the Italian word *millecose*, meaning "a thousand things". Literally anything edible can go in this soup. In Calabria they include a bean called *cicerchia* that is peculiar to the region.

INGREDIENTS

scant ¹/2 cup brown lentils
¹/2 ounce dried mushrooms
4 tablespoons olive oil
1 carrot, diced
1 celery stalk, diced
1 onion, finely chopped
1 garlic clove, finely chopped
a little chopped fresh Italian parsley
a good pinch of crushed red chiles (optional)
6¹/4 cups vegetable stock homemade, or
    with stock cubes
scant 1 cup each canned red kidney beans,
    cannellini beans and chickpeas, rinsed
    and drained
1 cup small pasta shapes, e.g. rigatoni,
    penne or penne rigate
salt and ground black pepper
freshly grated pecorino cheese, to serve
chopped Italian parsley, to garnish

Serves 4–6

1 Put the lentils in a medium saucepan, add 2 cups water and bring to a boil over high heat. Lower the heat to a gentle simmer and cook, stirring occasionally, for 15–20 minutes or until the lentils are just tender. Meanwhile, soak the dried mushrooms in ³/4 cup warm water for 15–20 minutes.

2 Turn the lentils into a strainer to drain, then rinse under the cold tap. Drain the soaked mushrooms and reserve the soaking liquid. Finely chop the mushrooms and set aside.

3 Heat the oil in a large saucepan and add the carrot, celery, onion, garlic, parsley and chiles, if using. Cook over low heat, stirring constantly, for 5–7 minutes.

4 Add the stock, then the mushrooms and their soaking liquid. Bring to a boil, then add the beans, chickpeas and lentils, with salt and pepper to taste. Cover, and simmer gently for 20 minutes.

5 Add the pasta and bring the soup back to a boil, stirring. Simmer, stirring frequently, until the pasta is *al dente*: 7–8 minutes or according to the instructions on the package. Season, then serve hot in soup bowls, with grated pecorino and chopped parsley.

COOK'S TIP

If you like, you can freeze the soup at the end of Step 4. To serve, thaw and bring to a boil, then add the pasta and simmer until it is just tender.

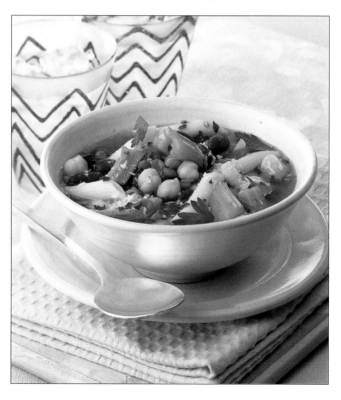

Zuppa di Vongole e Pastina

Clam and Pasta Soup

SUBTLY SWEET AND SPICY, this soup is substantial enough to be served on its own for lunch or supper. A crusty Italian loaf such as pugliese is the ideal accompaniment.

INGREDIENTS

2 tablespoons olive oil

1 onion, finely chopped

leaves from 1 fresh or dried thyme sprig, chopped, plus extra to garnish

2 garlic cloves, crushed

5–6 fresh basil leaves, plus extra to garnish

1/4–1/2 teaspoon crushed red chiles, to taste

4 cups fish stock

1 1/2 cups tomato sauce

1 teaspoon granulated sugar

scant 1 cup frozen peas

2/3 cup small pasta shapes, e.g. chifferini

8 ounces frozen shelled clams

salt and ground black pepper

Serves 4–6

1 Heat the oil in a large saucepan, add the onion and cook gently for about 5 minutes until softened, but not colored. Add the thyme, then stir in the garlic, basil leaves and chiles.

2 Add the stock, tomato sauce and sugar to the saucepan, with salt and pepper to taste. Bring to a boil, then lower the heat and simmer gently, stirring occasionally, for 15 minutes. Add the frozen peas and cook for another 5 minutes.

3 Add the pasta to the stock mixture and bring to a boil, stirring. Lower the heat and simmer, stirring frequently, until the pasta is only just *al dente*: about 5 minutes or according to the package instructions.

4 Turn the heat down to low, add the frozen or bottled clams and heat through for 2–3 minutes. Taste for seasoning. Serve hot in warmed bowls, garnished with basil and thyme.

COOK'S TIP

Frozen shelled clams are available at good fishmarkets and supermarkets; if you can't get them, use bottled or canned clams in natural juice (not vinegar). These both look and taste delicious and they are not too expensive. For a special occasion, stir some into the soup.

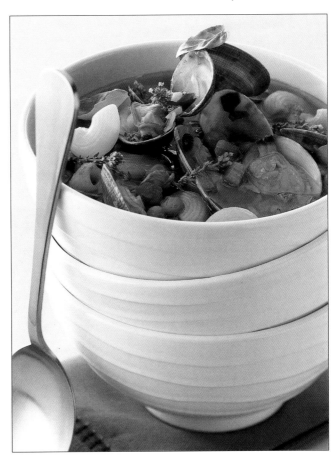

Minestrone di Orecchiette e Broccoli

Broccoli, Anchovy and Pasta Soup

THIS SOUP IS FROM PUGLIA in the south of Italy, where anchovies and broccoli are often used together.

INGREDIENTS

2 tablespoons olive oil

1 small onion, finely chopped

1 garlic clove, finely chopped

1/4–1/3 fresh red chile, seeded and
  finely chopped

2 drained canned anchovies

scant 1 cup tomato sauce

3 tablespoons dry white wine

5 cups vegetable stock

2 cups broccoli florets

1 3/4 cups orecchiette

salt and ground black pepper

freshly grated pecorino cheese,
  to serve

Serves 4

1 Heat the oil in a large saucepan. Add the onion, garlic, chile and anchovies and cook over low heat, stirring constantly, for 5–6 minutes.

2 Add the tomato sauce and wine, with salt and pepper to taste. Bring to a boil, cover the pan, then cook over low heat, stirring occasionally, for 12–15 minutes.

3 Pour in the stock. Bring to a boil, then add the broccoli and simmer for about 5 minutes. Add the pasta and bring back to a boil, stirring. Simmer, stirring frequently, until the pasta is *al dente*: 7–8 minutes or according to the instructions on the package. Taste for seasoning. Serve hot, in warmed bowls. Pass grated pecorino separately.

Brodo di Quadrucci e Piselli

Pasta Squares and Peas in Broth

THIS THICK SOUP IS FROM LAZIO, where it is traditionally made with fresh homemade pasta and peas. In this modern version, ready-made pasta is used with frozen peas, to save time.

INGREDIENTS

2 tablespoons butter

2 ounces pancetta or lean bacon,
  coarsely chopped

1 small onion, finely chopped

1 celery stalk, finely chopped

3 1/2 cups frozen peas

1 teaspoon tomato paste

1–2 teaspoons finely chopped fresh
  Italian parsley

4 cups chicken stock

11 ounces fresh lasagne sheets

about 2 ounces prosciutto
  (crudo if available), cut into cubes

salt and ground black pepper

freshly grated Parmesan cheese, to serve

Serves 4–6

1 Melt the butter in a large saucepan and add the pancetta or bacon, with the onion and celery. Cook over low heat, stirring constantly, for 5 minutes.

2 Add the peas and cook, stirring, for 3–4 minutes. Stir in the tomato paste and parsley, then add the chicken stock, with salt and pepper to taste. Bring to a boil. Cover, lower the heat and simmer for 10 minutes. Meanwhile, cut the lasagne sheets into 3/4-inch squares.

3 Taste the stock for seasoning. Drop in the pasta, stir and bring to a boil. Simmer for 2–3 minutes or until the pasta is *al dente*, then stir in the prosciutto. Serve hot in warmed bowls, with grated Parmesan passed separately.

COOK'S TIP

Take care when adding salt, because of the saltiness of the pancetta and the prosciutto.

Bean and Pasta Soup

THIS HEARTY MAIN MEAL soup sometimes goes by the simpler name of *Pasta e Fagioli*, while some Italians refer to it as *Minestrone di Pasta e Fagioli*. Traditional country recipes use dried beans and a ham bone, and require the soup to be cooked for a long time.

INGREDIENTS

1 onion
1 carrot
1 celery stalk
2 tablespoons olive oil
4 ounces pancetta or lean bacon, diced
7¹/₂ cups beef stock
1 cinnamon stick or a good pinch of
  ground cinnamon
scant 1 cup pasta shapes,
  e.g. conchiglie or corallini
1 can (14 ounces) borlotti beans, rinsed
  and drained, or see substitute below
1 thick slice cooked ham, about
  8 ounces, diced
salt and ground black pepper
coarsely shaved Parmesan cheese, to serve

Serves 4–6

1 Chop the vegetables. Heat the oil in a large saucepan, add the pancetta or bacon and cook, stirring, until lightly colored. Add the chopped vegetable mixture to the pan and cook for about 10 minutes, stirring frequently, until lightly colored. Pour in the stock, add the cinnamon with salt and pepper to taste, and bring to a boil. Cover and simmer gently for 15–20 minutes.

2 Add the pasta. Bring back to a boil, stirring constantly. Lower the heat and simmer, stirring frequently, for 5 minutes. Add the beans and diced ham and simmer until the pasta is *al dente*: 2–3 minutes or according to the instructions on the package.

3 Taste the soup for seasoning. Serve hot in warmed bowls, sprinkled with shavings of Parmesan.

VARIATIONS

• *Use spaghetti or tagliatelle instead of the small pasta shapes, breaking it into small pieces over the pan.*
• *Use cannellini or small navy beans instead of the borlotti. Alternatively, use dried beans that have been soaked, drained and boiled for 1 hour or until tender. Add them to the pan after the stock in Step 1.*
• *If you like, add 1 tablespoon tomato sauce or tomato paste or 1 large ripe tomato, peeled and chopped, with the beans and diced ham.*

Minestrone di Pasta e Ceci

Pasta and Chickpea Soup

A SIMPLE, COUNTRY-STYLE soup. The
shapes of the pasta and the beans
complement each other beautifully.

INGREDIENTS

1 onion
2 carrots
2 celery stalks
4 tablespoons olive oil
*1 can (14 ounces) chickpeas, rinsed
  and drained*
*1 can (7 ounces) cannellini beans, rinsed
  and drained*
2/3 cup tomato sauce
1/2 cup water
6 1/4 cups vegetable or chicken stock
2 fresh or dried rosemary sprigs
scant 2 cups conchiglie
salt and ground black pepper
freshly grated Parmesan cheese, to serve

Serves 4–6

1 Chop the onion, carrots and celery
finely, either in a food processor or
by hand.

2 Heat the oil in a large saucepan,
add the chopped vegetable
mixture and cook over low heat,
stirring frequently, for 5–7 minutes.

3 Add the chickpeas and cannellini
beans, stir well to mix, then cook
for 5 minutes. Stir in the tomato sauce
and water. Cook, stirring, for 2–3 minutes.

4 Add 2 cups of the stock, one of
the rosemary sprigs and salt and
pepper to taste. Bring to a boil, cover,
then simmer gently, stirring occasionally,
for 1 hour.

5 Pour in the remaining stock, add
the pasta and bring to a boil,
stirring. Lower the heat and simmer,
stirring frequently, until the pasta is
al dente: 7–8 minutes or according to
the instructions on the package. Taste
for seasoning. Remove the rosemary
sprig and serve the soup hot, in
warmed bowls, topped with grated
Parmesan and a few rosemary leaves.

VARIATIONS

• *You can use other pasta shapes, but
conchiglie are ideal because they scoop
up the chickpeas and beans.*
• *If you like, crush 1–2 garlic cloves and
fry them with the vegetables.*

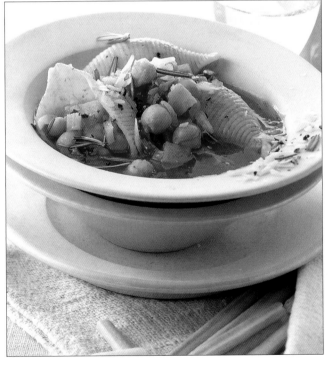

Minestrone alla Pugliese

Puglia-style Minestrone

THIS IS A TASTY SOUP for a Monday supper, because it can be made with the leftover carcass of Sunday's roast chicken. The sprinkling of salty ricotta salata at the finish is typical of Puglian cooking.

INGREDIENTS

1 roast chicken carcass
1 onion, quartered lengthwise
1 carrot, coarsely chopped
1 celery stalk, coarsely chopped
a few black peppercorns
1 small handful mixed fresh herbs
1 chicken stock cube
$1/2$ cup small pasta shapes, e.g. tubetti,
*   chifferini or pennette*
salt and ground black pepper
2 ounces ricotta salata cheese, coarsely
*   grated or crumbled and 2 tablespoons*
*   fresh mint leaves, to serve*

Serves 4

1 Break the chicken carcass into pieces and place these in a large saucepan. Add the onion, carrot, celery, peppercorns and herbs, then crumble in the stock cube and add a good pinch of salt. Cover the chicken generously with cold water (you will need about $6^1/4$ cups) and bring to a boil over high heat.

2 Lower the heat, half cover the pan and simmer gently for about 1 hour. Remove the pan from heat and let cool, then strain the liquid through a colander or strainer into a clean large saucepan.

3 Remove any meat from the chicken bones, cut it into bite-size pieces and set aside. Discard the carcass and flavoring ingredients.

4 Bring the stock in the pan to a boil, add the pasta and simmer, stirring frequently, until only just *al dente*: 5 – 6 minutes or according to the instructions on the package.

5 Add the pieces of chicken and heat through for a few minutes, by which time the pasta will be ready. Taste for seasoning. Serve hot in warmed bowls, sprinkled with the ricotta salata and mint leaves.

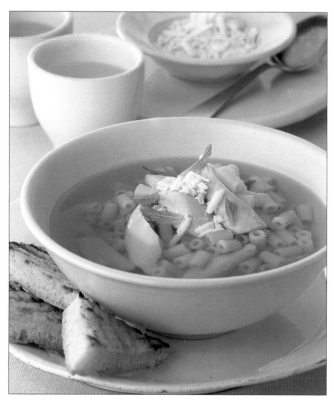

Zuppa di Lenticchie e Pastina

Lentil and Pasta Soup

THIS RUSTIC VEGETARIAN soup makes a warming winter meal and goes well with whole grain or crusty Italian bread.

INGREDIENTS

3/4 cup brown lentils

3 garlic cloves

4 cups water

3 tablespoons olive oil

2 tablespoons butter

1 onion, finely chopped

2 celery stalks, finely chopped

2 tablespoons sun-dried tomato paste

7 1/2 cups vegetable stock

a few fresh marjoram leaves

a few fresh basil leaves

leaves from 1 fresh thyme sprig

1/2 cup small pasta shapes, e.g. tubetti

salt and ground black pepper

tiny fresh herb leaves, to garnish

Serves 4–6

COOK'S TIP

Use green lentils instead of brown if you like, but the orange or red ones get mushy.

1 Put the lentils in a large saucepan. Smash 1 garlic clove (there's no need to peel it first) and add it to the lentils. Pour in the water and bring to a boil. Lower the heat to a gentle simmer and cook, stirring occasionally, for about 20 minutes or until the lentils are just tender. Pour the lentils into a strainer, remove the garlic and set it aside. Rinse the lentils under the cold water, then allow them to drain.

2 Heat 2 tablespoons of the oil with half the butter in a large saucepan. Add the onion and celery and cook over low heat, stirring frequently, for 5–7 minutes until softened.

3 Crush the remaining garlic, then peel and mash the reserved garlic. Add to the vegetables with the remaining oil, the tomato paste and the lentils. Stir, then add the stock, the fresh herbs and salt and pepper to taste. Bring to a boil, stirring. Simmer for 30 minutes, stirring occasionally.

4 Add the pasta and bring the water back to a boil, stirring. Simmer, stirring frequently, until the pasta is *al dente*: 7–8 minutes or according to the package instructions. Add the remaining butter and taste for seasoning. Serve hot in warmed bowls, sprinkled with the herb leaves.

Zuppa Casalinga

Farmhouse Soup

Root vegetables form the base of this chunky, minestrone-style main meal soup. You can vary the vegetables according to what you have to hand.

INGREDIENTS

2 tablespoons olive oil
I onion, coarsely chopped
3 carrots, cut into large chunks
6–7 ounces turnips, cut into large chunks
6 ounces rutabagas, cut into large chunks
I can (14 ounces) chopped Italian
 tomatoes
I tablespoon tomato paste
I teaspoon dried mixed herbs
I teaspoon dried oregano
$^{1}/_{2}$ cup dried peppers, washed and thinly
 sliced (optional)
$6^{1}/_{4}$ cups vegetable stock or water
$^{1}/_{2}$ cup small macaroni or conchiglie
I can (14 ounces) red kidney beans,
 rinsed and drained
2 tablespoons chopped fresh Italian parsley
salt and ground black pepper
freshly grated Parmesan cheese, to serve
Serves 4

1 Heat the oil in a large saucepan, add the onion and cook over low heat for about 5 minutes until softened. Add the fresh vegetables, canned tomatoes, tomato paste, dried herbs and dried peppers, if using. Stir in salt and pepper to taste. Pour in the stock or water and bring to a boil. Stir well, cover, lower the heat and simmer for 30 minutes, stirring occasionally.

COOK'S TIP

Packages of dried Italian peppers are sold in many supermarkets and in markets. They are piquant and firm with a "meaty" bite to them, which makes them ideal for adding substance to vegetarian soups.

2 Add the pasta and bring to a boil, stirring. Lower the heat and simmer, uncovered, until the pasta is only just *al dente*: about 5 minutes or according to the instructions on the package. Stir frequently.

3 Stir in the beans. Heat through for 2–3 minutes, then remove from heat and stir in the parsley. Taste the soup for seasoning. Serve hot in warmed soup bowls, with grated Parmesan handed separately.

Roasted Tomato and Pasta Soup

WHEN THE ONLY TOMATOES you can buy are not particularly flavorsome, make this soup. The roasting compensates for any lack of flavor in the tomatoes, and the soup has a wonderful smoky taste.

INGREDIENTS

I pound ripe Italian plum tomatoes, halved lengthwise
I large red bell pepper, quartered lengthwise and seeded
I large red onion, quartered lengthwise
2 garlic cloves, unpeeled
I tablespoon olive oil
5 cups vegetable stock or water
good pinch of granulated sugar
scant I cup small pasta shapes, e.g. tubetti or small macaroni
salt and ground black pepper
fresh basil leaves, to garnish

Serves 4

3 Add the remaining stock or water, the sugar and salt and pepper to taste. Bring to a boil, stirring.

4 Add the pasta and simmer, stirring frequently, until *al dente*: 7–8 minutes or according to the instructions on the package. Taste for seasoning. Serve hot in warmed bowls, garnished with the fresh basil.

COOK'S TIPS

• *You can roast the vegetables in advance, allow them to cool, then set aside them in a covered bowl in the refrigerator overnight before puréeing.*
• *The soup can be frozen without the pasta. Thaw and bring to a boil before adding the pasta.*

I Preheat the oven to 375°F. Spread out the tomatoes, red pepper, onion and garlic in a roasting pan and drizzle with the olive oil. Roast for 30–40 minutes until the vegetables are soft and charred, stirring and turning them after 15 minutes.

2 Turn the vegetables into a food processor, add about I cup of the stock or water and process until puréed. Scrape into a sieve placed over a large saucepan and press the purée through into the pan.

Pasta Soup with Chicken Livers

A SOUP THAT CAN BE served as either a first or main course. The fried fegatini are so delicious that even if you do not normally like chicken livers you will find yourself loving them in this soup.

INGREDIENTS

2/3 cup chicken livers, thawed if frozen
3 sprigs each fresh parsley, marjoram
    and sage
leaves from 1 fresh thyme sprig
5–6 fresh basil leaves
1 tablespoon olive oil
knob of butter
4 garlic cloves, crushed
1–2 tablespoons dry white wine
2 cans (11-ounce) condensed
    chicken consommé
2 cups frozen peas
1/2 cup pasta shapes, e.g. farfalle
2–3 scallions, diagonally sliced
salt and ground black pepper
Serves 4–6

1 Cut the chicken livers into small pieces with a sharp knife. Chop the herbs. Heat the oil and butter in a frying pan, add the garlic and herbs, with salt and pepper to taste, and fry gently for a few minutes. Add the livers, increase the heat to high and stir-fry for a few minutes until they change color and become dry. Pour the wine over the livers, cook until the wine evaporates, then remove the livers from heat and taste for seasoning.

2 Pour both cans of condensed chicken consommé into a large saucepan and add water to the condensed soup as directed on the labels. Add an extra can of water, then stir in a little salt and pepper to taste and bring to a boil.

3 Add the frozen peas to the pan and simmer for about 5 minutes, then add the small pasta shapes and bring the soup back to a boil, stirring. Allow to simmer, stirring frequently, until the pasta is only just *al dente*: about 5 minutes or according to the instructions on the package.

4 Add the fried chicken livers and scallions and heat through for 2–3 minutes. Taste for seasoning. Serve hot, in warmed bowls.

Meatball and Pasta Soup

EVEN THOUGH THIS SOUP comes from sunny Sicily, it is substantial enough for a hearty supper on a winter's day.

INGREDIENTS

2 cans (11-ounce) condensed
beef consommé
3/4 cup very thin pasta,
e.g. fidelini or spaghettini
fresh Italian parsley, to garnish
freshly grated Parmesan cheese, to serve

For the meatballs

1 very thick slice of white bread,
crusts removed
2 tablespoons milk
1 cup ground beef
1 garlic clove, crushed
2 tablespoons freshly grated
Parmesan cheese
2–3 tablespoons fresh Italian parsley
leaves, coarsely chopped
1 egg
nutmeg
salt and ground black pepper
Serves 4

1 Make the meatballs. Break the bread into a small bowl, add the milk and set aside to soak. Meanwhile, put the ground beef, garlic, Parmesan, parsley and egg in another large bowl. Grate fresh nutmeg liberally over the top and add salt and pepper to taste.

2 Squeeze the bread with your hands to remove as much milk as possible, then add the bread to the meatball mixture and mix everything together well with your hands. Wash your hands, rinse them under the cold tap, then form the mixture into tiny balls about the size of small marbles.

3 Pour both cans of consommé into a large saucepan, add water as directed on the labels, then add an extra can of water. Stir in salt and pepper to taste and bring to a boil.

4 Drop in the meatballs, then break the pasta into small pieces and add it to the soup. Bring the soup to a boil, stirring gently. Simmer, stirring frequently, until the pasta is *al dente*: 7–8 minutes or according to the instructions on the package. Taste for seasoning. Serve hot in warmed bowls, sprinkled with parsley and freshly grated Parmesan cheese.

Tomato Sauces

It was the Neapolitans who first discovered the delights of pasta and tomato sauce. Tomatoes originally came to Italy from the New World. They were yellow, which is why they were called golden apples (*pomodori*), and were originally used only as ornamental plants. They quickly took to the sunshine of southern Italy, however, and by the 18th century the red tomato was being enjoyed in salads. It wasn't long before they were partnered with pasta—and so began one of the most successful marriages in culinary history.

Tomato sauces, simple and uncooked or simmered for a while, are typically southern Italian. They go best with the dried commercially produced pasta of the south, and taste divine with those other wonderful southern ingredients—basil, garlic and olive oil. Most recipes in this chapter give advice on the best type of pasta to serve with the sauce, while some go further and include pasta as part of the recipe.

Spaghetti is the pasta most often used with tomato sauces, but all the sauces work well with a wide range of pasta, so feel free to mix and match.

La Pommarola

Fresh Tomato Sauce

THIS IS THE FAMOUS Neapolitan sauce that is made in summer when tomatoes are very ripe and sweet. It is very simple, so that nothing detracts from the flavor of the tomatoes themselves. It is served here with spaghetti, which is the traditional choice of pasta.

INGREDIENTS

1 1/2 pounds ripe Italian plum tomatoes
4 tablespoons olive oil
1 onion, finely chopped
12 ounces fresh or dried spaghetti
1 small handful fresh basil leaves
salt and ground black pepper
coarsely shaved Parmesan cheese, to serve

Serves 4

3 Meanwhile, cook the pasta according to the instructions on the package. Shred the basil leaves finely.

4 Remove the sauce from heat, stir in the basil and taste for seasoning. Drain the pasta, turn it into a warmed bowl, pour the sauce over and toss well. Serve immediately, with shaved Parmesan passed separately.

COOK'S TIPS

• *If good plum tomatoes are not available, substitute large ripe tomatoes which give excellent results.*
• *In Italy, cooks often make this sauce in bulk in the summer months and freeze it for later use. Let it cool, then freeze in usable quantities in rigid contalles. Thaw before reheating.*

VARIATIONS

Some Neapolitan cooks add a little crushed garlic with the onion and some use chopped fresh oregano or Italian parsley with the basil; it is a matter of personal taste.

1 With a sharp knife, cut a cross in the bottom (flower) end of each tomato. Bring a medium saucepan of water to a boil and remove from heat. Plunge a few of the tomatoes into the water, set aside for 30 seconds or so, then lift them out with a slotted spoon. Repeat with the remaining tomatoes, then peel off the skin and coarsely chop the flesh.

2 Heat the oil in a large saucepan, add the onion and cook over low heat, stirring frequently, for about 5 minutes until softened and lightly colored. Add the tomatoes, with salt and pepper to taste, bring to a simmer, then turn the heat down to low and cover the pan. Cook, stirring occasionally, for 30–40 minutes or until thick.

Rigatoni con Sugo di Pomodoro Invernale

Rigatoni with Winter Tomato Sauce

IN WINTER, WHEN FRESH tomatoes are not at their best, this is the sauce the Italians make. Canned tomatoes combined with *soffritto* (the sautéed mixture of chopped onion, carrot, celery and garlic) and herbs give a better flavor than winter tomatoes.

INGREDIENTS

1 onion
1 carrot
1 celery stalk
4 tablespoons olive oil
1 garlic clove, thinly sliced
a few leaves each fresh basil, thyme and
  oregano or marjoram
2 (14-ounce) cans chopped Italian
  plum tomatoes
1 tablespoon sun-dried tomato paste
1 teaspoon granulated sugar
6 tablespoons dry red or
  white wine (optional)
3 cups rigatoni
salt and ground black pepper
coarsely shaved Parmesan cheese, to serve

Serves 6–8

1 Chop the onion, carrot and celery stalk finely, either in a food processor or by hand.

2 Heat the olive oil in a medium saucepan, add the garlic slices and stir over very low heat for 1–2 minutes.

3 Add the chopped vegetables and the fresh herbs. Cook over low heat, stirring frequently, for 5–7 minutes until the vegetables have softened and are lightly colored.

4 Add the canned tomatoes, tomato paste and sugar, then stir in the wine, if using. Add salt and pepper to taste. Bring to a boil, stirring, then lower the heat to a gentle simmer. Cook, uncovered, for about 45 minutes, stirring occasionally.

5 Cook the pasta according to the instructions on the package. Drain it and turn it into a warmed bowl. Taste the sauce for seasoning, pour the sauce over the pasta and toss well. Serve immediately, with shavings of Parmesan passed separately. If you like, garnish with extra chopped herbs.

Tomato Sauces

Spaghetti with Tomatoes and Pancetta

THIS SAUCE COMES FROM **Spoleto** in Umbria. It is a fresh, light sauce in which the tomatoes are cooked for a short time, so it should only be made in summer when tomatoes have a good flavor.

INGREDIENTS

12 ounces ripe Italian plum tomatoes
5 ounces pancetta or lean bacon, diced
2 tablespoons olive oil
1 onion, finely chopped
12 ounces fresh or dried spaghetti
2–3 fresh marjoram sprigs, leaves stripped
salt and ground black pepper
freshly grated pecorino cheese,
  to serve
shredded fresh basil, to garnish
Serves 4

With a sharp knife, cut a cross in the bottom (flower) end of each plum tomato. Bring a medium saucepan of water to a boil and remove from heat. Plunge a few of the tomatoes into the water, set aside for 30 seconds or so, then lift them out with a slotted spoon and set aside. Repeat with the remaining tomatoes, then peel off the skin and finely chop the flesh.

COOK'S TIP

Try to find pancetta—bacon can be substituted but the sauce will not taste precisely the same. You can buy ready-diced pancetta in packages in super-markets. Alternatively, you can buy it thinly sliced, sometimes cut from a roll (arrotolata), and dice it yourself.

2 Put the pancetta or bacon in a medium saucepan with the oil. Stir over low heat until the fat is rendered. Add the onion and stir to mix. Cook gently for about 10 minutes, stirring.

3 Add the tomatoes, with salt and pepper to taste. Stir well and cook, uncovered, for about 10 minutes. Meanwhile, cook the pasta according to the instructions on the package.

4 Remove the sauce from heat, stir in the marjoram and taste for seasoning. Drain the pasta and turn it into a warmed bowl. Pour the sauce over the pasta and toss well. Serve immediately, sprinkled with shredded basil. Pass around grated pecorino.

Penne all'Arrabbiata

Penne with Tomato and Chili Sauce

THIS IS ONE OF ROME'S most famous
pasta dishes—penne tossed in a
tomato sauce flavored with chile.
Literally translated, *arrabbiata* means
"enraged" or "furious" but in this
context it should be translated as
"fiery". Make the sauce as hot as you
like by adding more chiles to taste.

INGREDIENTS

1 ounce dried porcini mushrooms

7 tablespoons butter

5 ounces pancetta or lean bacon, diced

1–2 dried red chiles, to taste

2 garlic cloves, crushed

*8 ripe Italian plum tomatoes, peeled
    and chopped*

*a few fresh basil leaves, torn, plus extra
    to garnish*

3 cups fresh or dried penne

²⁄₃ cup freshly grated Parmesan cheese

¹⁄₃ cup freshly grated pecorino cheese

salt

Serves 4

Soak the dried mushrooms in warm
water to cover for 15–20 minutes.
Drain, then squeeze dry with your
hands. Finely chop the mushrooms.

2 Melt 4 tablespoons of the butter
in a medium saucepan or skillet.
Add the pancetta or bacon and stir-fry
over medium heat until golden and
slightly crispy. Remove the pancetta
with a slotted spoon and set it aside.

3 Add the chopped mushrooms to
the pan and cook in the same
way. Remove and set aside with the
pancetta or bacon. Crumble 1 chile
into the pan, add the garlic and cook,
stirring, for a few minutes, until the
garlic turns golden.

4 Add the tomatoes and basil and
season with salt. Cook gently,
stirring occasionally, for 10–15 minutes.
Meanwhile, cook the penne in a pan of
salted boiling water, according to the
instructions on the package.

5 Add the pancetta or bacon and
the mushrooms to the tomato
sauce. Taste for seasoning, adding more
chiles if you prefer a hotter flavor. If
the sauce is too dry, stir in a little of the
pasta water.

6 Drain the pasta and turn it into a
warmed bowl. Dice the remaining
butter; add it to the pasta with the
cheeses, then toss until well coated.
Pour the tomato sauce over the pasta,
toss well and serve immediately, with a
few basil leaves sprinkled on top.

Spaghetti alla Puttanesca

Spaghetti with Tomatoes, Anchovies, Olives and Capers

FROM CAMPANIA IN THE SOUTH, this classic sauce has a strong flavor. *Alla puttanesca* means "prostitute style".

INGREDIENTS

2 tablespoons olive oil
1 small onion, finely chopped
1 garlic clove, finely chopped
4 drained canned anchovies
1/2 cup pitted black olives, sliced
1 tablespoon capers
1 can (14 ounces) chopped Italian
    plum tomatoes
3 tablespoons water
1 tablespoon chopped fresh Italian parsley
12 ounces fresh or dried spaghetti
salt and ground black pepper
Serves 4

1 Heat the oil in a medium saucepan and add the onion, garlic and drained anchovies. Cook over low heat, stirring constantly, for 5–7 minutes or until the anchovies break down to form a very soft pulp. Add the black olives and capers and stir-fry for a minute or so.

2 Add the tomatoes, water, half the parsley and salt and pepper to taste. Stir well and bring to a boil, then lower the heat and cover the pan. Simmer gently for 30 minutes, stirring occasionally. Meanwhile, cook the pasta according to the package instructions.

3 Drain the pasta and turn it into a warmed bowl. Taste the sauce for seasoning, pour it over the pasta and toss well. Serve immediately, with the remaining parsley sprinkled on top.

COOK'S TIP

Use good-quality, shiny black olives— Gaeta olives from Liguria are very good.

Bucatini all'Amatriciana

Bucatini with Tomato and Chili Sauce

AMATRICIANA IS A CLASSIC tomato sauce named after the town of Amatrice in the Sabine hills, Lazio. If you visit Rome, you will see it on many restaurant menus served with either bucatini or spaghetti.

INGREDIENTS

1 tablespoon olive oil
1 small onion, finely sliced
4 ounces smoked pancetta or
    lean bacon, diced
1 fresh red chile, seeded and cut into
    thin strips
1 can (14 ounces) chopped Italian
    plum tomatoes
2–3 tablespoons dry white wine
    or water
12 ounces bucatini
2–3 tablespoons freshly grated pecorino
    cheese, plus extra to serve (optional)
salt and ground black pepper
Serves 4

1 Heat the oil in a medium saucepan and cook the onion, pancetta and chile over low heat for 5–7 minutes, stirring. Add the tomatoes and wine or water, with salt and pepper to taste. Bring to a boil, stirring, then cover and simmer for 15–20 minutes, stirring occasionally. If the sauce is too dry, stir in a little of the pasta water.

2 Meanwhile, cook the pasta in a pan of salted boiling water according to the package instructions.

3 Drain the pasta and turn it into a warmed bowl. Taste the sauce for seasoning, pour it over the pasta and add the grated pecorino. Toss well. Serve immediately, with more grated pecorino passed separately if liked.

COOK'S TIP

Always take care when dealing with chiles. They contain a substance called capsaicin, which will irritate delicate skin, so it's a good idea to wear rubber gloves.

Tomato Sauces

Fusilli with Tomato and Balsamic Vinegar Sauce

THIS IS A MODERN CAL-ITAL recipe (Californian/Italian). The intense, sweet-sour flavor of balsamic vinegar gives a pleasant kick to a sauce made with canned tomatoes.

INGREDIENTS

2 cans (14-ounce) chopped Italian
  plum tomatoes
2 pieces of drained sun-dried tomato in
  olive oil, thinly sliced
2 garlic cloves, crushed
3 tablespoons olive oil
1 teaspoon granulated sugar
3 cups fresh or dried fusilli
3 tablespoons balsamic vinegar
salt and ground black pepper
coarsely shaved pecorino cheese and
  arugula salad, to serve

Serves 6–8

1 Put the canned and sun-dried tomatoes in a medium saucepan with the garlic, olive oil and sugar. Add salt and pepper to taste. Bring to a boil, stirring. Lower the heat and simmer for about 30 minutes until reduced.

2 Meanwhile, cook the pasta in salted boiling water according to the instructions on the package.

3 Add the balsamic vinegar to the sauce and stir to mix evenly. Cook for 1–2 minutes, then remove from heat and taste for seasoning.

4 Drain the pasta and turn it into a warmed bowl. Pour the sauce over the pasta and toss well. Serve immediately, with arugula salad and the shaved pecorino handed separately.

Linguine con Pesto di Pomodori Secchi

Linguine with Sun-dried Tomato Pesto

TOMATO PESTO WAS ONCE a rarity, but is becoming increasingly popular. To make it, sun-dried tomatoes are used instead of basil. The result is absolutely delicious.

INGREDIENTS

$^1/_3$ cup pine nuts

$^1/_3$ cup freshly grated Parmesan cheese

$^1/_2$ cup sun-dried tomatoes
in olive oil

1 garlic clove, coarsely chopped

4 tablespoons olive oil

12 ounces fresh or dried linguine

ground black pepper

coarsely shaved Parmesan cheese, to serve

basil leaves, to garnish

Serves 4

3 With the machine running, gradually add the olive oil through the feeder tube until it has all been incorporated evenly and the ingredients have formed a smooth-looking paste.

4 Cook the pasta according to the package instructions. Drain well, reserving a little of the cooking water. Turn the pasta into a warmed bowl, add the pesto and a few spoonfuls of the hot water and toss well. Serve immediately, garnish with basil leaves. Pass shavings of Parmesan separately.

1 Put the pine nuts in a small nonstick frying pan and toss over low to medium heat for 1–2 minutes or until the nuts are lightly toasted and golden.

2 Put the nuts in a food processor. Add the Parmesan, sun-dried tomatoes and garlic, with pepper to taste. Process until finely chopped.

COOK'S TIP

You can make this pesto up to 2 days in advance and keep it in a bowl in the refrigerator until ready to use. Pour a thin film of olive oil over the pesto in the bowl, then cover the bowl tightly with plastic wrap to prevent the pesto from flavoring other foods in the refrigerator.

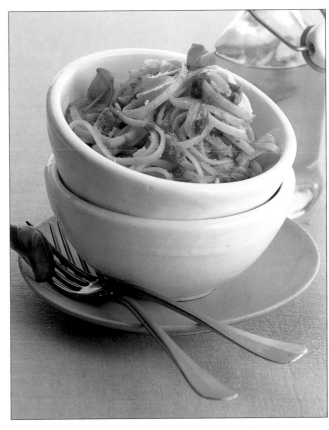

Cappelletti con Pomodoro e Panna

Cappelletti with Tomatoes and Cream

TOMATOES, CREAM AND FRESH BASIL are a winning combination. In this very quick and easy recipe, the sauce coats little pasta hats filled with soft cheeses to make a substantial supper dish for vegetarians. If you prefer a lighter dish, you can use the sauce to coat plain, unstuffed pasta. Small shapes such as penne, farfalle or conchiglie are best.

INGREDIENTS

1 2/3 cups tomato sauce

6 tablespoons dry white wine

2/3 cup heavy cream

2 1/2 cups fresh cappelletti

1 small handful of fresh basil leaves

4 tablespoons freshly grated
    Parmesan cheese

salt and ground black pepper

Serves 4–6

1 Pour the tomato sauce and wine into a medium saucepan and stir to mix. Bring to a boil over medium heat, then add the cream and stir until evenly mixed and bubbling. Turn the heat down to low and let simmer.

2 Cook the sacchettini until *al dente*: 5–7 minutes or according to the instructions on the package. Meanwhile, finely shred most of the basil leaves.

3 Drain the pasta well, return it to the pan and toss it with the grated Parmesan. Taste the sauce for seasoning, pour it over the pasta and toss well. Serve immediately, sprinkled with the shredded basil and whole basil leaves.

COOK'S TIPS

• *Cappelletti with a variety of fillings are available at supermarkets and Italian markets.*

• *Other stuffed pasta shapes, such as tortelloni, ravioli, or the more unusual sacchettini (little purses), can be used with this sauce.*

• *The tomato sauce can be made up to a day ahead, then chilled until ready to use. Reheat gently in a heavy saucepan while the pasta is cooking.*

La Crudaiola

Raw Tomato Sauce

THIS IS A WONDERFULLY simple uncooked tomato sauce that goes well with many different kinds of pasta, both long strands and short shapes. It is always made in summer when plum tomatoes have ripened on the vine in the sun and have their fullest flavor.

INGREDIENTS

1 1/4 pounds ripe Italian plum tomatoes

1 large handful fresh basil leaves

5 tablespoons extra virgin olive oil

4 ounces ricotta salata cheese, diced

1 garlic clove, crushed

salt and ground black pepper

coarsely shaved pecorino cheese, to serve

Serves 4

1 Coarsely chop the plum tomatoes, removing the cores and as many of the seeds as you can. Tear the basil leaves into shreds with your fingers.

2 Put all the ingredients (except the cheese) in a bowl, adding salt and pepper to taste, and stir well. Cover and let stand at room temperature for 1–2 hours to let the flavors mingle.

3 Taste the sauce to check the seasoning before tossing it with hot, freshly cooked pasta of your choice. Serve immediately with shavings of pecorino handed separately.

COOK'S TIPS

• *Ricotta salata is a salted and dried version of ricotta cheese. It is firmer than the traditional soft white ricotta, and can be easily diced, crumbled and even grated. It is available from some markets. If you can't find it, use feta cheese instead.*

• *Long pasta goes well with this sauce, especially bucatini or spaghetti, or you could serve it with short shapes, such as fusilli or orecchiette.*

Sugo Finto

Meaty Tomato Sauce

THE WORD FINTO means "mock" or "pretend", and this Roman sauce takes its name from the days when meat was scarce and expensive, so cooks would put a little meat fat in a tomato sauce to make it taste of meat. Sometimes meat stock was used for the same purpose.

INGREDIENTS

1 small onion
1 small carrot
2 celery stalks
2 garlic cloves
1 small handful fresh Italian parsley
2 ounces ham or bacon fat, finely chopped
4–6 tablespoons dry white wine,
  or more to taste
1 1/4 pounds ripe Italian plum
  tomatoes, chopped
salt and ground black pepper
Serves 4

1 Chop the onion, carrot and celery finely in a food processor. Add the garlic cloves and parsley and process until finely chopped. Alternatively, chop everything by hand.

2 Put the chopped vegetable mixture in a medium shallow saucepan or skillet with the ham fat and cook, stirring, over low heat for about 5 minutes. Add the wine, with salt and pepper to taste and simmer for 5 minutes, then stir in the tomatoes. Simmer for 40 minutes, stirring occasionally and adding a little hot water if the sauce seems too dry.

3 Have ready a large sieve placed over a large bowl. Carefully pour in the sauce and press it through the sieve with the back of a metal spoon, leaving behind the tomato skins and any tough pieces of vegetable that won't go through.

4 Return the sauce to the clean pan and heat it through, adding a little more wine or hot water if it is too thick. Taste the sauce for seasoning, then toss with hot, freshly cooked pasta of your choice.

COOK'S TIPS

• *Capelli d'angelo, preferably made without egg, is the traditional pasta to serve with* sugo finto, *but you can use tagliolini or tagliarini if you prefer.*
• *If you like, you can add about 1/4 ounce dried porcini mushrooms, soaked, drained and squeezed dry, when first cooking the other vegetables.*

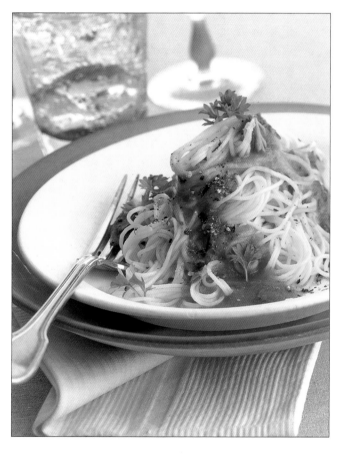

Farfalle al Sugo di Piselli

Farfalle with Tomatoes and Peas

THIS PRETTY SAUCE should be served with plain white pasta so that the red, green and white make it tricolor, the three colors of the Italian flag. Here farfalle (bow-tie shaped pasta) are used, but other pasta shapes will work just as well.

INGREDIENTS

1 tablespoon olive oil
5–6 lean bacon strips, cut crosswise
*   into small strips*
1 can (14 ounces) chopped Italian
*   plum tomatoes*
4 tablespoons water
3 cups farfalle
2 cups frozen peas
4 tablespoons mascarpone cheese
a few fresh basil leaves, shredded
salt and ground black pepper
freshly grated Parmesan cheese,
*   to serve*
basil leaves, to garnish
Serves 4

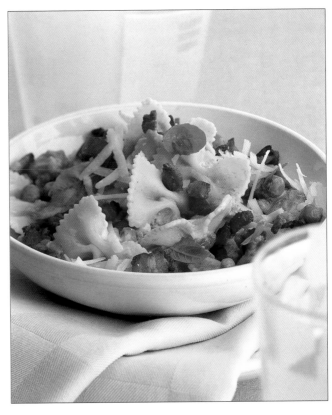

1 Heat the oil in a medium saucepan and add the bacon. Cook over low heat, stirring frequently, for 5–7 minutes.

2 Add the tomatoes and water, with salt and pepper to taste. Bring to a boil. Lower the heat, cover and simmer gently for about 15 minutes, stirring from time to time.

3 Meanwhile, cook the pasta in salted boiling water according to the instructions on the package.

4 Add the peas to the tomato sauce, stir well to mix and bring to a boil. Cover the pan and cook for 5–8 minutes, until the peas are cooked and the sauce is quite thick. Taste the sauce for seasoning.

5 Turn off the heat under the pan and add the mascarpone and shredded basil. Mix well, cover the pan and let stand for 1–2 minutes. Drain the pasta and turn it into a warmed bowl. Pour the sauce over the pasta and toss well. Serve immediately, garnished with basil, and pass some grated Parmesan separately.

Cream Sauces

The northern Italians love cream sauce with pasta. Its unctuous texture goes well with *pasta all'uovo*, pasta made with egg. The pasta in the north is often fresh rather than dried, and cream sauces complement it perfectly. The cream used in Italy is different from our fresh cream. Called *panna da cucina* (cream for cooking), it has a thin, almost runny, consistency and a slight tang. You can buy it fresh in Italy, but beyond its borders you are more likely to see long-life *panna da cucina* in Italian markets and specialty stores.

Oddly enough, the most famous cream sauce of all does not come from northern Italy, but from Rome. *Fettuccine all'Alfredo*—a simple dish of fresh fettuccine tossed in nothing more than cream, butter and grated Parmesan—is one of the best pasta dishes of all time, and very hard to beat. You will find the recipe in this chapter, plus many other simple sauces based on cream to rival Alfredo's creation. From classic favorites, such as *Spaghetti alla Carbonara* and *Vermicelli al Limone* to recipes using seasonal vegetables, such as asparagus and wild mushrooms, or more unusual ingredients, such as radicchio, there is plenty of choice.

Pasta with a cream sauce is always special and makes a good dinner party first course, but keep portions small, because flavors are rich.

Spaghetti alla Carbonara

Spaghetti with Eggs, Bacon and Cream

AN ALL-TIME FAVORITE that needs no introducing. This version has plenty of pancetta or bacon and is not too creamy, but you can vary the amounts as you please.

INGREDIENTS

2 tablespoons olive oil
1 small onion, finely chopped
8 pancetta or lean bacon strips, cut into
   1/2-inch strips
12 ounces fresh or dried spaghetti
4 eggs
4 tablespoons crème fraîche
4 tablespoons freshly grated Parmesan
   cheese, plus extra to serve
salt and ground black pepper
Serves 4

1 Heat the oil in a large saucepan or skillet, add the finely chopped onion and cook over low heat, stirring frequently, for about 5 minutes until softened but not colored.

2 Add the strips of pancetta or bacon to the onion in the pan and cook for about 10 minutes, stirring almost all the time. Meanwhile, cook the pasta in a pot of salted boiling water according to the instructions on the package until *al dente*.

3 Put the eggs, crème fraîche and grated Parmesan in a bowl. Grind in plenty of pepper, then beat everything together well.

4 Drain the pasta, turn it into the pan with the pancetta or bacon and toss well to mix. Turn the heat off under the pan. Immediately add the egg mixture and toss vigorously so that it cooks lightly and coats the pasta.

5 Quickly taste for seasoning, then divide among four warmed bowls and sprinkle with black pepper. Serve immediately, with extra grated Parmesan passed separately.

Fusilli di Bosco

Fusilli with Wild Mushrooms

A VERY RICH DISH WITH AN earthy flavor and lots of garlic, this makes an ideal main course for vegetarians, especially if it is followed by a crisp green salad.

INGREDIENTS

5 ounces wild mushrooms preserved
   in olive oil
2 tablespoons butter
2 cups fresh wild mushrooms, sliced if large
1 teaspoon finely chopped fresh thyme
1 teaspoon finely chopped fresh marjoram
   or oregano, plus extra herbs to serve
4 garlic cloves, crushed
3 cups fresh or dried fusilli
scant 1 cup panna da cucina or
   heavy cream
salt and ground black pepper
Serves 4

1 Drain about 1 tablespoon of the oil from the mushrooms into a medium saucepan. Slice or chop the preserved mushrooms into bite-size pieces, if they are large.

2 Add the butter to the oil in the pan and heat over low heat until sizzling. Add the preserved and the fresh mushrooms, the chopped herbs and the garlic, with salt and pepper to taste. Simmer over medium heat, stirring frequently, for about 10 minutes or until the fresh mushrooms are soft and tender. Meanwhile, cook the pasta in salted boiling water according to the instructions on the package.

3 As soon as the mushrooms are cooked, increase the heat to high and toss the mixture with a wooden spoon to boil off any excess liquid. Pour in the cream and bring to a boil, stirring, then taste and add more salt and pepper if needed.

4 Drain the pasta and turn it into a warmed bowl. Pour the sauce over the pasta and toss well. Serve immediately, sprinkled with finely chopped fresh herbs.

Farfalle Verdi e Rosa

Pink and Green Farfalle

IN THIS MODERN RECIPE, pink shrimp and green zucchini combine prettily with cream and pasta bows to make a substantial main course. Serve with crusty Italian rolls or chunks of warm crusty bread.

INGREDIENTS

$^1/_4$ cup butter

2–3 scallions, very thinly sliced on the diagonal

12 ounces zucchini, thinly sliced on the diagonal

4 tablespoons dry white wine

$2^3/_2$ cups farfalle

5 tablespoons crème fraîche

$1^1/_3$ cups peeled cooked shrimp, thawed and thoroughly dried if frozen

1 tablespoon finely chopped fresh marjoram or Italian parsley, or a mixture

salt and ground black pepper

Serves 4

1 Melt the butter in a large saucepan, add the scallions and cook over low heat, stirring frequently, for about 5 minutes until softened. Add the zucchini, with salt and pepper to taste, and stir-fry for 5 minutes. Pour over the wine and let it bubble, then cover and simmer for 10 minutes.

VARIATION

Use penne instead of the farfalle, and asparagus tips instead of the zucchini.

2 Cook the pasta in a large pot of salted boiling water according to the instructions on the package. Meanwhile, add the crème fraîche to the zucchini mixture and simmer for about 10 minutes until well reduced.

3 Add the shrimp to the zucchini mixture, heat through gently and taste for seasoning. Drain the pasta and turn it into a warmed bowl. Add the sauce and chopped herbs and toss well. Serve immediately.

Penne ai Gamberetti con Pernod

Penne with Shrimp and Pernod

THIS IS A MODERN RECIPE, typical of those found on menus in the most innovative Italian restaurants. The Pernod and dill go well together, but you could use white wine and basil.

INGREDIENTS

scant 1 cup panna da cucina or heavy cream

1 cup fish stock

3 cups penne

2–3 tablespoons Pernod

$1^1/_3$ cups peeled cooked shrimp, thawed and thoroughly dried if frozen

2 tablespoons chopped fresh dill, plus extra to garnish

salt and ground black pepper

Serves 4

1 Put the cream and the fish stock in a medium saucepan and bring to a boil. Lower the heat and simmer, stirring occasionally, for 10–15 minutes, until reduced by about half. Meanwhile, cook the pasta in a large pot of salted boiling water according to the instructions on the package.

2 Add the Pernod and shrimp to the cream sauce, with salt and pepper to taste, if necessary. Heat the shrimp through very gently. Drain the pasta and turn it into a warmed bowl. Pour the sauce over the pasta, add the dill and toss well. Serve immediately, sprinkled with chopped dill.

Pipe Rigate with Peas and Ham

3 Add about half the cream, increase the heat to high and let the cream bubble, stirring constantly, until it thickens and coats the peas. Remove from heat, stir in the prosciutto and taste for seasoning.

4 Cook the pasta according to the instructions on the package. Turn into a colander and drain well.

5 Immediately melt the remaining butter with the cream in the pan in which the pasta was cooked. Add the pasta and toss over medium heat until it is evenly coated. Pour in the sauce, toss lightly to mix with the pasta and heat through. Serve immediately, sprinkled with fresh herbs.

PRETTILY FLECKED WITH PINK and green, this is a lovely dish for a spring or summer supper party.

INGREDIENTS

2 tablespoons butter
1 tablespoon olive oil
1 1/4–1 1/2 cups frozen peas, thawed
1 garlic clove, crushed
2/3 cup chicken stock, dry white wine
  or water
2 tablespoons chopped fresh Italian parsley
3/4 cup panna da cucina or heavy cream
4 ounces prosciutto crudo, shredded
3 cups pipe rigate
salt and ground black pepper
chopped fresh herbs, to garnish
Serves 4

1 Melt half the butter with the olive oil in a medium saucepan until foaming. Add the thawed frozen peas and the crushed garlic to the pan, followed by the chicken stock, wine or water.

2 Sprinkle in the chopped parsley and add salt and pepper to taste. Cook over medium heat, stirring frequently, for 5–8 minutes or until most of the liquid has been absorbed.

COOK'S TIPS

• *Prosciutto is quite expensive, but it tastes very good in this dish. To cut the cost you could use ordinary cooked ham or pancetta.*
• *If you can't get pipe rigate, use conchiglie or orecchiette instead, all of which trap the peas.*

Alfredo's Fettuccine

THIS SIMPLE RECIPE WAS invented by a Roman restaurateur called Alfredo, who became famous for serving it with a gold fork and spoon.

INGREDIENTS

$^1/_4$ cup butter

scant 1 cup panna da cucina or
   heavy cream

$^2/_3$ cup freshly grated Parmesan cheese,
   plus extra to serve

12 ounces fresh fettuccine

salt and ground black pepper

Serves 4

1 Melt the butter in a large saucepan or skillet. Add the cream and bring it to a boil. Simmer for 5 minutes, stirring, then add the Parmesan, with salt and pepper to taste, and turn off the heat under the pan.

2 Bring a large pot of salted water to a boil. Drop in the pasta all at once and quickly bring back to a boil, stirring occasionally. Cook until *al dente*: 2–3 minutes, or according to the instructions on the package. Drain well.

3 Turn on the heat under the pan of cream to low, add the pasta all at once and toss until it is coated in the sauce. Taste for seasoning. Serve immediately, with extra grated Parmesan passed separately.

COOK'S TIPS

• With so few ingredients, it is particularly important to use only the best-quality ones for this dish to be a success. Use good unsalted butter and top-quality Parmesan cheese. The best is Parmigiano-Reggiano—available from Italian markets—which has its name stamped on the rind. Grate it only just before using.

• Fresh fettuccine is traditional, so either make it yourself or buy it from an Italian delicatessen. If you cannot get fettuccine, you can use tagliatelle instead.

Linguine al Prosciutto e Mascarpone

Linguine with Ham and Mascarpone

MASCARPONE CHEESE masquerades as cream in this recipe. Its thick, unctuous consistency makes it perfect for sauces. Have the water boiling, ready for the pasta, before you start making the sauce, because everything cooks so quickly.

INGREDIENTS

2 tablespoons butter
³/4 cup mascarpone cheese
3¹/2 ounces cooked ham, cut into
  thin strips
2 tablespoons milk
3 tablespoons freshly grated Parmesan
  cheese, plus extra to serve
1¹/4 pounds fresh linguine
salt and ground black pepper
Serves 6

1 Melt the butter in a medium saucepan, add the ham, mascarpone and milk and stir well over low heat until the mascarpone has melted. Add 1 tablespoon of the grated Parmesan and plenty of pepper and stir well.

2 Cook the pasta in a large pot of salted boiling water for 2–3 minutes, until *al dente*.

3 Drain the cooked pasta well and turn it into a warmed bowl. Pour the sauce over the pasta, add the remaining Parmesan and toss well.

4 Taste for seasoning and serve the pasta immediately, with a pepper grinder and extra grated Parmesan passed separately.

Farfalle alla Crema di Gorgonzola

Farfalle with Gorgonzola Cream

SWEET AND SIMPLE, this sauce has a nutty tang from the blue cheese. It is also good with long pasta, such as spaghetti or trenette.

INGREDIENTS

3 cups farfalle
6 ounces Gorgonzola cheese, any rind
  removed, diced
²/3 cup panna da cucina or heavy cream
pinch of granulated sugar
2 teaspoons finely chopped fresh sage, plus
  fresh sage leaves (some whole, some
  shredded) to garnish
salt and ground black pepper
Serves 4

1 Cook the pasta until *al dente*: 8–10 minutes or according to the instructions on the package.

2 Meanwhile, put the Gorgonzola and cream in a medium saucepan. Add the sugar and plenty of ground black pepper and heat gently, stirring frequently, until the cheese has melted. Remove the pan from heat.

3 Drain the cooked pasta well and return it to the pot in which it was cooked. Pour the sauce into the pot with the pasta.

4 Add the chopped sage to the pasta and toss over medium heat until the pasta is evenly coated. Taste for seasoning, adding salt if necessary, then divide among four warmed bowls. Garnish each portion with sage and serve immediately.

Vermicelli with Lemon

FRESH AND TANGY, THIS MAKES an excellent first course for a dinner party. It doesn't rely on fresh seasonal ingredients, so it is good at any time of year. It is also a recipe to remember when you're pushed for time, because the sauce can easily be made in the time it takes to cook the pasta.

INGREDIENTS

12 ounces vermicelli
juice of 2 large lemons
$1/4$ cup butter
scant 1 cup panna da cucina or
  heavy cream
$1^1/3$ cups freshly grated Parmesan cheese
salt and ground black pepper
Serves 4

1 Cook the pasta in salted boiling water according to the instructions on the package.

2 Meanwhile, pour the lemon juice into a medium saucepan. Add the butter and cream, then salt and pepper to taste.

3 Bring to a boil, then lower the heat and simmer for about 5 minutes, stirring occasionally, until the cream reduces slightly.

4 Drain the pasta and return it to the pot. Add the grated Parmesan, then taste the sauce for seasoning and pour it over the pasta. Toss quickly over medium heat until the pasta is evenly coated with the sauce, then divide among four warmed bowls and serve immediately.

COOK'S TIP

Lemons vary in the amount of juice they yield. On average, a large fresh lemon will yield 4–6 tablespoons. The lemony flavor of this dish is quite tangy—you can use less juice if you prefer.

VARIATIONS

• *Use spaghettini or spaghetti, or even small pasta shapes, such as fusilli, farfalle or orecchiette.*
• *For an even tangier taste, add a little grated lemon zest to the sauce when you add the butter and the cream to the pan in Step 2.*

Spaghetti allo Zafferano

Spaghetti with Saffron

A QUICK AND EASY DISH THAT makes a delicious midweek supper. The ingredients are all staples that you are likely to have in the refrigerator, so this recipe is perfect for impromptu meals.

INGREDIENTS

12 ounces spaghetti

a few saffron strands

2 tablespoons water

5 ounces cooked ham, cut into matchsticks

scant 1 cup panna da cucina or
heavy cream

2/3 cup freshly grated Parmesan cheese,
plus extra to serve

2 egg yolks

salt and ground black pepper

Serves 4

3 Add the strips of ham to the pan containing the saffron. Stir in the cream and Parmesan, with a little salt and pepper to taste. Heat gently, stirring all the time. When the cream starts to bubble around the edges, remove the sauce from the heat and add the egg yolks. Beat well to mix, then taste for seasoning.

4 Drain the pasta and turn it into a warmed bowl. Immediately pour the sauce over the pasta and toss well. Serve immediately, with extra grated Parmesan passed separately.

COOK'S TIPS

• *Individual envelopes or tubes of saffron powder, enough for four servings, are sold at Italian markets and some super-markets, and one tube can be used for this sauce instead of the saffron strands. Simply sprinkle in the powder in Step 3, when adding salt and pepper.*

• *Use a heavy pan for heating the cream so that it does not stick on the bottom. Make sure you beat the sauce immediately after the eggs are added.*

1 Cook the pasta in a large pot of salted boiling water according to the instructions on the package.

2 Meanwhile, put the saffron strands in a saucepan, add the water and bring to a boil immediately. Remove the pan from heat and allow to stand for a while.

Garganelli agli Asparagi e Panna

Garganelli with Asparagus and Cream

A LOVELY RECIPE FOR LATE spring when bunches of fresh young asparagus are on sale in shops and markets everywhere.

INGREDIENTS

1 bunch fresh young asparagus,
*   9–11 ounces*
3 cups garganelli
2 tablespoons butter
scant 1 cup panna da cucina or
*   heavy cream*
2 tablespoons dry white wine
1–1 1/3 cups freshly grated
*   Parmesan cheese*
2 tablespoons chopped fresh mixed herbs,
*   such as basil, Italian parsley, chervil,*
*   marjoram and oregano*
salt and ground black pepper
Serves 4

3 Cook the pasta according to the instructions on the package. Meanwhile, put the butter and cream in a medium saucepan, add salt and pepper to taste and bring to a boil. Simmer for a few minutes until the cream reduces and thickens, then add the asparagus, wine and about half the grated Parmesan. Taste for seasoning and keep on low heat.

4 Drain the pasta when cooked and turn it into a warmed bowl. Pour the sauce over the pasta, sprinkle with the fresh herbs and toss well. Serve immediately, topped with the remaining grated Parmesan.

COOK'S TIPS

• *When buying asparagus look for thin stalks, which will be sweet and tender. Don't buy asparagus with thick or woody stalks, which will be tough.*
• *Garganelli all'uovo (with egg) are just perfect for this dish. You can buy packages of this pasta in Italian markets.*
• *Penne (quills) or penne rigate (ridged quills) are an alternative pasta for this recipe. They are similar in shape and size to garganelli.*

1 Trim off and throw away the woody ends of the asparagus—after trimming, you should have about 7 ounces asparagus spears. Cut the spears diagonally into pieces that are roughly the same length and shape as the garganelli.

2 Blanch the asparagus spears in salted boiling water for 2 minutes, the tips for 1 minute. Immediately after blanching drain the asparagus spears and tips, rinse in cold water and set aside.

Tagliatelle al Radicchio con Panna

Tagliatelle with Radicchio and Cream

3 Add the butter, onion and garlic to the pan and stir-fry for 5 minutes more. Add the radicchio and toss for 1–2 minutes until wilted.

4 Pour in the cream and add the grated Parmesan, with salt and pepper to taste. Stir for 1–2 minutes, until the cream is bubbling and the ingredients are evenly mixed. Taste the sauce for seasoning.

THIS IS A MODERN RECIPE that is very quick and easy to make. It is deliciously rich, and makes a good dinner party first course.

INGREDIENTS

8 ounces tagliatelle
3–3 1/2 ounces pancetta or
 lean bacon, diced
2 tablespoons butter
1 onion, finely chopped
1 garlic clove, crushed
1 head of radicchio, about 4–6 ounces,
 finely shredded
2/3 cup panna da cucina or heavy cream
2/3 cup freshly grated Parmesan cheese
salt and ground black pepper
Serves 4

1 Cook the pasta according to the instructions on the package.

2 Meanwhile, put the pancetta or bacon in a medium saucepan and heat gently until the fat is rendered. Increase the heat slightly and stir-fry the pancetta or bacon for 5 minutes.

5 Drain the pasta and turn it into a warmed bowl. Pour the sauce over and toss well. Serve immediately.

COOK'S TIP

In Italy, cooks use a type of radicchio called radicchio di Treviso. It is very striking to look at, having long leaves that are dramatically striped in dark red and white. Radicchio di Treviso is available in some supermarkets and specialty green-markets, but if you cannot get it you can use the round radicchio instead, which is very easy to obtain.

Fish
and
Shellfish

I t is not surprising that seafood sauces are often served with pasta along the Italian coastline, and on the islands of Sicily and Sardinia, but they're very popular inland, too. Clams, mussels, tuna, shrimp, anchovies, salmon, scallops and squid are the most common fish and shellfish used, but cooks in coastal areas also create unique pasta dishes using the local catch. These are hard to replicate elsewhere.

Sometimes seafood is cooked with tomatoes, sometimes with a cream-based sauce, so the look and taste of seafood pasta can vary considerably from one dish to another. Intense flavors are found in Sicilian recipes, such as *Spaghetti alla Siracusana* and *Spaghetti alla Bottarga*, while the popular modern classic *Penne, Panna e Salmone* is mild and creamy. *Spaghetti alla Caprese*, which comes from the island of Capri, is fresh and light.

Spaghetti is the traditional pasta to serve with seafood sauces, since so many of them are based on olive oil and tomatoes. It remains the all-time favorite, but other shapes work equally well. When partnered with seafood, pasta proves its versatility.

Vermicelli alla Napoletana

Vermicelli with Clam Sauce

THIS RECIPE TAKES ITS name from the city of Naples, where both fresh tomato sauce and seafood are traditionally served with vermicelli. Here the two are combined to make a very tasty dish.

INGREDIENTS

2¼ pounds fresh hard-shell clams
1 cup dry white wine
2 garlic cloves, bruised
1 large handful fresh Italian parsley
2 tablespoons olive oil
1 small onion, finely chopped
8 ripe Italian plum tomatoes, peeled,
  seeded and finely chopped
½–1 fresh red chile, seeded and
  finely chopped
12 ounces vermicelli
salt and ground black pepper
Serves 4

1 Scrub the clams thoroughly under cold running water and discard any that are open or that do not close when sharply tapped against the work surface.

2 Pour the wine into a large saucepan, add the garlic cloves and half the parsley, then the clams. Cover tightly with the lid and bring to a boil over high heat. Cook for about 5 minutes, shaking the pan frequently, until the clams have opened.

3 Turn the clams into a large colander set over a bowl and let the liquid drain through. Set aside the clams until cool enough to handle, then remove about two-thirds of them from their shells, pouring the clam liquid into the bowl of cooking liquid. Discard any clams that have failed to open. Set both shelled and unshelled clams aside, keeping the unshelled clams warm in a bowl covered with a lid.

4 Heat the oil in a saucepan, add the onion and cook gently, stirring frequently, for about 5 minutes until softened and lightly colored. Add the tomatoes, then strain in the clam cooking liquid. Add the chile and salt and pepper to taste.

5 Bring to a boil, half cover the pan and simmer gently for 15–20 minutes. Meanwhile, cook the pasta according to the package instructions. Chop the remaining parsley finely.

6 Add the shelled clams to the tomato sauce, stir well and heat through very gently for 2–3 minutes.

7 Drain the cooked pasta well and turn it into a warmed bowl. Taste the sauce for seasoning, then pour the sauce over the pasta and toss everything together well. Garnish with the reserved clams, sprinkle the parsley over the pasta and serve immediately.

Conchiglie di Mare
Seafood Conchiglie

THIS IS A VERY SPECIAL MODERN dish, a warm salad composed of scallops, pasta and fresh arugula flavored with roasted pepper, chile and balsamic vinegar. It makes a substantial and impressive dinner party first course, or a main course for a light lunch.

INGREDIENTS

8 large fresh sea scallops
2³/4 cups conchiglie
1 tablespoon olive oil
1 tablespoon butter
1/2 cup dry white wine
3¹/2 ounces arugula leaves, stalks trimmed
salt and ground black pepper

For the vinaigrette

4 tablespoons extra virgin olive oil
1 tablespoon balsamic vinegar
1 piece bottled roasted pepper, drained and
   finely chopped
1–2 fresh red chiles, seeded and chopped
1 garlic clove, crushed
1–2 teaspoons honey, to taste

Serves 4

1 Cut each scallop into 2–3 pieces. If the corals are attached, pull them off and cut each piece in half. Season the scallops and corals with salt and pepper.

2 To make the vinaigrette, put the oil, vinegar, chopped pepper and chiles in a cup with the garlic and honey and whisk well.

3 Cook the pasta according to the instructions on the package.

4 Meanwhile, heat the oil and butter in a nonstick frying pan until sizzling. Add half the scallops and toss over high heat for 2 minutes. Remove with a slotted spoon and keep warm. Cook the remaining scallops in the same way.

5 Add the wine to the liquid remaining in the pan and stir over high heat until the mixture has reduced to a few tablespoons. Remove from heat and keep warm.

6 Drain the pasta and turn it into a warmed bowl. Add the arugula, scallops, the reduced cooking juices and the vinaigrette and toss well to combine. Serve immediately.

COOK'S TIPS

• *Use only fresh scallops for this dish—they are available all year round in most fishmarkets and from fish counters in supermarkets. Frozen scallops tend to be watery and tasteless, and often prove to be rubbery when cooked.*
• *For a more formal presentation, arrange the arugula leaves in a circle on each of four individual serving plates. Toss the pasta, scallops, reduced cooking juices and vinaigrette together and spoon into the center of the arugula leaves.*

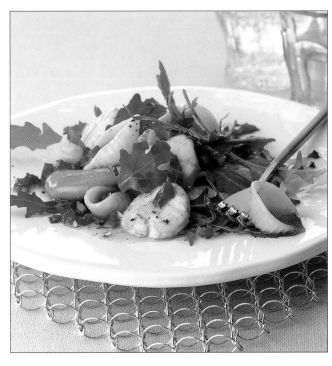

Spaghetti alla Siracusana

Spaghetti with Anchovies and Olives

THE STRONG FLAVORS of this dish are typical of Sicilian cuisine.

INGREDIENTS

3 tablespoons olive oil

1 large red bell pepper, seeded and
   finely chopped

1 small eggplant, finely chopped

1 onion, finely chopped

8 ripe Italian plum tomatoes, peeled, seeded
   and finely chopped

2 garlic cloves, finely chopped

$1/2$ cup dry red or white wine

$1/2$ cup water

1 handful fresh herbs, such as basil, Italian
   parsley and rosemary

11 ounces spaghetti

2 ounces canned anchovies, coarsely chopped,
   plus extra whole anchovies to garnish

12 pitted black olives

1–2 tablespoons capers, to taste

salt and ground black pepper

Serves 4

1 Heat the oil in a saucepan and add all the finely chopped vegetables and garlic. Cook gently, stirring frequently, for 10–15 minutes until the vegetables are soft. Pour in the wine and water, add the fresh herbs and pepper to taste and bring to a boil. Lower the heat and simmer, stirring occasionally, for 10–15 minutes. Meanwhile, cook the pasta in a large pot of salted boiling water according to the instructions on the package.

2 Add the chopped anchovies, olives and capers to the sauce, heat through for a few minutes and taste for seasoning. Drain the pasta and turn it into a warmed bowl. Pour the sauce over the pasta, toss well and serve immediately.

COOK'S TIP

If the anchovies are omitted, this makes a good sauce for vegetarians.

Spaghetti alla Caprese

Spaghetti with Tuna, Anchovies, Olives and Mozzarella

THIS RECIPE FROM CAPRI is fresh, light and full of flavor, so serve it as soon as it is cooked to enjoy it at its best.

INGREDIENTS

11 ounces spaghetti

2 tablespoons olive oil

6 ripe Italian plum tomatoes, chopped

1 teaspoon granulated sugar

1 jar (2 ounces) anchovies in olive oil, drained

4 tablespoons dry white wine

$1/2$ cup pitted black olives, quartered
   lengthwise

1 can (7 ounces) tuna in olive oil, drained

$4^1/2$-ounce package mozzarella cheese,
   drained and diced

salt and ground black pepper

fresh basil leaves, to garnish

Serves 4

1 Cook the pasta according to the instructions on the package. Meanwhile, heat the oil in a medium saucepan. Add the tomatoes, sugar and pepper to taste, and toss over medium heat for a few minutes until the tomatoes soften and the juices run. Snip a few anchovies at a time into the pan of tomatoes with kitchen scissors.

2 Add the wine, tuna and olives and stir once or twice until they are just evenly mixed into the sauce. Add the mozzarella and heat through without stirring. Taste and add salt if necessary. Drain the pasta and turn it into a warmed bowl. Pour the sauce over, toss gently and sprinkle with basil leaves. Serve immediately.

Orecchiette con Acciughe e Broccoli

Orecchiette with Anchovies and Broccoli

WITH ITS ROBUST FLAVORS, this pasta dish is typical of southern Italian and Sicilian cooking. Anchovies, pine nuts, garlic and pecorino cheese are all very popular ingredients. Serve with crusty Italian bread for a light lunch or supper.

INGREDIENTS

2 cups broccoli florets
^{1}/2 cup pine nuts
3 cups orecchiette
4 tablespoons olive oil
I small red onion, thinly sliced
I jar (2 ounces) anchovies in olive oil
I garlic clove, crushed
^{2}/3 cup freshly grated
    pecorino cheese
salt and ground black pepper
Serves 4

COOK'S TIP

Orecchiette (little ears) from Puglia are a special type of pasta with a chewy texture. You can get them in Italian markets, or use conchiglie instead.

1 Break the broccoli florets into small sprigs and cut off the stalks. If the stalks are large, chop or slice them. Cook the broccoli florets and stalks in a saucepan of boiling salted water for 2 minutes, then drain and refresh under cold running water. Allow to drain on paper towels.

2 Put the pine nuts in a dry nonstick frying pan and toss over low to medium heat for 1–2 minutes or until the nuts are lightly toasted and golden. Remove and set aside.

3 Cook the pasta according to the instructions on the package.

4 Meanwhile, heat the oil in a skillet, add the red onion and fry gently, stirring frequently, for about 5 minutes until softened. Add the anchovies with their oil, then add the garlic and fry over medium heat, stirring frequently, for 1–2 minutes until the anchovies break down into a paste. Add the broccoli and plenty of pepper and toss over the heat for a minute or two until the broccoli is hot. Taste for seasoning.

5 Drain the pasta and turn it into a warmed bowl. Add the broccoli mixture and grated pecorino and toss well to combine. Sprinkle the pine nuts over the top and serve immediately.

Trenette ai Frutti di Mare

Trenette with Shellfish

COLORFUL AND DELICIOUS, this typical Genoese dish is ideal for a dinner party. The sauce is quite runny, so serve it with crusty bread and spoons as well as forks.

INGREDIENTS

3 tablespoons olive oil

1 small onion, finely chopped

1 garlic clove, crushed

1/2 fresh red chile, seeded and chopped

*1 can (7 ounces) chopped Italian
    plum tomatoes*

2 tablespoons chopped fresh Italian parsley

14 ounces fresh hard-shell clams

14 ounces fresh mussels

4 tablespoons dry white wine

3 1/2 cups trenette

a few fresh basil leaves

*2/3 cup peeled cooked shrimp, thawed and
    thoroughly dried if frozen*

salt and ground black pepper

chopped fresh herbs, to garnish

Serves 4

1 Heat 2 tablespoons of the oil in a skillet or medium saucepan. Add the onion, garlic and chile and cook over medium heat for 1–2 minutes, stirring constantly. Stir in the tomatoes, half the parsley and pepper to taste. Bring to a boil, lower the heat, cover and simmer for 15 minutes.

2 Meanwhile, scrub the clams and mussels under cold running water. Discard any that are open or that do not close when sharply tapped against the work surface.

3 In a large saucepan, heat the remaining oil. Add the clams and mussels, with the rest of the parsley and toss over high heat for a few seconds. Pour in the wine, then cover tightly. Cook for about 5 minutes, shaking the pan frequently, until the clams and mussels have opened.

4 Remove the pan from heat and transfer the clams and mussels to a bowl with a slotted spoon, discarding any shellfish that have failed to open.

5 Strain the cooking liquid into a measuring cup and set aside. Reserve eight clams and four mussels in their shells for the garnish, then remove the rest from their shells.

6 Cook the pasta according to the instructions on the package. Meanwhile, add 1/2 cup of the reserved seafood liquid to the tomato sauce. Bring to a boil over high heat, stirring. Lower the heat, tear the basil leaves and add the shrimp with the shelled clams and mussels. Stir well, then taste for seasoning.

7 Drain the pasta and turn it into a warmed bowl. Add the seafood sauce and toss well to combine. Serve in individual bowls, sprinkle with herbs and garnish each portion with two reserved clams and one mussel in their shells.

Spaghetti alle Vongole

Spaghetti with Clam Sauce

THIS IS ONE OF ITALY'S most famous pasta dishes, sometimes translated as "white clam sauce" to distinguish it from that other classic, clams in tomato sauce. It is how they serve clams with pasta in Venice.

INGREDIENTS

2¼ pounds fresh hard-shell clams
4 tablespoons olive oil
3 tablespoons chopped fresh Italian parsley
½ cup dry white wine
12 ounces spaghetti
2 garlic cloves
salt and ground black pepper
Serves 4

1 Scrub the clams under cold running water, discarding any that are open or that do not close when sharply tapped against the work surface.

2 Heat half the oil in a large saucepan, add the clams and 1 tablespoon of the parsley and cook over high heat for a few seconds. Pour in the wine, then cover tightly. Cook for about 5 minutes, shaking the pan frequently, until the clams have opened. Meanwhile, cook the pasta in salted boiling water according to the instructions on the package.

3 Using a slotted spoon, transfer the clams to a bowl, discarding any that have failed to open. Strain the liquid and set it aside. Put eight clams in their shells to one side for the garnish, then remove the rest from their shells.

4 Heat the remaining oil in the clean pan. Fry the whole garlic cloves over medium heat until golden, crushing them with the back of a spoon. Remove the garlic with a slotted spoon and discard.

5 Add the shelled clams to the oil remaining in the pan, gradually add some of the strained liquid from the clams, then add plenty of pepper. Cook for 1–2 minutes, gradually adding more liquid as the sauce reduces. Add the remaining parsley and cook for 1–2 minutes.

6 Drain the pasta, add it to the pan and toss well. Serve in individual dishes, scooping the shelled clams from the bottom of the pan and placing some of them on top of each serving. Garnish with the reserved clams in their shells and serve immediately.

Penne with Shrimp and Artichokes

THIS IS A GOOD DISH TO MAKE in late spring or early summer, when greenish-purple baby artichokes appear in shops and on market stalls.

INGREDIENTS

juice of ¹/2 lemon
4 baby globe artichokes
6 tablespoons olive oil
2 garlic cloves, crushed
2 tablespoons chopped fresh mint
2 tablespoons chopped fresh Italian parsley
3 cups penne
8–12 peeled cooked large or jumbo shrimp,
* each cut into 2–3 pieces*
2 tablespoons butter
salt and ground black pepper
Serves 4

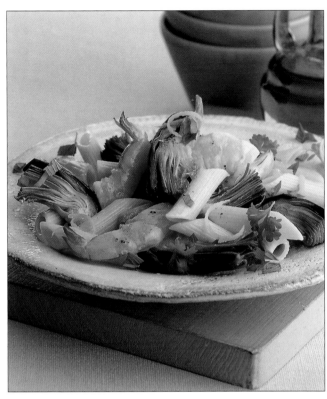

1 Have ready a bowl of cold water to which you have added the lemon juice. To prepare the artichokes, cut off the artichoke stalks, if any, and cut across the tops of the leaves. Peel off and discard any tough or discolored outer leaves.

2 Cut the artichokes lengthwise into quarters and remove any hairy chokes from their centers. Finally, cut the pieces of artichoke lengthwise into ¹/4-inch slices and put these in the bowl of acidulated water.

3 Drain the slices of artichoke and pat them dry. Heat the olive oil in a nonstick frying pan and add the artichokes, the crushed garlic and half the mint and parsley to the pan.

4 Season with plenty of salt and pepper. Cook over low heat, stirring frequently, for about 10 minutes or until the artichokes feel tender when pierced with a sharp knife.

5 Meanwhile, cook the pasta in a large pot of salted boiling water according to the instructions on the package.

6 Add the shrimp to the artichokes, stir well to mix, then heat through gently for 1–2 minutes.

7 Drain the pasta and turn it into a warmed bowl. Add the butter and toss until it has melted. Spoon the artichoke mixture over the pasta and toss to combine. Serve immediately, sprinkled with the remaining herbs.

Pesce con Fregola

Fish with Fregola

THIS SARDINIAN SPECIALITY is a cross between a soup and a stew. Serve it with crusty Italian country bread to mop up the juices.

INGREDIENTS

5 tablespoons olive oil

4 garlic cloves, finely chopped

$1/2$ small fresh red chile, seeded and finely chopped

1 large handful fresh Italian parsley, coarsely chopped

1 red snapper, about 1 pound, cleaned, with head and tail removed

1 ocean perch or porgy, about $1 1/4$ pounds, cleaned, with head and tail removed

12 ounces–1 pound thick cod fillet

1 can (14 ounces) chopped Italian plum tomatoes

$1 1/2$ cups fregola

salt and ground black pepper

Serves 4–6

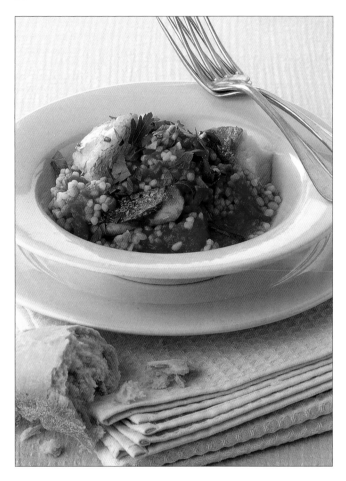

1 Heat 2 tablespoons of the olive oil in a large flameproof casserole. Add the chopped garlic and chile, with about half the chopped fresh parsley. Fry over medium heat, stirring occasionally, for about 5 minutes.

2 Cut all the fish into large chunks—including the skin and the bones in the case of the snapper and mullet—and add the pieces to the casserole as you cut them. Sprinkle the pieces with another 2 tablespoons of the olive oil and fry for a few minutes more.

3 Add the tomatoes, then fill the empty can with water and pour this into the pan. Bring to a boil. Stir in salt and pepper to taste, lower the heat and cook for 10 minutes, stirring occasionally.

4 Add the fregola and simmer for 5 minutes, then add 1 cup water and the remaining oil. Simmer for 15 minutes, until the fregola is *al dente*.

5 If the sauce becomes too thick, add more water, then taste for seasoning. Serve hot, in warmed bowls, sprinkled with the remaining parsley.

COOK'S TIPS

• *You can make the basic fish sauce several hours in advance or even the day before, bringing it to a boil and adding the fregola just before serving.*

• *Fregola is a tiny pasta shape from Sardinia. If you can't get it, use a tiny soup pasta (pastina), such as corallini or seme de melone.*

Farfalle al Sugo di Tonno
Farfalle with Tuna

A QUICK AND SIMPLE DISH that makes
a good weekday supper if you
have canned tomatoes and tuna in
the pantry.

INGREDIENTS

2 tablespoons olive oil

1 small onion, finely chopped

1 garlic clove, finely chopped

1 can (14 ounces) chopped Italian
plum tomatoes

3 tablespoons dry white wine

8–10 pitted black olives, cut into rings

2 teaspoons chopped fresh oregano or
1 teaspoon dried oregano, plus extra fresh
oregano to garnish

3 1/2 cups farfalle

1 can (6 ounces) tuna in olive oil

salt and ground black pepper

Serves 4

1 Heat the olive oil in a medium skillet
or saucepan, add the onion and garlic
and fry gently for 2–3 minutes, until
the onion is soft and golden.

2 Add the plum tomatoes and bring
to a boil, then add the white wine
and simmer for a minute or so. Stir in
the olives and oregano, with salt and
pepper to taste, then cover and cook
for 20–25 minutes, stirring from time
to time.

3 Meanwhile, cook the pasta in a
large pot of salted boiling water
according to the instructions
on the package.

4 Drain the canned tuna and flake
it with a fork. Add the tuna to the
sauce with about 4 tablespoons of the
water used for cooking the pasta. Taste
and adjust the seasoning.

5 Drain the cooked pasta well and
turn it into a warmed large serving
bowl. Pour the tuna sauce over the top
and toss to mix. Serve immediately,
garnished with sprigs of oregano.

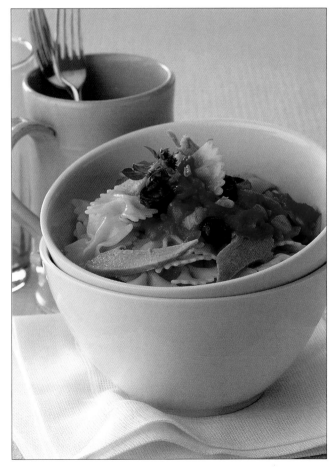

Paglia e Fieno con Salsa di Gamberi e Vodka

Paglia e Fieno with Shrimp and Vodka

THE COMBINATION OF SHRIMP, vodka and pasta may seem unusual, but it has become something of a modern classic in Italy. Here it is stylishly presented with two-colored pasta, but the sauce goes equally well with short shapes such as penne, rigatoni and farfalle.

INGREDIENTS

2 tablespoons olive oil
1/4 large onion, finely chopped
1 garlic clove, crushed
1–2 tablespoons sun-dried tomato paste
scant 1 cup panna da cucina or
   heavy cream
12 ounces fresh or dried paglia e fieno
12 large raw shrimp, peeled and chopped
2 tablespoons vodka
salt and ground black pepper
Serves 4

1 Heat the oil in a medium saucepan, add the onion and garlic and cook gently, stirring frequently, for about 5 minutes or until softened.

2 Add the tomato paste and stir for 1–2 minutes, then add the cream and bring to a boil, stirring. Season with salt and pepper to taste and let the sauce bubble until it starts to thicken slightly. Remove from heat.

3 Cook the pasta according to the instructions on the package. When it is almost ready, add the shrimp and vodka to the sauce; toss quickly over medium heat for 2–3 minutes or until the shrimp turn pink.

4 Drain the pasta and turn it into a warmed bowl. Pour the sauce over and toss well. Divide among warmed bowls and serve immediately.

COOK'S TIP

This sauce is best served as soon as it is ready, otherwise the shrimp will overcook and become tough. Make sure that the pasta has only a minute or two of cooking time left before adding the shrimp to the sauce.

Penne, Panna e Salmone

Penne with Cream and Smoked Salmon

THIS MODERN WAY OF serving pasta is popular all over Italy. The three essential ingredients combine together beautifully, and the dish is very quick and easy to make.

INGREDIENTS

3 cups penne
4 ounces thinly sliced smoked salmon
2–3 fresh thyme sprigs
2 tablespoons butter
2/3 cup heavy cream
salt and ground black pepper
Serves 4

1 Cook the pasta in a pot of salted boiling water according to the instructions on the package.

2 Meanwhile, using kitchen scissors, cut the smoked salmon into thin strips, about 1/4-inch wide. Strip the leaves from the thyme sprigs.

3 Melt the butter in a large saucepan. Stir in the cream with a quarter of the salmon and thyme leaves, then season with pepper. Heat gently for 3–4 minutes, stirring constantly. Do not allow to boil. Taste for seasoning.

4 Drain the pasta and toss it in the cream and salmon sauce. Divide among four warmed bowls and top with the remaining salmon and thyme leaves. Serve immediately.

VARIATION

Although penne is traditional with this sauce, it also goes very well with fresh ravioli stuffed with spinach and ricotta.

Spaghetti alla Bottarga

Spaghetti with Bottarga

ALTHOUGH THIS MAY SEEM an unusual recipe, with bottarga (salted and air-dried mullet or tuna roe) as the principal ingredient, it is very well known in Sardinia—and also in Sicily and parts of southern Italy. It is simplicity itself to make and tastes very, very good.

INGREDIENTS

12 ounces fresh or dried spaghetti

4 tablespoons olive oil

2–3 garlic cloves, peeled

ground black pepper

4–6 tablespoons grated bottarga, to taste

Serves 4

1 Cook the pasta according to the instructions on the package.

2 Meanwhile, heat half the olive oil in a large saucepan. Add the garlic and cook gently, stirring, for a few minutes. Remove the pan from heat, scoop out the garlic with a slotted spoon and discard.

3 Drain the pasta very well. Return the pan of garlic-flavored oil to the heat and add the pasta. Toss well, season with pepper and moisten with the remaining oil, or more to taste. Divide the pasta among four warmed bowls, sprinkle the grated bottarga over the top and serve immediately.

COOK'S TIP

You can buy bottarga in Italian markets. Small jars of ready-grated bottarga are convenient, but the best flavor comes from vacuum-packed slices of mullet bottarga. This is very easy to grate on a box grater. Keep any leftover bottarga tightly wrapped in the refrigerator, so that it does not flavor other foods.

Spaghetti alla Carrettiera

Spaghetti with Tuna, Mushrooms and Bacon

THE TERM ALLA CARRETTIERA means "cart-driver's style". The Romans lay claim to this recipe, but so do the Neapolitans and Sicilians, so there are many different versions of it.

INGREDIENTS

1/2 ounce dried porcini mushrooms
3/4 cup warm water
2 tablespoons olive oil
1 garlic clove
3 ounces pancetta or lean bacon, cut into
*   1/4-inch strips*
3 cups button mushrooms, chopped
14 ounces fresh or dried spaghetti
1 can (7 ounces) tuna in olive oil, drained
salt and ground black pepper
freshly grated Parmesan cheese, to serve
Serves 4

1 Put the porcini in a small bowl. Pour over the warm water and allow to soak for 15–20 minutes.

2 Heat the oil in a large saucepan, add the garlic clove and cook gently for about 2 minutes, crushing it with a wooden spoon to release the flavor. Remove the garlic and discard. Add the pancetta or bacon to the oil remaining in the pan and cook for 3–4 minutes, stirring occasionally.

3 Meanwhile, drain the dried mushrooms, reserving the soaking liquid, and chop them finely.

4 Add both types of mushroom to the pan and cook, stirring, for 1–2 minutes, then add 6 tablespoons of the reserved liquid from soaking the dried mushrooms, with salt and pepper to taste. Simmer for 10 minutes, stirring occasionally. Meanwhile, cook the pasta according to the instructions on the package, adding the remaining soaking liquid from the mushrooms to the pasta cooking water.

5 Add the drained canned tuna to the mushroom sauce and fold it in gently. Taste for seasoning.

6 Drain the cooked pasta well and turn it into a warmed serving bowl. Pour the sauce over the top, toss well and sprinkle liberally with some freshly grated Parmesan. Serve immediately, with more Parmesan passed separately.

Capelli d'Angelo all'Aragosta

Capelli d'Angelo with Lobster

THIS IS A SOPHISTICATED, stylish dish for a special occasion. Some cooks make the sauce with champagne rather than sparkling white wine, especially when they are planning to serve champagne with the meal.

INGREDIENTS

meat from the body, tail and claws of
   1 cooked lobster
juice of 1/2 lemon
3 tablespoons butter
4 fresh tarragon sprigs, leaves stripped
   and chopped
4 tablespoons heavy cream
6 tablespoons sparkling dry white wine
4 tablespoons fish stock
11 ounces fresh capelli d'angelo
salt and ground black pepper
about 2 teaspoons sevruga caviar,
   to garnish (optional)

Serves 4

1 Cut the lobster meat into small pieces and put it in a bowl. Sprinkle with the lemon juice. Melt the butter in a skillet or large saucepan, add the lobster meat and tarragon and stir over the heat for a few seconds. Add the cream and stir for a few seconds more, then pour in the wine and stock, with salt and pepper to taste. Simmer for 2 minutes, then remove from heat and cover.

2 Cook the pasta according to the instructions on the package. Drain well, reserving a few spoonfuls of the cooking water.

3 Place the pan of lobster sauce over medium to high heat, add the pasta and toss for just long enough to combine and heat through; moisten with a little of the reserved water from the pasta. Serve immediately in warmed bowls, sprinkled with sevruga caviar if you like.

COOK'S TIP

To remove the meat from a lobster, place the lobster on a board with its underbelly facing uppermost. With a large sharp knife, cut the lobster in half lengthwise. Spoon out the green liver and any pink roe (coral) and reserve these, then remove and discard the gravel sac (stomach). Pull the white tail meat out from either side of the shell and discard the black intestinal vein. Crack the claws with a nutcracker just below the pincers and remove the meat from the base. Pull away the small pincer, taking the white membrane with it, then remove the meat from this part of the shell. Pull the meat from the large pincer shell.

Linguine al Granchio

Linguine with Crab

THIS RECIPE COMES FROM Rome. It makes a very rich and tasty first course on its own, or can be served for a lunch or supper with crusty Italian bread. Some cooks like a finer sauce, and force the crabmeat through a sieve after pounding. If you choose to follow their example, be warned—it's hard work.

INGREDIENTS

about 9 ounces fresh crabmeat
3 tablespoons olive oil
1 small handful fresh Italian parsley,
* coarsely chopped, plus extra to garnish*
1 garlic clove, crushed
12 ounces ripe Italian plum tomatoes,
* peeled and chopped*
4–6 tablespoons dry white wine
12 ounces fresh or dried linguine
salt and ground black pepper

Serves 4

1 Put the crabmeat in a mortar and pound to a rough pulp with a pestle. If you do not have a pestle and mortar, use a sturdy bowl and the end of a rolling pin. Set aside.

2 Heat 2 tablespoons of the oil in a large saucepan. Add the parsley and garlic, with salt and pepper to taste, and fry for a few minutes until the garlic begins to brown.

3 Add the tomatoes, pounded crabmeat and wine, cover the pan and simmer gently for 15 minutes, stirring occasionally.

4 Meanwhile, cook the pasta according to the instructions on the package, draining it the moment it is *al dente*, and reserving a little of the cooking water.

5 Return the pasta to the clean pan, add the remaining oil and toss quickly over medium heat until the oil coats the strands.

6 Add the tomato and crab mixture to the pasta and toss again, adding a little of the reserved cooking water if you think it necessary. Adjust the seasoning to taste. Serve hot, in warmed bowls, sprinkled with parsley.

COOK'S TIP

For this recipe you will need the very freshest crabmeat. Fish markets will have freshly-picked crabmeat sold by weight, and the fish counters at supermarkets also provide it. Use both the white and dark meat.

Tagliatelle con Capesante

Tagliatelle with Scallops

SCALLOPS AND BRANDY MAKE this a relatively expensive dish, but it is so delicious that you will find it well worth the cost. Serve it for a dinner party first course.

INGREDIENTS

7 ounces sea scallops, sliced
2 tablespoons all-purpose flour
3 tablespoons butter
2 scallions, cut into thin rings
1/2–1 small fresh red chile, seeded and very
   finely chopped
2 tablespoons finely chopped fresh
   Italian parsley
4 tablespoons brandy
7 tablespoons fish stock
10 ounces fresh spinach-flavored
   tagliatelle
salt and ground black pepper

Serves 4

1 Toss the scallops in the flour, then shake off the excess. Bring a large pot of salted water to a boil, ready for cooking the pasta.

2 Meanwhile, melt the butter in a skillet or large saucepan. Add the scallions, finely chopped chile and half the parsley and fry, stirring frequently, for 1–2 minutes over medium heat. Add the scallops and toss over the heat for 1–2 minutes.

3 Pour the brandy over the scallops, then set it alight with a match. As soon as the flames have died down, stir in the fish stock and salt and pepper to taste. Mix well. Simmer for 2–3 minutes, then cover the pan and remove it from heat.

4 Add the pasta to a boiling water and cook it according to the instructions on the package. Drain, add to the sauce and toss over medium heat until mixed. Serve at once, in warmed bowls sprinkled with the remaining parsley.

COOK'S TIP

Buy fresh scallops if possible. Fresh scallops always have a better texture and flavor than frozen scallops, which tend to be watery.

Spaghetti con Seppie e Piselli

Spaghetti with Squid and Peas

IN TUSCANY, SQUID IS often cooked with peas in a tomato sauce. This recipe is a variation on the theme, and it works very well.

INGREDIENTS

1 pound prepared squid
2 tablespoons olive oil
1 small onion, finely chopped
1 can (14 ounces) chopped Italian
   plum tomatoes
1 garlic clove, finely chopped
1 tablespoon red wine vinegar
1 teaspoon granulated sugar
2 teaspoons finely chopped fresh rosemary
1 cup frozen peas
12 ounces fresh or dried spaghetti
1 tablespoon chopped fresh Italian parsley
salt and ground black pepper

Serves 4

1 Cut the prepared squid into strips about 1/4-inch wide. Finely chop any tentacles.

2 Heat the oil in a skillet or medium saucepan, add the finely chopped onion and cook gently, stirring, for about 5 minutes, until softened. Add the squid, tomatoes, garlic, red wine vinegar and sugar.

3 Add the rosemary, and salt and pepper to taste. Bring to a boil, stirring, then cover and simmer gently for 20 minutes. Uncover the pan, add the peas and cook for 10 minutes. Meanwhile, cook the pasta according to the instructions on the package, then drain and turn it into a warmed bowl. Pour the sauce over the pasta, add the parsley, then toss well and serve.

Spaghetti con Salmone e Gamberi

Spaghetti with Salmon and Shrimp

THIS IS A LOVELY FRESH-TASTING pasta dish, perfect for an al fresco meal in summer. Serve it as a main course lunch with warm crusty Italian bread and a dry white wine.

INGREDIENTS

11-ounce salmon fillet

scant 1 cup dry white wine

a few fresh basil sprigs, plus extra basil
   leaves, to garnish

6 ripe Italian plum tomatoes, peeled and
   finely chopped

2/3 cup heavy cream

3 cups fresh or dried spaghetti

2/3 cup peeled cooked shrimp, thawed and
   thoroughly dried if frozen

salt and ground black pepper

Serves 4

1 Put the salmon skin-side up in a wide shallow pan. Pour the wine over, then add the basil sprigs to the pan and sprinkle the fish with salt and pepper. Bring the wine to a boil, cover the pan and simmer gently for no more than 5 minutes. Using a spatula, lift the fish out of the pan and set aside to cool a little.

2 Add the tomatoes and cream to the liquid remaining in the pan and bring to a boil. Stir well, then lower the heat and simmer, uncovered, for 10–15 minutes. Meanwhile, cook the pasta according to the instructions on the package.

3 Flake the fish into large chunks, discarding the skin and any bones. Add the fish to the sauce with the shrimp, shaking the pan until the fish and shellfish are well coated. Taste the sauce for seasoning.

4 Drain the pasta and turn it into a warmed bowl. Pour the sauce over the pasta and toss to combine. Serve immediately, garnished with fresh basil leaves.

COOK'S TIP

Check the salmon fillet carefully for small bones when you are flaking the flesh. Although the salmon is already filleted, you will always find a few stray "pin" bones. Pick them out carefully using tweezers or your fingertips.

Tagliolini con Vongole e Cozze

Tagliolini with Clams and Mussels

SERVED ON WHITE CHINA, this makes a stunning looking dish for a dinner party first course. The sauce can be prepared a few hours ahead of time, then the pasta cooked and the dish assembled at the last minute.

INGREDIENTS

1 pound fresh mussels
1 pound fresh hard-shell clams
4 tablespoons olive oil
1 small onion, finely chopped
2 garlic cloves, finely chopped
1 large handful fresh Italian parsley, plus
    extra chopped parsley to garnish
3/4 cup dry white wine
1 cup fish stock
1 small fresh red chile, seeded and chopped
12 ounces squid ink tagliolini or tagliatelle
salt and ground black pepper
Serves 4

1 Scrub the mussels and clams under cold running water and discard any that are open or damaged, or that do not close when sharply tapped against the work surface.

2 Heat half the oil in a large pot, add the onion and cook gently for about 5 minutes until softened. Sprinkle in the garlic, then add about half the parsley sprigs, with salt and pepper to taste. Add the mussels and clams and pour in the wine. Cover with the lid and bring to a boil over a high heat. Cook for about 5 minutes, shaking the pan frequently, until the shellfish have opened.

3 Turn the mussels and clams into a fine strainer set over a bowl and let the liquid drain through. Discard the aromatics in the sieve, together with any mussels or clams that have failed to open. Return the liquid to the clean pot and add the fish stock. Chop the remaining parsley finely and add it to the liquid with the chopped chile. Bring to a boil, then lower the heat and simmer, stirring, for a few minutes until slightly reduced. Turn off the heat.

4 Remove and discard the top shells from about half the mussels and clams. Put all the mussels and clams in the pan of liquid and seasonings, then cover the pan tightly and set aside.

5 Cook the pasta according to the instructions on the package.

6 Drain well, then return to the clean pot; toss with the remaining olive oil. Put the pot of shellfish over a high heat and toss to quickly heat the shellfish through and combine with the liquid and seasonings.

7 Divide the pasta among four warmed plates, spoon the shellfish mixture over and around, then serve immediately, sprinkled with parsley.

Meat
and
Poultry

When we think of a meat sauce to serve with pasta, our minds automatically turn to Bolognese sauce, or *ragù alla Bolognese*, as it is correctly called in Italian. Thanks to Italian emigrés, Bolognese sauce has become one of the most famous pasta sauces outside Italy, especially in the United States and Great Britain. Beef, pork and pancetta simmered with wine and tomatoes until rich, intensely meaty and satisfying, is very hard to beat. Unfortunately, this superb sauce is almost always served with spaghetti outside Italy, which is incorrect. It should be teamed with tagliatelle.

Many meat sauces hail from the north of Italy, especially from the region of Emilia-Romagna, where both fresh meat and the famous hams, salame and sausages are enjoyed in abundance. The actual quantity of meat in the sauce is never very large, however, and the size of the pieces must be small or the sauce will simply slide off the pasta. The egg-enriched pasta of the northern regions is good with meat sauces because it holds the sauce well, but it is by no means the only possibility. Long, thin types of pasta such as spaghetti and vermicelli allow flavor to cling subtly because they do not hold a great deal of sauce with each forkful, a point worth considering when a meat sauce is very rich.

Tagliatelle alla Bolognese

Tagliatelle with Meat Sauce

THIS RECIPE IS AN authentic meat sauce—ragù—from the city of Bologna in Emilia-Romagna. It is very rich, and is always served with tagliatelle, never with spaghetti.

INGREDIENTS

1 pound fresh or dried tagliatelle
salt and ground black pepper
freshly grated Parmesan cheese, to serve

For the Bolognese meat sauce
1 onion
2 carrots
2 celery stalks
2 garlic cloves
2 tablespoons butter
1 tablespoon olive oil
4¹/₂-ounces pancetta or lean bacon, diced
9 ounces lean ground beef
9 ounces lean ground pork
¹/₂ cup dry white wine
2 cans (14-ounce) crushed Italian plum tomatoes
2–3 cups beef stock, homemade or from stock cubes
scant ¹/₂ cup panna da cucina or heavy cream
Serves 6–8

2 Add the ground beef and pork, lower the heat and cook gently for 10 minutes, stirring frequently and breaking up any lumps in the meat with a wooden spoon. Stir in salt and pepper to taste, then add the wine and stir again. Simmer for about 5 minutes, or until reduced.

4 Pour the cream into the sauce, stir well to mix, then simmer, without a lid, for another 30 minutes, stirring frequently. Meanwhile, cook the pasta according to the package instructions. Taste the sauce to check the seasoning. Drain the cooked pasta and turn it into a warmed bowl. Pour the sauce over the pasta and toss well. Serve immediately, sprinkled with grated Parmesan.

1 Make the meat sauce. Chop all the fresh vegetables finely. Heat the butter and oil in a large skillet or saucepan until sizzling. Add the vegetables and the pancetta or bacon and cook over medium heat, stirring frequently, for 10 minutes or until the vegetables have softened.

3 Add the canned tomatoes and 1 cup of the beef stock and bring to a boil. Stir the sauce well, then lower the heat. Half cover the pan with a lid and let simmer very gently for 2 hours. Stir occasionally during this time and add more stock as it becomes absorbed.

VARIATION

Some cooks add a few chopped chicken livers when frying the meat at the beginning of Step 2. This gives the sauce a stronger, almost gamey, flavor.

Spaghetti con Polpettine

Spaghetti with Meatballs

MEATBALLS SIMMERED in a sweet and spicy tomato sauce are truly delicious with spaghetti. Children love them and you can easily leave out the chiles.

INGREDIENTS

12 ounces ground beef

1 egg

4 tablespoons coarsely chopped fresh Italian parsley

1/2 teaspoon crushed dried red chiles

1 thick slice white bread, crusts removed

2 tablespoons milk

about 2 tablespoons olive oil

1 1/4 cups tomato sauce

1 3/4 cups vegetable stock

1 teaspoon granulated sugar

12 ounces–1 pound fresh or dried spaghetti

salt and ground black pepper

freshly grated Parmesan cheese, to serve

Serves 6–8

1 Put the ground beef in a large bowl. Add the egg, and half the parsley and crushed chiles. Season with plenty of salt and pepper.

2 Tear the bread into small pieces and place in a small bowl. Moisten with the milk. Allow to soak for a few minutes, then squeeze out the excess milk and crumble the bread over the meat mixture. Mix everything together with a wooden spoon, then use your hands to squeeze and knead the mixture until it becomes smooth and quite sticky.

3 Wash your hands, rinse them under the cold tap, then pick up small pieces of the mixture and roll them between your palms to make about 40-60 small balls. Place the meatballs on a tray for about 30 minutes.

4 Heat the oil in a large nonstick frying pan. Cook the meatballs in batches until browned on all sides. Pour the tomato sauce and stock into a large saucepan. Heat gently, then add the remaining chiles and the sugar, with salt and pepper to taste. Add the meatballs to the sauce mixture, then bring to a boil. Lower the heat and cover. Simmer for 20 minutes.

5 Cook the pasta according to the package instructions. When it is *al dente*, drain and turn it into a warmed large bowl. Pour the sauce over the pasta and toss gently. Sprinkle with the remaining parsley and serve with grated Parmesan passed separately.

Ragù d'Agnello e Peperoni

Lamb and Sweet Pepper Sauce

THIS SIMPLE SAUCE is a speciality of the Abruzzo-Molise region, east of Rome, where it is traditionally served with *maccheroni alla chitarra*—square-shaped long macaroni.

INGREDIENTS

4 tablespoons olive oil

9 ounces boneless lamb neck fillet, diced quite small

2 garlic cloves, finely chopped

2 bay leaves, torn

1 cup dry white wine

4 ripe Italian plum tomatoes, peeled and chopped

2 large red bell peppers, seeded and diced

salt and ground black pepper

Serves 4–6

1 Heat half the olive oil in a medium skillet or saucepan, add the small pieces of lamb and sprinkle with a little salt and pepper. Cook the meat over medium to high heat for about 10 minutes, stirring often, until it is browned on all sides.

2 Sprinkle in the garlic and add the bay leaves, then pour in the wine and let it bubble until reduced.

3 Add the remaining oil, the tomatoes and the peppers; stir to mix with the lamb. Season again. Cover with the lid and simmer over low heat for 45–55 minutes or until the lamb is very tender. Stir occasionally during cooking and moisten with water if the sauce becomes too dry. Remove the bay leaves from the sauce before serving it with pasta.

COOK'S TIPS

• *The peppers don't have to be red. Use yellow, orange or green if you prefer; either one color or a mixture.*

• *If you need to add water to the sauce towards the end of cooking, take it from the pot used for cooking the pasta.*

• *You can make your own fresh maccheroni alla chitarra or buy the dried pasta from an Italian delicatessen. Alternatively, this sauce is just as good with ordinary long or short macaroni. You will need 12–15 ounces.*

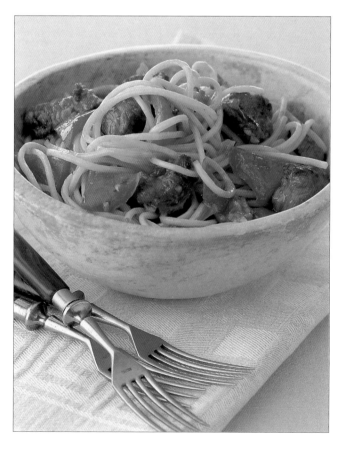

Fusilli with Sausage

SPICY HOT SAUSAGE and tomato sauce combine with spirals of pasta to make this really tasty dish from southern Italy. Pecorino cheese, with its strong and salty flavor, is the perfect accompaniment. Serve for an informal supper party with a full-bodied red wine and crusty country bread.

INGREDIENTS

14 ounces spicy pork sausages
2 tablespoons olive oil
1 small onion, finely chopped
2 garlic cloves, crushed
1 large yellow bell pepper, seeded and cut
  into strips
1 teaspoon paprika
1 teaspoon dried mixed herbs
1–2 teaspoons chili sauce
1 can (14 ounces) Italian plum tomatoes
1–1 1/4 cups vegetable stock, homemade
  or from stock cubes
2 3/4 cups fresh or dried fusilli
salt and ground black pepper
freshly grated pecorino cheese, to serve
Serves 4

1 Broil the sausages for 10–12 minutes, until they are browned on all sides, then drain them on paper towels.

2 Heat the oil in a large skillet or saucepan, add the onion and garlic and cook over low heat, stirring frequently, for 5–7 minutes until soft. Add the yellow pepper, paprika, herbs and chili sauce to taste. Cook gently for 5–7 minutes, stirring occasionally.

3 Pour in the canned tomatoes, breaking them up with a wooden spoon, then add salt and pepper to taste and stir well. Cook over medium heat for 10–12 minutes, adding the vegetable stock gradually as the sauce reduces.

4 While the tomato sauce is cooking, cut the broiled sausages diagonally into 1/2-inch pieces.

5 Add the sausage pieces to the sauce, reduce the heat to low and cook for 10 minutes. Meanwhile, cook the pasta according to the instructions on the package.

6 Taste the sauce for seasoning. Drain the pasta and add it to the pan of sauce. Toss well, then divide among four warmed bowls. Sprinkle each serving with a little grated pecorino and serve immediately, with more pecorino passed separately.

Malloreddus

Sardinian Sausage and Pasta

IN SARDINIA THEY CALL this dish simply "malloreddus", which is the local name for the type of pasta traditionally used to make it.

INGREDIENTS

2 tablespoons olive oil

6 garlic cloves

7 ounces Italian pure pork sausage,
  diced small

2 small handfuls fresh basil leaves

1 can (14 ounces) chopped Italian
  plum tomatoes

water, see method

a good pinch of saffron threads

1 tablespoon granulated sugar

3 cups malloreddus (gnocchi sardi)

1 cup freshly grated pecorino
  sardo cheese

salt and ground black pepper

Serves 4–6

1 Heat the oil in a medium skillet or saucepan. Add the garlic, sausage and half the basil leaves. Fry, stirring frequently, until the sausage is browned all over. Remove and discard the garlic. Add the tomatoes. Fill the empty can with water, pour it into the pan, then stir in the saffron, sugar, 1 teaspoon salt and pepper to taste. Bring to a boil, lower the heat and simmer for 20–30 minutes, stirring occasionally.

2 Meanwhile, cook the pasta in a pot of salted boiling water according to the package instructions.

3 Drain the pasta and turn it into a warmed bowl. Taste the sauce for seasoning, pour it over the pasta and toss well. Add about one-third of the grated pecorino and the remaining basil and toss well to mix again. Serve immediately, with the remaining pecorino sprinkled on top.

COOK'S TIP

In Sardinia, a special type of sausage is used for malloreddus. It is flavored with anise and black pepper and is called sartizzu sardo. A good alternative to sartizzu sardo would be the piquant salsiccia piccante. If, however, you prefer a slightly milder flavor, try luganega, which is much more widely available. Some butchers make their own Italian-style sausage on the premises, in which case you can always ask the butcher if he will season it for you with anise and black pepper if you want to try and create the authentic taste for yourself.

Rigatoni alla Bresàola e Peperoni

Rigatoni with Bresàola and Peppers

BRESÀOLA—CURED RAW BEEF—is usually served thinly sliced as an antipasto. Here its strong, almost gamey, flavor is used to good effect.

INGREDIENTS

2 tablespoons olive oil

1 small onion, finely chopped

5 ounces bresàola, cut into thin strips

1 small handful fresh basil leaves

4 bell peppers (red and orange or yellow), diced

1/2 cup dry white wine

1 can (14 ounces) chopped plum tomatoes

4 cups rigatoni

2/3 cup freshly shaved Parmesan cheese

1 small handful fresh basil leaves

salt and ground black pepper

Serves 6

1 Heat the oil in a medium saucepan, add the onion and *bresàola*. Cover the pan and cook over low heat for 5–8 minutes, until the onion has softened. Stir in the basil leaves, then add the peppers, wine, 1 teaspoon salt and plenty of pepper. Stir well, then simmer for 10–15 minutes.

2 Add the canned tomatoes to pan and increase the heat to high. Bring to a boil, stirring, then lower the heat and replace the lid. Simmer gently, stirring occasionally, for 20 minutes or until the peppers are very soft and quite creamy. Meanwhile, cook the pasta in a pot of salted boiling water according to the instructions on the package.

3 Drain the cooked pasta and turn it into a warmed bowl. Taste the sauce for seasoning, then pour it over the pasta and add about half the Parmesan. Toss well and serve immediately, with the remaining Parmesan sprinkled on top.

Bucatini alla Posillipo

Bucatini with Sausage and Pancetta

THIS IS A VERY RICH and satisfying main course dish. It hardly needs grated Parmesan cheese as an accompaniment, but you can pass some around in a separate bowl if you wish.

INGREDIENTS

4 ounces pork sausage-meat
1 can (14 ounces) Italian plum tomatoes
1 tablespoon olive oil
1 garlic clove, crushed
4 ounces pancetta or lean bacon,
    coarsely chopped
2 tablespoons chopped fresh Italian parsley
14 ounces bucatini
4–5 tablespoons panna da cucina or
    heavy cream
2 egg yolks
salt and ground black pepper
Serves 4

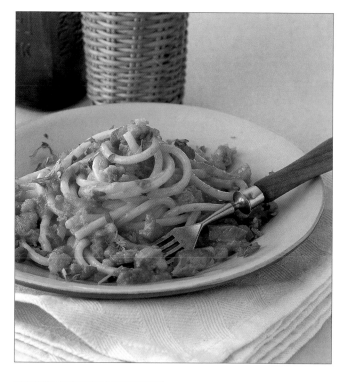

1 Remove any skin from the sausage-meat and break the meat up coarsely with a knife. Purée the tomatoes in a food processor or blender.

2 Heat the oil in a medium skillet or saucepan, add the garlic and fry over low heat for 1–2 minutes. Remove the garlic with a slotted spoon and discard it.

3 Add the pork sausage-meat and pancetta or bacon and cook over medium heat for 3–4 minutes. Stir constantly with a wooden spoon to break up the sausage-meat—it will become brown and look crumbly.

4 Add the puréed tomatoes to the pan with half the parsley and salt and pepper to taste. Stir well and bring to a boil, scraping up any sediment from the sausage-meat that has stuck to the bottom of the pan.

5 Lower the heat, cover and simmer for 30 minutes, stirring from time to time. Taste the sausage-meat sauce for seasoning.

6 Meanwhile, cook the pasta according to the instructions on the package. Put the cream and egg yolks in a warmed large bowl and mix with a fork. As soon as the pasta is *al dente*, drain it well and add it to the bowl of cream mixture. Toss until the pasta is coated, then pour the sausage-meat sauce over the pasta and toss again. Serve immediately, sprinkled with the remaining parsley.

COOK'S TIPS

• *To save time puréeing the tomatoes, use tomato sauce.*
• *For authenticity, buy salsiccia a metro, a pure pork sausage sold by the length at Italian delicatessens.*
• *Bucatini is a long hollow pasta that looks like hard drinking straws; spaghetti works equally well.*

Rigatoni con Ragù di Maiale

Rigatoni with Pork

THIS IS AN EXCELLENT meat sauce using ground pork rather than the more usual ground beef. Here it is served with rigatoni, a short tubular pasta shape, but you could serve it with tagliatelle or spaghetti to make a pork version of Bolognese.

INGREDIENTS

1 small onion
1/2 carrot
1/2 celery stalk
2 garlic cloves
2 tablespoons butter
2 tablespoons olive oil
5 ounces ground pork
4 tablespoons dry white wine
1 can (14 ounces) chopped Italian
*   plum tomatoes*
a few fresh basil leaves, plus extra basil
*   leaves, to garnish*
3 1/2 cups rigatoni
salt and ground black pepper
freshly shaved Parmesan cheese,
*   to serve*
Serves 4

1 Chop all the fresh vegetables finely, either in a food processor or by hand. Heat the butter and oil in a large skillet or saucepan until just sizzling, add the chopped vegetables and cook over medium heat, stirring frequently, for 3–4 minutes.

2 Add the ground pork and cook gently for 2–3 minutes, breaking up any lumps in the meat with a wooden spoon.

3 Lower the heat and fry for another 2–3 minutes, stirring frequently, then stir in the wine. Mix in the tomatoes, whole basil leaves, salt to taste and plenty of pepper. Bring to a boil, then lower the heat, cover and simmer for 40 minutes, stirring from time to time.

4 Cook the pasta according to the instructions on the package. Just before draining it, add a ladleful or two of the cooking water to the sauce. Stir well, then taste the sauce for seasoning.

5 Drain the pasta, add it to the pan of sauce and toss well. Serve immediately, sprinkled with the basil and shaved Parmesan.

VARIATION

To give the sauce a more intense flavor, soak 1/2 ounce dried porcini mushrooms in 3/4 cup warm water for 15–20 minutes, then drain, chop and add with the meat.

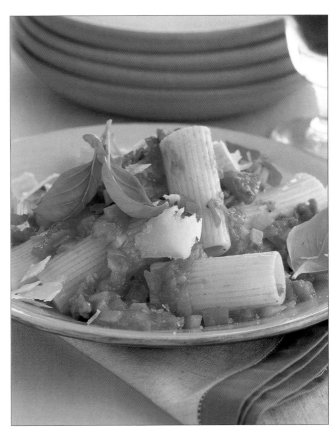

Eliche con Salsiccie e Radicchio

Eliche with Sausage and Radicchio

SAUSAGE AND RADICCHIO may seem odd companions, but the combined flavor of these ingredients is really delicious. This robust and hearty dish makes a good main course.

INGREDIENTS

2 tablespoons olive oil
1 onion, finely chopped
7 ounces Italian pure pork sausage
$3/4$ cup tomato sauce
6 tablespoons dry white wine
$2^3/4$ cups eliche
2 ounces radicchio leaves
salt and ground black pepper
Serves 4

1 Heat the olive oil in a large, deep skillet or saucepan. Add the finely chopped onion and cook over low heat, stirring frequently, for about 5 minutes or until softened.

2 Snip the end off the sausage skin and squeeze the sausage-meat into the pan. With a wooden spoon, stir the sausage-meat to mix it with the oil and onion and break it up into small pieces.

3 Continue to fry the mixture, increasing the heat if necessary, until the sausage-meat is brown all over and looks crumbly. Stir in the tomato sauce, then sprinkle in the wine, with salt and pepper to taste. Simmer over low heat, stirring occasionally, for 10–12 minutes.

4 Meanwhile, cook the pasta according to the instructions on the package. Just before draining the pasta, add a ladleful or two of the cooking water to the sausage sauce and stir it in well. Taste the sauce to check the seasoning.

5 Finely shred the radicchio leaves. Drain the cooked pasta and turn it into the pan of sausage sauce. Add the shredded radicchio and toss well to combine everything thoroughly. Serve immediately.

COOK'S TIPS

• *The best sausage to use is the one you buy from the Italian delicatessen called* salsiccia puro suino. *It is made from 100 percent pure pork plus flavorings and seasonings.*
• *If you can get it, use the long, tapering* radicchio di Treviso *for this dish; otherwise the tightly furled, round radicchio can be used.*

Spaghetti with Ground Beef Sauce

SPAGHETTI BOLOGNESE is not an authentic Italian dish. It was "invented" by Italian emigrés in America in the sixties in response to popular demand for a spaghetti dish with meat sauce. This is a rich, spicy version.

INGREDIENTS

2 tablespoons olive oil
1 onion, finely chopped
1 garlic clove, crushed
1 teaspoon dried mixed herbs
1/4 teaspoon cayenne pepper
12 ounces–1 pound ground beef
1 can (14 ounces) chopped Italian
   plum tomatoes
3 tablespoons tomato ketchup
1 tablespoon sun-dried tomato paste
1 teaspoon Worcestershire sauce
1 teaspoon dried oregano
1 3/4 cups beef or vegetable stock,
   homemade or using a stock cube
3 tablespoons red wine
14 ounces–1 pound spaghetti
salt and ground black pepper
freshly grated Parmesan cheese, to serve

Serves 4–6

2 Stir in the canned tomatoes, ketchup, sun-dried tomato paste, Worcestershire sauce, oregano and plenty of black pepper. Pour in the stock and red wine and bring to a boil, stirring. Cover the pan, lower the heat and let the sauce simmer for 30 minutes, stirring occasionally.

3 Cook the pasta according to the instructions on the package. Drain well and divide among warmed bowls. Taste the sauce and add a little salt if necessary, then spoon it on top of the pasta and sprinkle with a little grated Parmesan. Serve immediately, with grated Parmesan passed separately.

1 Heat the oil in a medium saucepan, add the onion and garlic and cook over low heat, stirring frequently, for about 5 minutes, until softened. Stir in the mixed herbs and cayenne and cook for 2–3 minutes more. Add the ground beef and cook gently for about 5 minutes, stirring frequently and breaking up any lumps in the meat with a wooden spoon.

Tortellini con Prosciutto

Tortellini with Ham

THIS IS A VERY EASY RECIPE that can be made quickly from pantry ingredients. It is therefore ideal for an after-work supper.

INGREDIENTS

9-ounce package tortellini alla carne
   (meat-filled tortellini)
2 tablespoons olive oil
1 small onion, finely chopped
4 ounces cooked ham, diced
²/₃ cup strained crushed Italian
   plum tomatoes
scant ¹/₂ cup panna da cucina or
   heavy cream
generous 1 cup freshly grated
   Parmesan cheese
salt and ground black pepper
Serves 4

1 Cook the pasta according to the instructions on the package.

2 Meanwhile, heat the oil in a large skillet or saucepan, add the onion and cook over low heat, stirring frequently, for about 5 minutes, until softened. Add the ham and cook, stirring occasionally, until it darkens.

3 Add the strained crushed tomatoes. Fill the empty carton with water and pour it into the pan. Stir well, then add salt and pepper to taste. Bring to a boil, lower the heat and simmer the sauce for a few minutes, stirring occasionally, until it has reduced slightly. Stir in the cream. Drain the pasta well and add it to the sauce.

4 Add a handful of grated Parmesan to the pan. Stir, toss well and taste for seasoning. Serve in warmed bowls, topped with the remaining Parmesan.

COOK'S TIP

Cartons of strained crushed tomatoes are handy for making quick sauces.

Ragù al Vino Rosso

Bolognese Sauce with Red Wine

THIS IS A VERSATILE meat sauce. You can toss it with freshly cooked pasta—the quantity here is enough for 1 pound tagliatelle, spaghetti or a short pasta shape such as penne or fusilli—or alternatively you can layer it in a baked dish like lasagne.

INGREDIENTS

1 medium onion
1 small carrot
1 celery stalk
2 garlic cloves
3 tablespoons olive oil
14 ounces ground beef
¹/₂ cup red wine
scant 1 cup tomato sauce
1 tablespoon tomato purée
1 teaspoon dried oregano
1 tablespoon chopped fresh Italian parsley
1¹/₂ cups beef stock
8 small plum tomatoes (optional)
salt and ground black pepper
Serves 4–6

1 Chop all the vegetables finely, either in a food processor or by hand. Heat the oil in a large saucepan, add the chopped vegetable mixture and cook over low heat, stirring frequently, for 5–7 minutes.

2 Add the ground beef and cook for 5 minutes, stirring frequently and breaking up any lumps in the meat with a wooden spoon.

3 Stir in the wine and mix well. Cook for 1–2 minutes, then add the tomato sauce, tomato purée, herbs and 4 tablespoons of the stock. Season with salt and pepper to taste. Stir well and bring to a boil.

4 Cover the pan, and cook over low heat for 30–40 minutes, stirring, adding more stock as necessary. Add the tomatoes, if using, and simmer for 5-10 minutes more. Taste for seasoning and toss with hot, freshly cooked pasta, or use in baked pasta dishes.

Fettuccine al Prosciutto e Piselli

Fettuccine with Ham and Peas

THIS SIMPLE DISH MAKES a very good first course for six people, or a main course for three to four. The ingredients are all easily available from the supermarket, so the recipe makes an ideal impromptu supper.

INGREDIENTS

1/4 cup butter

1 small onion, finely chopped

1 3/4 cups fresh or frozen peas

scant 1/2 cup chicken stock, homemade or
with stock cubes

1/2 teaspoon granulated sugar

3/4 cup dry white wine

12 ounces fresh fettuccine

3-ounce piece cooked ham, cut into
bite-size chunks

1 1/3 cups freshly grated Parmesan cheese

salt and ground black pepper

Serves 3–6

1 Melt the butter in a medium skillet or saucepan, add the onion and cook over low heat for about 5 minutes, or until softened but not colored. Add the peas, stock and sugar, with salt and pepper to taste.

2 Bring to a boil, then lower the heat and simmer for 3–5 minutes or until the peas are tender. Add the wine, increase the heat and boil until the wine has reduced.

3 Cook the pasta according to the instructions on the package. When it is almost ready, add the ham to the sauce, with about a third of the grated Parmesan. Heat through, stirring, then taste for seasoning.

4 Drain the pasta and turn it into a warmed large bowl. Pour the sauce over the pasta and toss well. Serve immediately, sprinkled with the remaining grated Parmesan.

Pappardelle with Rabbit Sauce

THIS RICH-TASTING DISH comes from the north of Italy, where rabbit sauces for pasta are very popular.

INGREDIENTS

1/2 ounce dried porcini mushrooms

3/4 cup warm water

1 small onion

1/2 carrot

1/2 celery stalk

2 bay leaves

2 tablespoons butter

1 tablespoon olive oil

1 1/2 ounces pancetta or lean bacon, chopped

1 tablespoon coarsely chopped fresh Italian parsley, plus extra to garnish

9 ounces boneless rabbit meat

6 tablespoons dry white wine

1 can (7 ounces) chopped Italian plum tomatoes or scant 1 cup tomato sauce

11 ounces fresh or dried pappardelle

salt and ground black pepper

Serves 4

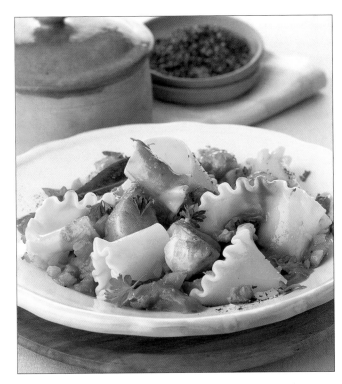

1 Put the dried mushrooms in a bowl, pour over the warm water and allow to soak for 15–20 minutes. Finely chop the vegetables, either in a food processor or by hand. Make a tear in each bay leaf, so that they will release their flavor when added to the sauce.

2 Heat the butter and oil in a skillet or medium saucepan until just sizzling. Add the chopped vegetables, pancetta or bacon and the parsley and cook for about 5 minutes.

3 Add the pieces of rabbit and fry on both sides for 3–4 minutes. Pour the wine over and let it reduce for a few minutes, then add the tomatoes or tomato sauce. Drain the mushrooms and pour the soaking liquid into the pan. Chop the mushrooms and add them to the mixture, with the bay leaves and salt and pepper to taste. Stir well, cover and simmer for 35–40 minutes, until the rabbit is tender, stirring occasionally.

4 Remove the pan from heat and lift out the pieces of rabbit with a slotted spoon. Cut them into bite-size chunks and stir them into the sauce. Remove and discard the bay leaves. Taste the sauce and add more salt and pepper, if needed. Cook the pasta according to the instructions on the package. Meanwhile, reheat the sauce. Drain the pasta and toss with the sauce in a warmed bowl. Serve immediately, sprinkled with parsley.

Farfalle con Pollo e Pomodorini

Farfalle with Chicken and Cherry Tomatoes

QUICK TO PREPARE and easy to cook, this colorful dish is full of flavor. Serve it for a midweek supper, with a green salad to follow.

INGREDIENTS

12 ounces skinless chicken breast fillets, cut
into bite-size pieces
4 tablespoons Italian dry vermouth
2 teaspoons chopped fresh rosemary, plus
4 fresh rosemary sprigs, to garnish
1 tablespoon olive oil
1 onion, finely chopped
3¹/₂-ounce piece Italian salami, diced
2¹/₂ cups farfalle
1 tablespoon balsamic vinegar
14-ounces cherry tomatoes
good pinch of crushed dried red chiles
salt and ground black pepper
Serves 4

1 Put the pieces of chicken in a large bowl, pour in the dry vermouth and sprinkle with half the chopped rosemary and salt and pepper to taste. Stir well and set aside.

2 Heat the oil in a large skillet or saucepan, add the onion and salami and fry over medium heat for about 5 minutes, stirring frequently.

3 Cook the pasta according to the instructions on the package.

4 Add the chicken and vermouth to the onion and salami, increase the heat to high and fry for 3 minutes or until the chicken is white on all sides. Sprinkle the vinegar over the chicken.

5 Add the cherry tomatoes and dried chiles. Stir well and simmer for a few minutes more. Taste the sauce for seasoning.

6 Drain the pasta and turn it into the skillet or saucepan. Add the remaining chopped rosemary and toss to mix the pasta and sauce together. Serve immediately in warmed bowls, garnished with the rosemary sprigs.

COOK'S TIP

The tomatoes look good left whole, but if you prefer you can crush them with the back of a wooden spoon while they are simmering in the pan.

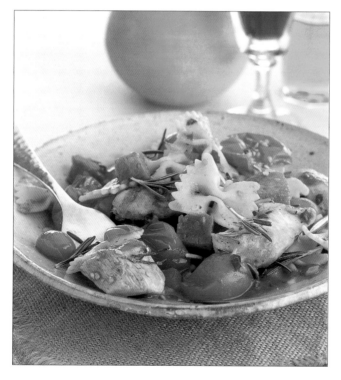

Penne alla Rusticana

Penne with Chicken, Broccoli and Cheese

THE COMBINATION OF BROCCOLI, garlic and Gorgonzola is very good, and goes especially well with chicken.

INGREDIENTS

scant 1 cup broccoli florets, divided into
    tiny sprigs
1/4 cup butter
2 skinless chicken breast fillets, cut into
    thin strips
2 garlic cloves, crushed
3 1/2 cups penne
1/2 cup dry white wine
scant 1 cup panna da cucina *or*
    heavy cream
3 1/2 ounces Gorgonzola cheese, rind
    removed and diced small
salt and ground black pepper
freshly grated Parmesan cheese, to serve

Serves 4

1 Plunge the broccoli into a saucepan of boiling salted water. Bring back to a boil and boil for 2 minutes, then drain in a colander and refresh under cold running water. Shake well to remove the surplus water and set aside to drain completely.

2 Melt the butter in a large skillet or saucepan, add the chicken and garlic, with salt and pepper to taste, and stir well. Fry over medium heat for 3 minutes or until the chicken becomes white. Meanwhile, start cooking the pasta according to the instructions on the package.

3 Pour the wine and cream over the chicken mixture in the pan, stir to mix, then simmer, stirring occasionally, for about 5 minutes, until the sauce has reduced and thickened. Add the broccoli, increase the heat and toss to heat it through and mix it with the chicken. Taste for seasoning.

4 Drain the pasta and add it to the sauce. Add the Gorgonzola and toss well. Serve with grated Parmesan.

VARIATION

Use leeks instead of broccoli if you prefer. Fry them with the chicken.

Pappardelle al Pollo e Porcini

Pappardelle with Chicken and Mushrooms

RICH AND CREAMY, this is a good supper party dish.

INGREDIENTS

1/2 ounce dried porcini mushrooms
3/4 cup warm water
2 tablespoons butter
I small leek or 4 scallions, chopped
I garlic clove, crushed
I small handful fresh Italian parsley,
   coarsely chopped
1/2 cup dry white wine
I cup chicken stock
14 ounces fresh or dried pappardelle
2 skinless chicken breast fillets, cut into
   thin strips
7 tablespoons mascarpone cheese
salt and ground black pepper
fresh basil leaves, shredded, to garnish

Serves 4

I Put the dried mushrooms in a bowl. Pour in the warm water and allow to soak for 15–20 minutes. Turn into a fine sieve set over a bowl and squeeze the mushrooms with your hands to release as much liquid as possible.

2 Chop the mushrooms finely and set aside the strained soaking liquid until required.

3 Melt the butter in a medium skillet or saucepan, add the chopped mushrooms, garlic, parsley and leek or scallions, with salt and pepper to taste. Cook over low heat, stirring frequently, for about 5 minutes, then pour in the wine and stock and bring to a boil. Lower the heat and simmer for about 5 minutes or until the liquid has reduced and is thickened.

4 Meanwhile, start cooking the pasta in salted boiling water according to the package instructions, adding the reserved soaking liquid from the mushrooms to the water.

5 Add the chicken strips to the sauce and simmer for 5 minutes or until just tender. Add the mascarpone a spoonful at a time, stirring well after each addition, then add one or two spoonfuls of the water used for cooking the pasta. Taste for seasoning.

6 Drain the pasta and turn it into a warmed large bowl. Add the chicken and sauce and toss well. Serve immediately, topped with the shredded basil leaves.

VARIATIONS

• Add I cup sliced button or cremini mushrooms with the chicken.
• Add blanched sprigs of broccoli before the mascarpone in Step 5.

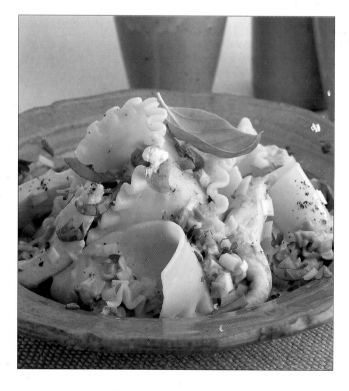

Conchiglie coi Fegatini alle Erbe

Conchiglie with Chicken Livers and Herbs

FRESH HERBS AND CHICKEN livers are a good combination, often used together on crostini in Tuscany. Here they are tossed with pasta shells to make a very tasty supper dish.

INGREDIENTS

¹/4 cup butter

4 ounces pancetta or lean bacon, diced

9 ounces frozen chicken livers, thawed, drained and diced

2 garlic cloves, crushed

2 teaspoons chopped fresh sage

2³/4 cups conchiglie

²/3 cup dry white wine

4 ripe Italian plum tomatoes, peeled and diced

1 tablespoon chopped fresh Italian parsley

salt and ground black pepper

Serves 4

1 Melt half the butter in a medium skillet or saucepan, add the pancetta or bacon and fry over medium heat for a few minutes, until it is lightly colored but not crisp.

2 Add the chicken livers, garlic, half the sage and plenty of pepper. Increase the heat and toss the livers for about 5 minutes, until they change color all over. Meanwhile, start cooking the pasta according to the instructions on the package.

3 Pour the wine over the chicken livers in the pan and let it sizzle, then lower the heat and simmer gently for 5 minutes. Add the remaining butter to the pan. As soon as it has melted, add the diced tomatoes, toss to mix, then add the remaining sage and the parsley. Stir well. Taste and add salt if needed.

4 Drain the pasta and turn it into a warmed bowl. Pour the sauce over and toss well. Serve immediately.

Vegetables
and
Vegetarian

Pasta really comes into its own when it is served with a vegetable sauce. After all, when pasta was first "invented" it was a food for the poor, and vegetables were often all they could afford.

Vegetable sauces are invariably simple, in fact the simpler the better. Modern recipes often consist of nothing more elaborate than chopped or sliced raw vegetables "cooked" by the heat of freshly drained pasta. Color, crunch and flavor are all retained, along with maximum nutritive value.

Almost all the recipes in this chapter can be cooked in a very short time, making them perfect for quick after-work suppers. Not all of them contain vegetables; some simply consist of butter and herbs, cheese and pepper, garlic and oil. These are the easiest of all pasta sauces to make, and some of the best.

Traditional vegetable sauces come from the south of Italy, where commercially-dried pasta is favored over the fresh. Generally speaking, dried pasta does seem to be the best choice for serving with vegetables, but for extra nutritional value there is no reason why fresh, egg-enriched pasta cannot be used.

Trenette alla Genovese

Trenette with Pesto, Green Beans and Potatoes

IN LIGURIA, IT IS TRADITIONAL to serve pesto with trenette, green beans and diced potatoes. The ingredients for making fresh pesto are quite expensive, so the green beans and potatoes are added to help make the pesto go further.

INGREDIENTS

about 40 fresh basil leaves

2 garlic cloves, thinly sliced

1 1/2 tablespoons pine nuts

3 tablespoons freshly grated Parmesan cheese, plus extra to serve

2 tablespoons freshly grated pecorino cheese, plus extra to serve

4 tablespoons extra virgin olive oil

2 potatoes, total weight about 9 ounces

3 1/2 ounces green beans

12 ounces trenette

salt and ground black pepper

Serves 4

1 Put the basil leaves, garlic, pine nuts and cheeses in a blender or food processor and process for about 5 seconds. Add half the olive oil and a pinch of salt and process for 5 seconds more. Stop the machine, remove the lid and scrape down the side of the bowl. Add the remaining oil and process for 5–10 seconds.

2 Cut the potatoes in half length-wise. Slice each half crosswise into 1/4-inch thick slices. Trim the beans, then cut them into 3/4-inch pieces. Plunge the potatoes and beans into a large saucepan of salted boiling water and boil, uncovered, for 5 minutes.

3 Add the pasta, bring the water back to a boil, stir well, then cook for 5–7 minutes or until the pasta is *al dente*.

4 Meanwhile, put the pesto in a large bowl and add 3–4 tablespoons of the water used for cooking the pasta. Mix well.

5 Drain the pasta and vegetables, add them to the pesto and toss well. Serve immediately on warmed plates, with extra grated Parmesan and pecorino passed separately.

COOK'S TIPS

• *Don't worry if the potatoes break up during cooking—this will add to the creaminess of the finished dish.*

• *The pesto can be made up to 2–3 days in advance and kept in a bowl in the refrigerator until needed. Pour a thin film of olive oil over the surface of the pesto and cover the bowl tightly with plastic wrap before refrigerating.*

• *Trenette is the traditional Ligurian pasta that is served with pesto, but if you find it difficult to obtain you can use bavette or linguine instead. The two-colored paglia e fieno would be another good choice.*

Paglia e Fieno with Sun-dried Tomatoes and Radicchio

THIS IS A LIGHT, MODERN PASTA dish of the kind served in fashionable restaurants. It is the presentation that sets it apart, not the preparation, which is very quick and easy.

INGREDIENTS

3 tablespoons pine nuts
12 ounces paglia e fieno
3 tablespoons extra virgin olive oil
2 tablespoons sun-dried tomato paste
2 pieces drained sun-dried tomatoes in olive oil, cut into very thin slivers
1 1/2 ounces radicchio leaves, finely shredded
4 – 6 scallions, thinly sliced into rings
salt and ground black pepper

Serves 4

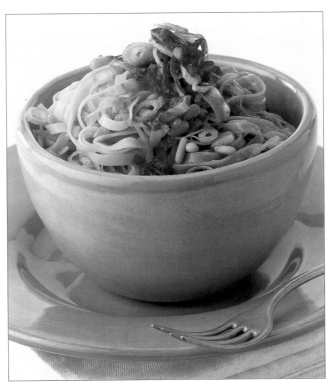

1 Put the pine nuts in a nonstick frying pan and toss over low to medium heat for 1–2 minutes or until they are lightly toasted and golden. Remove and set aside.

2 Cook the pasta according to the package instructions, keeping the colors separate by using two pans.

5 Arrange a portion of green and white pasta in each of four warmed bowls, then spoon the sun-dried tomato and radicchio mixture in the center. Sprinkle the scallions and toasted pine nuts decoratively over the top and serve immediately. Before eating, each diner should toss the sauce ingredients with the pasta to mix well.

3 While the pasta is cooking, heat 1 tablespoon of the oil in a medium skillet or saucepan. Add the sun-dried tomato paste and the sun-dried tomatoes, then stir in 2 ladlefuls of the water used for cooking the pasta. Simmer until the sauce is slightly reduced, stirring constantly.

4 Mix in the shredded radicchio, then taste and season if necessary. Keep on low heat. Drain the paglia e fieno, keeping the colors separate, and return the noodles to the pans in which they were cooked. Add about 1 tablespoon oil to each pan and toss over medium to high heat until the pasta is glistening with the oil.

COOK'S TIP

If you find the presentation too fussy, you can toss the sun-dried tomato and radicchio mixture with the pasta in one large warmed bowl before serving, then serve it sprinkled with the scallions and toasted pine nuts.

Penne con Salsa di Carciofi

Penne with Artichokes

ARTICHOKES ARE A VERY popular vegetable in Italy, and are often used in sauces for pasta. This sauce is garlicky and richly flavored, the perfect dinner party first course during the globe artichoke season.

INGREDIENTS

juice of 1/2–1 lemon
2 globe artichokes
2 tablespoons olive oil
1 small fennel bulb, thinly sliced,
* with feathery tops reserved*
1 onion, finely chopped
4 garlic cloves, finely chopped
1 handful fresh Italian parsley,
* coarsely chopped*
1 can (14 ounces) chopped Italian
* plum tomatoes*
2/3 cup dry white wine
3 cups penne
2 teaspoons capers, chopped
salt and ground black pepper
freshly grated Parmesan cheese, to serve

Serves 6

1 Have ready a bowl of cold water to which you have added the juice of half a lemon. Cut off the artichoke stalks, then discard the outer leaves until the pale inner leaves that are almost white at the base remain.

2 Cut off the tops of these leaves so that the base remains. Cut the base in half lengthwise, then force the hairy choke out of the center with the tip of the knife and discard. Cut the artichokes lengthwise into 1/4-inch slices, adding them immediately to the bowl of acidulated water.

3 Bring a large saucepan of water to a boil. Add a good pinch of salt, then drain the artichokes and add them immediately to the water. Boil for 5 minutes, drain and set aside.

4 Heat the oil in a large skillet or saucepan and add the fennel, onion, garlic and parsley. Cook over low to medium heat, stirring frequently, for about 10 minutes, until the fennel has softened and is lightly colored.

5 Add the tomatoes and wine, with salt and pepper to taste. Bring to a boil, stirring, then lower the heat, cover the pan and simmer for 10–15 minutes. Stir in the artichokes, replace the lid and simmer for 10 minutes more. Meanwhile, cook the pasta in salted boiling water according to the instructions on the package.

6 Drain the pasta, reserving a little of the cooking water. Stir the capers into the sauce, then taste for seasoning and add the remaining lemon juice if you like.

7 Turn the pasta into a warmed large bowl, pour the sauce over and toss well to mix, adding a little of the reserved cooking water if you like a runnier sauce. Serve immediately, garnished with the reserved fennel fronds. Pass around a bowl of grated Parmesan separately.

Spaghetti alla Bellini

Spaghetti with Eggplant

THIS FAMOUS DISH IS NAMED after the Sicilian composer. You may also come across it called Spaghetti alla Norma, after Bellini's opera.

INGREDIENTS

4 tablespoons olive oil

1 garlic clove, coarsely chopped

1 pound ripe Italian plum tomatoes, peeled
   and chopped

vegetable oil for shallow frying

12 ounces eggplant, diced small

14 ounces fresh or dried spaghetti

1 handful fresh basil leaves, shredded

4 ounces ricotta salata cheese,
   coarsely grated

salt and ground black pepper

Serves 4–6

1 Heat the olive oil, add the garlic and cook over low heat, stirring constantly, for 1–2 minutes. Stir in the tomatoes, then add salt and pepper to taste. Cover and simmer for 20 minutes.

2 Meanwhile, pour oil into a deep frying pan to a depth of about 1/2-inch. Heat the oil until hot but not smoking, then fry the eggplant cubes in batches for 4–5 minutes until tender and lightly browned. Remove the eggplant with a slotted spoon and drain on paper towels.

3 Cook the pasta according to the instructions on the package. Meanwhile, stir the fried eggplant into the tomato sauce and warm through. Taste for seasoning.

4 Drain the pasta and turn it into a warmed bowl. Add the sauce, with the shredded basil and a generous handful of the grated ricotta salata. Toss well and serve immediately, with the remaining ricotta sprinkled on top.

COOK'S TIP

Some cooks sprinkle eggplant with salt and let them sit for 20–30 minutes. This is said to help remove any bitterness, but it is not necessary if the eggplant are young and fresh.

Chiaroscuro

Black Pasta with Ricotta

THIS IS DESIGNER PASTA at its most dramatic, the kind of dish you are most likely to see at a fashionable Italian restaurant. Serve it for a smart dinner party first course—it will be a great talking point.

INGREDIENTS

11 ounces black pasta
4 tablespoons ricotta cheese, as fresh
*   as possible*
4 tablespoons extra virgin olive oil
1 small fresh red chile, seeded and
*   finely chopped*
1 small handful fresh basil leaves
salt and ground black pepper

Serves 4

1 Cook the pasta in salted boiling water according to the instructions on the package. Meanwhile, put the ricotta in a bowl, add salt and pepper to taste and use a little of the hot water from the pasta pan to mix it to a smooth, creamy consistency. Taste for seasoning.

2 Drain the pasta. Heat the oil gently in the clean pan and add the pasta with the chile and salt and pepper to taste. Toss quickly over high heat to combine.

3 Divide the pasta equally among four warmed bowls, then top with the ricotta. Sprinkle with the basil leaves and serve immediately. Each diner tosses their own portion of pasta and cheese.

COOK'S TIP

Black pasta is made with squid ink. If you prefer, use green spinach-flavored pasta or red tomato-flavored pasta.

Paglia e Fieno alle Noci e Gorgonzola

Paglia e Fieno with Walnuts and Gorgonzola

CHEESE AND NUTS ARE popular ingredients for pasta sauces. The combination is very rich, so reserve this dish for a dinner party first course. It needs no accompaniment other than a good dry white wine.

INGREDIENTS

10 ounces paglia e fieno
2 tablespoons butter
1 teaspoon finely chopped fresh sage or
*   ¹/₂ teaspoon dried sage, plus fresh sage*
*   leaves, to garnish (optional)*
4 ounces torta di Gorgonzola
*   cheese, diced*
3 tablespoons mascarpone cheese
5 tablespoons milk
¹/₂ cup walnut halves, ground
2 tablespoons freshly grated Parmesan cheese
freshly ground black pepper

Serves 4

1 Cook the pasta in a large pot of salted boiling water, according to the instructions on the package. Meanwhile, melt the butter in a large skillet or saucepan over low heat, add the sage and stir it around. Sprinkle in the diced *torta di Gorgonzola* and then add the mascarpone. Stir the ingredients with a wooden spoon until the cheeses start to melt. Pour in the milk and keep stirring.

2 Sprinkle in the walnuts and grated Parmesan and add plenty of black pepper. Continue to stir over low heat until the mixture forms a creamy sauce. Do not allow it to boil or the nuts will taste bitter, and do not cook the sauce for longer than a few minutes or the nuts will discolor it.

3 Drain the pasta, turn it into a warmed bowl, then add the sauce and toss well. Serve immediately, with more black pepper ground on top. Garnish with the sage leaves, if desired.

COOK'S TIP

Ground nuts are sold in packages in supermarkets, but you will get a better flavor if you buy walnut halves and grind them yourself in a food processor.

Vegetables and Vegetarian

Conchiglie con Verdure Arrostite

Conchiglie with Roasted Vegetables

NOTHING COULD BE SIMPLER—or more delicious—than tossing freshly cooked pasta with roasted vegetables. The flavor is superb.

INGREDIENTS

1 red bell pepper, seeded and cut into
   1/2-inch squares
1 yellow or orange bell pepper, seeded and
   cut into 1/2-inch squares
1 small eggplant, coarsely diced
2 zucchini, coarsely diced
5 tablespoons extra virgin olive oil
1 tablespoon chopped fresh
   Italian parsley
1 teaspoon dried oregano or marjoram
9 ounces baby Italian plum tomatoes,
   cored and halved lengthwise
2 garlic cloves, coarsely chopped
3–3 1/2 cups conchiglie
salt and ground black pepper
4–6 fresh marjoram or oregano sprigs,
   to garnish

Serves 4–6

1 Preheat the oven to 375°F. Rinse the prepared peppers, eggplant and zucchini in a strainer or colander under cold running water, drain, then turn the vegetables into a large roasting pan.

2 Pour 3 tablespoons of the olive oil over the vegetables and sprinkle with the fresh and dried herbs. Add salt and pepper to taste and stir well. Roast for about 30 minutes, stirring two or three times.

3 Stir the halved tomatoes and chopped garlic into the vegetable mixture, then roast for 20 minutes more, stirring once or twice. Meanwhile, cook the pasta according to the instructions on the package.

4 Drain the pasta and turn it into a warmed bowl. Add the roasted vegetables and the remaining oil and toss well. Serve the pasta and vegetables hot in warmed bowls, sprinkling each portion with a few herb flowers.

COOK'S TIP

Pasta and roasted vegetables are very good served cold, so if you have any of this dish left over, cover it tightly with plastic wrap, chill in the refrigerator overnight and serve it the next day as a salad. It would also make a particularly good salad to take on a picnic.

Green Vegetable Sauce

ALTHOUGH DESCRIBED AS *SUGO* in Italian, this is not a true "sauce", because it does not have any liquid apart from the oil and melted butter. It is more a medley of vegetables. Tossed with freshly cooked pasta, it is ideal for a fresh and light lunch or supper. Allow about 1 pound dried pasta for this amount of sauce.

INGREDIENTS

2 carrots

1 zucchini

3 ounces green beans

1 small leek

2 ripe Italian plum tomatoes

1 handful fresh Italian parsley

2 tablespoons butter

3 tablespoons extra virgin olive oil

$^1/_2$ teaspoon granulated sugar

1 cup frozen peas

salt and ground black pepper

Serves 4

3 Stir in the zucchini, green beans, peas and plenty of salt and pepper. Cover and cook over low to medium heat for 5–8 minutes, until the vegetables are tender, stirring occasionally.

4 Stir in the parsley and chopped plum tomatoes and adjust the seasoning to taste. Serve at once, tossed with freshly cooked pasta of your choice.

1 Dice the carrots and the zucchini finely. Trim the green beans, then cut them into $^3/_4$-inch lengths. Slice the leek thinly. Peel and dice the tomatoes. Chop the Italian parsley and set aside.

2 Melt the butter in the oil in a medium skillet or saucepan. When the mixture sizzles, add the prepared leek and carrots. Sprinkle the sugar over and fry, stirring frequently, for about 5 minutes.

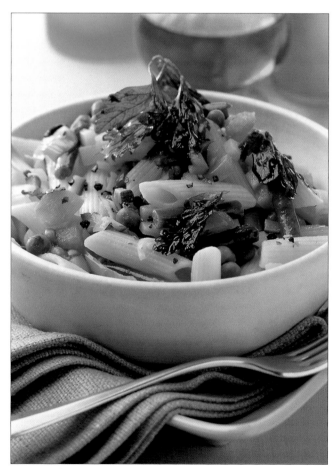

Spaghettini all'Aglio Arrostito

Spaghettini with Roasted Garlic

ROASTED GARLIC TASTES sweet and is milder than you would expect.

INGREDIENTS

1 whole head of garlic
14 ounces fresh or dried spaghettini
1/2 cup extra virgin olive oil
salt and ground black pepper
coarsely shaved Parmesan cheese, to serve

Serves 4

1 Preheat the oven to 350°F. Place the garlic in an oiled baking pan and roast it for 30 minutes.

2 Cook the pasta in a large pot of salted boiling water according to the instructions on the package.

3 Allow the garlic to cool, then lay it on its side and slice off the top third with a sharp knife.

4 Hold the garlic over a bowl and dig out the flesh from each clove with the point of the knife. When all the flesh has been added to the bowl, pour in the oil and add plenty of black pepper. Mix well.

5 Drain the pasta and return it to the clean pot. Pour in the oil and garlic mixture and toss the pasta vigorously over medium heat until all the strands are thoroughly coated. Serve immediately, with shavings of Parmesan handed separately.

VARIATION

For a fiery finish, sprinkle crushed, dried red chiles over the pasta when tossing it with the oil and garlic.

COOK'S TIP

Although you can now buy roasted garlic in supermarkets, it is best to roast it yourself for this simple recipe, so that it melts into the olive oil and coats the strands of pasta beautifully.

Elicoidali di Mezzanotte

Elicoidali with Cheese and Cream

MEZZANOTE MEANS MIDDLE of the night, which is when this rich and filling dish is traditionally eaten after a night out. It is very quick, so if you have a carton of ricotta in the refrigerator it also makes a simple evening meal.

INGREDIENTS

3 1/2 cups elicoidali

3 egg yolks

7 tablespoons freshly grated
    Parmesan cheese

scant 1 cup ricotta cheese

4 tablespoons panna da cucina or
    heavy cream

nutmeg

3 tablespoons butter

salt and ground black pepper

Serves 4

1 Cook the pasta according to the instructions on the package.

2 Meanwhile, mix the egg yolks, grated Parmesan and ricotta together in a bowl. Add the cream and mix with a fork.

3 Grate in nutmeg to taste, then season with plenty of black pepper and a little salt. Drain the pasta thoroughly when cooked. Return the clean pot to the heat. Melt the butter, add the drained pasta and toss vigorously over medium heat.

4 Turn off the heat under the pot and add the ricotta mixture. Stir well with a large spoon for 10–15 seconds until all the pasta is coated in sauce. Serve immediately, in warmed individual bowls.

COOK'S TIP

Elicoidali are a short tubular pasta with curved ridges. If you can't get them, use rigatoni, which have straight ridges.

Chitarra Spaghetti with Butter and Herbs

THIS IS A VERSATILE RECIPE. You can use just one favorite herb or several— basil, Italian parsley, rosemary, thyme, marjoram or sage would all work well. Square-shaped spaghetti is traditional for this type of sauce, but you can use ordinary spaghetti or spaghettini, or even linguine.

INGREDIENTS

14 ounces fresh or dried spaghetti
  alla chitarra
2 good handfuls mixed fresh herbs, plus
  extra herb leaves and flowers,
  to garnish
1/2 cup butter
salt and ground black pepper
freshly grated Parmesan cheese, to serve
Serves 4

VARIATION

If you like the flavor of garlic with herbs, add 1–2 crushed garlic cloves when melting the butter.

1 Cook the pasta according to the instructions on the package.

2 Chop the herbs coarsely or finely, whichever you prefer.

3 When the pasta is almost *al dente*, melt the butter in a large skillet or saucepan. As soon as it sizzles, drain the pasta and add it to the pan, then sprinkle in the herbs and salt and pepper to taste.

4 Toss over medium heat until the pasta is coated in the oil and herbs. Serve immediately in warmed bowls, sprinkled with extra herb leaves and flowers. Pass around grated Parmesan separately.

Spaghetti with Cheese and Pepper

THIS IS A ROMAN DISH, always made with spaghetti. It is remarkably easy to cook, and tastes wonderful.

INGREDIENTS

14 ounces fresh or dried spaghetti
1 1/3 cup freshly grated pecorino
  (preferably Pecorino Romano) cheese
1 teaspoon coarsely ground black pepper
extra virgin olive oil, to taste
salt
Serves 4

1 Cook the pasta according to the instructions on the package.

2 As soon as the pasta is *al dente*, drain it, leaving it a little moister than usual, and turn it into a large warmed bowl.

3 Add the cheese, pepper and salt to taste. Toss well to mix, then moisten with as much olive oil as you like. Serve immediately.

Vegetables and Vegetarian

Rigatoni with Wild Mushrooms

THIS IS A GOOD SAUCE to make from pantry ingredients because it doesn't rely on anything fresh, apart from the fresh herbs.

INGREDIENTS

2 1/2-ounce packages dried porcini
  mushrooms
3/4 cup warm water
2 tablespoons olive oil
2 shallots, finely chopped
2 garlic cloves, crushed
a few sprigs of fresh marjoram, leaves
  stripped and finely chopped, plus extra
  to garnish
1 handful fresh Italian parsley, chopped
2 tablespoons butter, diced
1 can (14 ounces) chopped Italian
  plum tomatoes
3 1/2 cups rigatoni
1/3 cup freshly grated Parmesan cheese,
  plus extra to serve
salt and ground black pepper
Serves 4–6

1 Put the dried mushrooms in a bowl, pour the warm water over and soak for 15–20 minutes. Turn into a fine sieve set over a bowl and squeeze the mushrooms to release as much liquid as possible. Reserve the mushrooms and the strained liquid.

2 Heat the oil in a medium skillet and fry the shallots, garlic and herbs over low heat, stirring frequently, for about 5 minutes. Add the mushrooms and butter and stir until the butter has melted. Season well.

3 Stir in the tomatoes and the reserved liquid from the soaked mushrooms. Bring to a boil, then cover, lower the heat and simmer for about 20 minutes, stirring occasionally. Meanwhile, cook the pasta according to the instructions on the package.

4 Taste the sauce for seasoning. Drain the pasta, reserving some of the cooking water, and turn it into a warmed large bowl. Add the sauce and the grated Parmesan and toss to mix. Add a little cooking water if you prefer a runnier sauce. Serve immediately, garnished with marjoram and with more Parmesan passed separately.

VARIATIONS

• If you have a bottle of wine open, add a splash with the canned tomatoes.
• For a richer sauce, add a few spoonfuls of panna da cucina, cream or mascarpone to the sauce just before serving.

Eliche col Pesto

Eliche with Pesto

BOTTLED PESTO IS a useful standby, but if you have a food processor, it is very easy to make your own.

INGREDIENTS

1 1/3 cups fresh basil leaves, plus
   fresh basil leaves, to garnish
2–4 garlic cloves
4 tablespoons pine nuts
1/2 cup extra virgin olive oil
1 1/3 cups freshly grated Parmesan cheese,
   plus extra to serve
1/3 cup freshly grated pecorino cheese
3 1/2 cups eliche
salt and ground black pepper

Serves 4

1 Put the basil leaves, garlic and pine nuts in a blender or food processor. Add 4 tablespoons of the olive oil. Process until the ingredients are finely chopped, then stop the machine, remove the lid and scrape down the sides of the bowl.

2 Turn the machine on again and slowly pour the remaining oil in a thin, steady stream through the feeder tube. You may need to stop the machine and scrape down the sides of the bowl once or twice to make sure everything is evenly mixed.

3 Scrape the mixture into a large bowl and beat in the cheeses with a wooden spoon. Taste and add salt and pepper if necessary.

4 Cook the pasta according to the instructions on the package. Drain it well, then add it to the bowl of pesto and toss well. Serve immediately, garnished with the fresh basil leaves. Pass grated Parmesan separately.

COOK'S TIP

Pesto can be made up to 2–3 days in advance. To store pesto, transfer it to a small bowl and pour a thin film of olive oil over the surface. Cover it tightly with plastic wrap and keep it in the refrigerator.

Spaghetti Aglio e Olio

Spaghetti with Garlic and Oil

IN ROME THEY RUN THE words together to pronounce the name of this dish as "spaghetti-ayo-e-oyo" or simply "ayo-e-oyo". Sometimes it is given its full name of *Spaghetti Aglio, Olio e Peperoncino* because chile—peperoncino—is always included to give the dish some bite.

INGREDIENTS

14 ounces fresh or dried spaghetti
6 tablespoons extra virgin olive oil
2–4 garlic cloves, crushed
1 dried red chile
1 small handful fresh Italian parsley,
   coarsely chopped
salt

Serves 4

1 Cook the pasta according to the package instructions, adding plenty of salt to the water. (See Cook's Tips.)

2 Meanwhile, heat the oil very gently in a small frying pan or saucepan. Add the crushed garlic and whole dried chile and stir over low heat until the garlic is just beginning to brown. Remove the chile and discard.

3 Drain the pasta and turn it into a warmed large bowl. Pour on the oil and garlic mixture, add the parsley and toss vigorously until the pasta glistens. Serve immediately.

Pasta con Funghi

Pasta with Mushrooms

SERVED WITH WARM CRUSTY Italian bread, this makes an excellent vegetarian supper dish.

INGREDIENTS

1/2 ounce dried porcini mushrooms

3/4 cup warm water

3 tablespoons olive oil

2 garlic cloves, finely chopped

1 handful fresh Italian parsley, coarsely chopped

2 large pieces drained sun-dried tomato in olive oil, sliced into thin strips

1/2 cup dry white wine

2 cups cremini mushrooms, thinly sliced

2 cups vegetable stock

4 cups short pasta shapes, e.g. ruote, penne, fusilli or eliche

salt and ground black pepper

arugula and/or fresh Italian parsley, to garnish

Serves 4

1 Put the dried porcini mushrooms in a bowl, pour the warm water over and allow to soak for 15–20 minutes. Turn into a fine sieve set over a bowl and squeeze the porcini with your hands to release as much liquid as possible. Reserve the strained soaking liquid. Chop the porcini finely.

2 Heat the oil and cook the garlic, parsley, sun-dried tomato strips and porcini over low heat, stirring frequently, for about 5 minutes.

3 Stir in the wine, simmer for a few minutes until reduced, then stir in the cremini mushrooms. Pour in the stock and simmer, uncovered, for 15–20 minutes more, until the liquid has reduced and the sauce is quite thick and rich.

4 Cook the pasta according to the instructions on the package.

5 Taste the mushroom sauce for seasoning. Drain the pasta, reserving a little of the cooking liquid, and turn it into a warmed large bowl. Add the mushroom sauce and toss well, thinning the sauce if necessary with some of the pasta cooking water. Serve immediately, sprinkled liberally with chopped arugula and/or parsley.

VARIATION

Fresh wild mushrooms can be used instead of cremini mushrooms, but they are seasonal and often expensive. A cheaper alternative is to use a carton of mixed wild mushrooms. These are sold in many supermarkets.

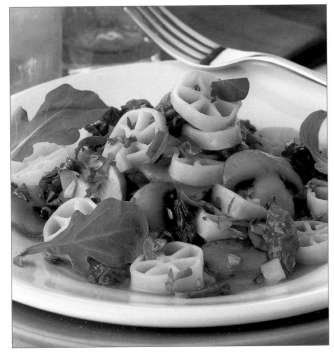

Pizzoccheri della Valtellina

Buckwheat Noodles with Cabbage, Potatoes and Cheese

THIS IS A VERY UNUSUAL PASTA dish from Valtellina in the Italian Alps. The buckwheat noodles are unique to this area, and the dish takes its name from them.

INGREDIENTS

14 ounces Savoy cabbage, cut into
   1/2-inch strips
2 potatoes, total weight about 7 ounces,
   cut into 1/4-inch slices
14 ounces pizzoccheri
6 tablespoons butter
1 generous handful fresh sage
   leaves, shredded
2 garlic cloves
7 ounces fontina cheese, rind removed and
   thinly sliced
2–3 tablespoons freshly grated Parmesan
   cheese, plus extra to serve
salt and ground black pepper
Serves 6

Bring a very large pot of salted water to a boil. Add the cabbage and potatoes and boil for 5 minutes.

2 Add the pasta, stir well and let the water return to a boil. Lower the heat and simmer for 15 minutes, or according to the instructions on the package, until the pasta is *al dente*.

3 A few minutes before the pasta is ready, melt the butter in a small saucepan. Add the sage and whole garlic cloves and fry over low to medium heat until the garlic is golden and sizzling. Lift the garlic out of the pan and discard it. Set the sage and garlic butter aside.

4 Drain the pasta and vegetables. Pour a quarter of the mixture into a warmed large bowl and arrange about a third of the fontina slices on top. Repeat these layers until all the ingredients have been used, then sprinkle with the grated Parmesan. Pour the sage and garlic butter over the top and serve immediately, with extra Parmesan handed separately.

COOK'S TIPS

• *Look for packages of dried pizzoccheri pasta in Italian markets.*
• *Fontina is a mountain cheese with a sweet, nutty taste that is quite widely available, but if you cannot get it, look for Taleggio, Gruyère or Emmental—they are all similar cheeses. Cooks in the mountain regions of northern Italy would probably use either bitto or casera cheese, but these are not so easy to obtain outside the region.*
• *When in season, Swiss chard is used instead of cabbage, as is spinach.*

Fettuccine al Burro e Parmigiano

Fettuccine with Butter and Parmesan

VERY FEW INGREDIENTS are needed to make up this incredibly simple dish. It comes from northern Italy, where butter and cheese are the most popular ingredients for serving with pasta. Children love it.

INGREDIENTS

14 ounces fresh or dried fettuccine
1/4 cup unsalted butter, cubed
1 1/3 cups freshly grated Parmesan cheese
salt and ground black pepper
Serves 4

Cook the pasta in a pot of salted boiling water according to the instructions on the package. Drain thoroughly, then turn into a warmed bowl.

2 Add the butter and Parmesan a third at a time, tossing the pasta after each addition until it is evenly coated. Season to taste and serve.

Sugo di Melanzane

Eggplant Sauce

FULL OF FLAVOR, THIS EXCELLENT vegetarian sauce goes well with any short pasta shape. It can also be layered with sheets of pasta and béchamel or cheese sauce to make a delicious vegetarian lasagne.

INGREDIENTS

2 tablespoons olive oil
1 small fresh red chile
2 garlic cloves
2 handfuls fresh Italian parsley, coarsely chopped
1 pound eggplant, coarsely chopped
1 handful fresh basil leaves
scant 1 cup water
1 vegetable stock cube
8 ripe Italian plum tomatoes, peeled and finely chopped
4 tablespoons red wine
1 teaspoon granulated sugar
1 envelope saffron powder
1/2 teaspoon ground paprika
salt and ground black pepper
Serves 4–6

1 Heat the oil in a large skillet or saucepan and add the whole chile, whole garlic cloves and half the chopped parsley. Smash the garlic cloves with a wooden spoon to release their juice, then cover the pan and cook the mixture over low to medium heat for about 10 minutes, stirring occasionally.

2 Remove and discard the chile. Add the eggplant to the pan with the rest of the parsley and all the basil. Pour in half the water. Crumble in the stock cube and stir until it is dissolved, then cover and cook, stirring frequently, for about 10 minutes.

3 Add the tomatoes, wine, sugar, saffron and paprika, with salt and pepper to taste, then pour in the remaining water. Stir well, replace the lid and cook for 30–40 minutes more, stirring occasionally. Taste for seasoning and serve with pasta or use as suggested in a baked dish. If you like, garnish with extra chopped parsley.

COOK'S TIP

Italian cooks often sprinkle a little Italian seasoning into sauces like this one. It is very good for accentuating savory flavors, and is well worth keeping in the pantry.

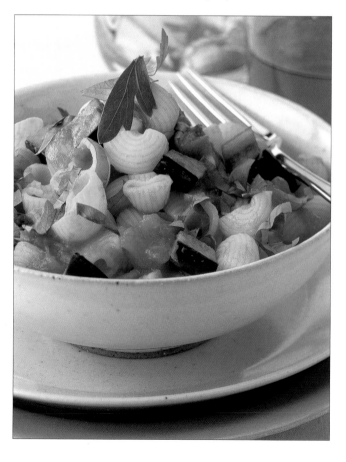

Orecchiette with Arugula

THIS HEARTY DISH IS FROM PUGLIA in the south-east of Italy. Serve it as a main course with country bread. Some specialty markets and super-markets sell a farmhouse-style Italian loaf called *pugliese*, which would be the most appropriate.

INGREDIENTS

3 tablespoons olive oil
1 small onion, finely chopped
11 ounces canned chopped Italian plum
  tomatoes or tomato sauce
1/2 teaspoon dried oregano
pinch of cayenne pepper
2 tablespoons red or white wine (optional)
2 potatoes, total weight about
  7 ounces, diced
2 3/4 cups orecchiette
2 garlic cloves, finely chopped
5 ounces arugula leaves, stalks
  removed, shredded
scant 1/2 cup ricotta cheese
salt and ground black pepper
freshly grated pecorino cheese, to serve
Serves 4–6

1 Heat 1 tablespoon of the olive oil in a medium saucepan, add half the finely chopped onion and cook gently, stirring frequently, for about 5 minutes, until softened. Add the canned tomatoes or tomato sauce, oregano and cayenne pepper to the onion. Pour the wine over, if using, and add a little salt and pepper to taste. Cover the pan and simmer for about 15 minutes, stirring occasionally.

2 Bring a large pot of salted water to a boil. Add the potatoes and pasta. Stir well and let the water return to a boil. Lower the heat and simmer for 15 minutes, or according to the instructions on the package, until the pasta is cooked.

3 Heat the remaining oil in a large skillet or saucepan, add the rest of the onion and the garlic and fry for 2–3 minutes, stirring occasionally. Add the arugula, toss over the heat for about 2 minutes, until wilted, then stir in the tomato sauce and the ricotta. Mix well.

4 Drain the pasta and potatoes, add both to the pan of sauce and toss to mix. Taste for seasoning and serve immediately in warmed bowls, with grated pecorino handed separately.

COOK'S TIP

Orecchiette are always slightly chewy. When making this dish it is traditional to cook them in the same pan as the potatoes, but if you are not sure of getting the timing right, cook them separately.

Baked Pasta

Like Bolognese sauce, lasagne, macaroni cheese and cannelloni have become so popular outside Italy that we seldom stop to consider the origins of these delicious pasta dishes. A kind of layered pasta pie was mentioned by the Roman gastronome Apicius in the first century A.D., so we know that lasagne, at least, has a very long history. In the Renaissance, sumptuous layered pasta dishes, often molded into fanciful shapes, were popular with the wealthy. Nowadays, *pasta al forno*, as baked pasta dishes are called in Italy, are more often eaten at family meals, especially on occasions when large numbers must be catered for. Baked dishes can be prepared in advance and are easy to serve.

This chapter introduces classic dishes and regional favorites with modern adaptations. In calculating serving quantities, it is assumed the dish will be a main course, but smaller portions can be served as a first course, which is more traditional in Italy.

Spaghetti Tetrazzini

Spaghetti and Turkey in Cheese Sauce

AN ITALIAN-AMERICAN RECIPE, Spaghetti Tetrazzini makes an excellent family meal. It is quite filling and rich, so serve it with a tossed green salad.

INGREDIENTS

6 tablespoons butter

12 ounces turkey breast fillet, cut into thin strips

2 pieces bottled roasted pepper, drained, rinsed, dried and cut into thin strips

6 ounces spaghetti

1/2 cup all-purpose flour

3 3/4 cups hot milk

1 1/3 cups freshly grated Parmesan cheese

1/4–1/2 teaspoon mustard powder

salt and ground black pepper

Serves 4–6

1 Melt about a third of the butter in a saucepan, add the turkey and sprinkle with a little salt and plenty of pepper. Toss the turkey over medium heat for about 5 minutes, until the meat turns white, then add the roasted pepper strips and toss to mix. Remove with a slotted spoon and set aside.

2 Preheat the oven to 350°F. Cook the pasta according to the instructions on the package.

3 Meanwhile, melt the remaining butter over low heat in the pan in which the turkey was cooked. Sprinkle in the flour and cook, stirring, for 1–2 minutes, then increase the heat to medium.

4 Add the hot milk a little at a time, whisking vigorously after each addition. Bring to a boil and cook, stirring, until the sauce is smooth and thick. Add two thirds of the grated Parmesan, then whisk in mustard, salt and pepper to taste. Remove the sauce from heat.

5 Drain the pasta and return it to the clean pot. Mix in half the cheese sauce, then spoon the mixture around the edge of a baking dish. Stir the turkey mixture into the remaining cheese sauce and spoon into the center of the dish. Sprinkle the remaining Parmesan evenly over the tetrazzini and bake for 15–20 minutes, until the cheese topping is just crisp. Serve hot.

Lasagne di Mare

Shellfish Lasagne

THIS IS A LUXURY LASAGNE suitable for an informal supper or lunch party. It is quite expensive to make, but the flavor is superb, so put it on your list for special occasion meals.

INGREDIENTS

4–6 fresh sea scallops

1 pound peeled raw large shrimp

1 garlic clove, crushed

6 tablespoons butter

1/2 cup all-purpose flour

2 1/2 cups hot milk

scant 1/2 cup panna da cucina or heavy cream

1/2 cup dry white wine

2 envelopes saffron powder

good pinch of cayenne pepper

4 1/2 ounces fontina cheese, thinly sliced

1 cup freshly grated Parmesan cheese

6–8 fresh egg lasagne sheets

salt and ground black pepper

Serves 4–6

1 Preheat the oven to 375°F. Cut the scallops and shrimp into bite-size pieces and spread out in a dish. Sprinkle with the garlic and salt and pepper to taste. Melt about a third of the butter in a medium saucepan, add the scallops and shrimp and toss over medium heat for 1–2 minutes or just until the shrimp turn pink. Remove the shellfish with a slotted spoon and set aside.

2 Add the remaining butter to the pan and melt over low heat. Sprinkle in the flour and cook, stirring, for 1–2 minutes, then increase the heat to medium and add the hot milk a little at a time, whisking vigorously after each addition. Bring to a boil and cook, stirring, until the sauce is smooth and very thick. Whisk in the cream, wine, saffron powder, cayenne and salt and pepper to taste, then remove the sauce from heat.

3 Spread about a third of the sauce over the bottom of a baking dish. Arrange half the fontina slices over the sauce and sprinkle with about a third of the grated Parmesan. Scatter about half the shellfish evenly on top, then cover with half the lasagne sheets. Repeat the layers, then cover with the remaining sauce and Parmesan.

4 Bake the lasagne for 30–40 minutes or until the topping is golden brown and bubbling. Let stand for 10 minutes before serving.

Lasagne ai Funghi e Zucchine

Mushroom and Zucchini Lasagne

THIS IS THE PERFECT main-course lasagne for vegetarians. Adding dried porcini to fresh cremini mushrooms intensifies the "mushroomy" flavor and gives the whole dish more substance. Serve with crusty Italian bread.

INGREDIENTS

$^1/_2$ ounce dried porcini mushrooms

$^3/_4$ cup warm water

2 tablespoons olive oil

6 tablespoons butter

1 pound zucchini, thinly sliced

1 onion, finely chopped

6 cups (about 1 pound) cremini
mushrooms, thinly sliced

2 garlic cloves, crushed

1 recipe Winter Tomato Sauce

2 teaspoons chopped fresh marjoram or
1 teaspoon dried marjoram, plus extra
fresh leaves, to garnish

6–8 precooked lasagne sheets

$^2/_3$ cup freshly grated
Parmesan cheese

salt and ground black pepper

For the white sauce

3 tablespoons butter

$^1/_3$ cup all-purpose flour

$3^3/_4$ cups hot milk

nutmeg

Serves 6

1 Put the dried porcini mushrooms in a bowl. Pour over the warm water and allow to soak for 15–20 minutes. Turn the porcini and liquid into a fine sieve set over a bowl and squeeze the mushrooms with your hands to release as much liquid as possible. Chop the mushrooms finely and set aside. Strain the soaking liquid through a fine sieve and reserve half for the sauce.

2 Preheat the oven to 375°F. Heat the olive oil with 2 tablespoons of the butter in a large skillet or saucepan.

3 Add about half the zucchini slices to the pan and season with salt and pepper to taste. Cook the zucchini over medium heat, turning the slices frequently, for 5–8 minutes until they are lightly colored on both sides. Remove the zucchini from the pan with a slotted spoon and allow to drain on paper towels. Repeat with the remaining zucchini.

4 Melt half the remaining butter in the fat remaining in the pan, then cook the finely chopped onion, stirring, for 1–2 minutes. Add half of the fresh mushrooms and the crushed garlic to the pan and sprinkle with a little salt and pepper to taste.

5 Toss the mushrooms over high heat for 5 minutes or so, until the mushrooms are juicy and tender. Transfer to a bowl with a slotted spoon, then repeat with the remaining butter and mushrooms.

6 Make the white sauce. Melt the butter in a large saucepan, add the flour and cook, stirring, over medium heat for 1–2 minutes.

7 Add the hot milk a little at a time, whisking well after each addition. Bring to a boil and cook, stirring, until the sauce is smooth and thick. Grate in fresh nutmeg to taste and season with a little salt and pepper. Whisk well, then remove the sauce from heat.

8 Place the tomato sauce in a blender or food processor with the reserved porcini soaking liquid and blend to a pureé. Add the zucchini to the bowl of fried mushrooms, then stir in the porcini and marjoram.

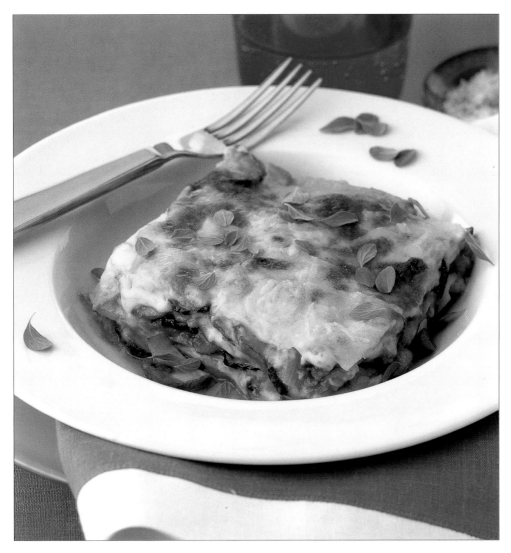

10 Top with about a third of the white sauce, then about half the lasagne sheets. Repeat these layers, then top with the remaining tomato sauce and white sauce and sprinkle with the grated Parmesan cheese.

11 Bake the lasagne for 35–40 minutes, or until the pasta feels tender when pierced with a skewer. Allow to stand for about 10 minutes before serving. If you like, sprinkle each serving with marjoram leaves.

9 Adjust the seasoning to taste, then spread a third of the tomato sauce in a baking pan. Add half the vegetable mixture, spreading it evenly.

COOK'S TIPS

• The amount of pasta will depend on the size and shape of the pasta sheets and your baking dish; you may need to break the pasta to fit.
• This dish is time-consuming to prepare, but well worth the effort. You can make the tomato sauce in advance and chill it for up to 2 days, until you are ready to assemble the lasagne, or you can freeze it. Make sure that you allow it to thaw completely before using.

Lasagne con Polpettine

Lasagne with Meatballs

THIS IS AN UNUSUAL RECIPE for lasagne because there is both a meat sauce and meatballs. The result is very rich and satisfying, making it an ideal dish for an informal winter lunch or supper party. It takes a long time to make, so prepare it the day before and bake it on the day.

INGREDIENTS
11 ounces ground beef
11 ounces ground pork
1 large egg
1 cup fresh white bread crumbs
5 tablespoons freshly grated
*   Parmesan cheese*
2 tablespoons chopped fresh Italian parsley
2 garlic cloves, crushed
4 tablespoons olive oil
1 onion, finely chopped
1 carrot, finely chopped
1 celery stalk, finely chopped
2 cans (14 ounces) chopped Italian
*   plum tomatoes*
2 teaspoons dried oregano or basil
6–8 fresh lasagne sheets, or precooked
*   if necessary*
salt and ground black pepper

For the béchamel sauce
3 cups milk
1 bay leaf
1 fresh thyme sprig
1/4 cup butter
1/2 cup all-purpose flour
nutmeg
Serves 6–8

1 First make the meatballs. Put 6 ounces each of the ground beef and pork in a large bowl. Add the egg, bread crumbs, 2 tablespoons of the grated Parmesan, half the parsley and garlic and plenty of salt and pepper.

2 Mix everything together with a wooden spoon, then use your hands to squeeze and knead the mixture until it becomes smooth and quite sticky.

3 Wash your hands, rinse under the cold tap, then pick up small pieces of the mixture and roll them between your palms to make about 60 very small balls. Place the balls on a tray and chill for about 30 minutes.

4 Meanwhile, put the milk for the béchamel sauce in a saucepan. Make a tear in the bay leaf, then add the leaf and thyme sprig to the milk and bring it to a boil. Remove from heat, cover and let infuse.

5 Make the meat sauce. Heat half the oil in a medium skillet or saucepan, add the onion, carrot, celery and remaining garlic and stir over low heat for about 5 minutes. until softened. Add the remaining ground beef and pork and cook gently for 10 minutes, stirring frequently and breaking up any lumps in the meat.

6 Stir in salt and pepper to taste, then add the tomatoes, remaining parsley and the oregano or basil. Stir well, cover and simmer gently for 45 minutes to 1 hour, stirring occasionally.

7 Meanwhile, heat the remaining oil in a large, nonstick frying pan. When hot, cook the meatballs in batches over medium to high heat for 5–8 minutes, until browned on all sides. Shake the pan from time to time so that the meatballs roll around. As they cook, transfer the meatballs to paper towels to drain.

8 Preheat the oven to 375°F. Make the béchamel sauce. Strain the milk to remove the bay leaf and thyme sprig. Melt the butter in a medium saucepan, add the flour and cook, stirring, for 1–2 minutes.

9 Add the milk a little at a time, whisking vigorously after each addition. Bring to a boil and cook, stirring constantly, until the sauce is smooth and thick. Grate in a little nutmeg to taste and season with salt and pepper. Whisk well, then remove from heat.

10 Spread about a third of the meat sauce in the bottom of a large, shallow baking dish.

11 Add half the meatballs, spread with a third of the béchamel and cover with half the lasagne sheets. Repeat these layers, then top with the remaining meat sauce and béchamel.

12 Sprinkle the remaining grated Parmesan evenly over the surface and bake for 30–40 minutes or until golden brown and bubbling. Allow the lasagne to stand for 10 minutes before serving. If you like, garnish each serving with extra chopped parsley.

VARIATION

In the south of Italy, where this type of lasagne is popular, they often add salami, chopped hard-boiled eggs, mozzarella and ricotta cheese to the layers.

COOK'S TIPS

• *Homemade lasagne does not need precooking, but if you have bought fresh pasta check the instructions on the package.*
• *To prevent cooked lasagne sheets from sticking together, rinse them under cold running water, then return to the pan with enough cold water to cover. Drain well on paper towels before using.*

Frittata di Vermicelli

Vermicelli Omelette

A FRITTATA IS A FLAT BAKED omelette. Here it is made with vegetables and herbs, but you can put anything you like in it. Ham, sausage, salami, chicken, mushrooms, zucchini and eggplant are just a few suggestions, or you could simply add mixed herbs. Frittata is absolutely delicious cold. Cut into wedges, it is excellent food for picnics.

INGREDIENTS

2 ounces vermicelli

6 eggs

4 tablespoons panna da cucina or
    heavy cream

I handful fresh basil leaves, shredded

I handful fresh Italian parsley, chopped

I cup freshly grated Parmesan cheese

2 tablespoons butter

I tablespoon olive oil

I onion, finely sliced

3 large pieces bottled roasted red pepper,
    drained, rinsed, dried and cut into strips

I garlic clove, crushed

salt and ground black pepper

arugula leaves, to serve

Serves 4–6

Preheat the oven to 375°F. Cook the pasta in a pot of salted boiling water for 8 minutes.

2 Meanwhile, break the eggs into a bowl and add the cream and herbs. Whisk in about two-thirds of the grated Parmesan and add salt and pepper to taste.

3 Drain the pasta well and allow to cool; snip it into short lengths with scissors. Add to the egg mixture and whisk again. Set aside.

4 Melt the butter in the oil in a large, ovenproof nonstick frying pan. Add the onion and cook gently, stirring frequently, for 5 minutes until softened. Add the peppers and garlic.

5 Pour the egg and pasta mixture into the pan and stir well. Cook over low to medium heat, without stirring, for 3–5 minutes or until the frittata is just set underneath. Sprinkle over the remaining Parmesan and bake in the oven for 5 minutes or until set. Before serving, allow to stand for at least 5 minutes. Cut into wedges and serve warm or cold, with arugula.

Lasagne from Bologna

THIS IS THE CLASSIC *lasagne al forno*.
It is based on a rich, meaty filling, as
you would expect from an authentic
Bolognese recipe.

INGREDIENTS

1 recipe Bolognese Meat Sauce
2/3–1 cup hot beef stock, or water with
    stock cube
12 precooked dried lasagne sheets
2/3 cup freshly grated
    Parmesan cheese

For the white sauce
1/4 cup butter
1/2 cup all-purpose flour
3 3/4 cups hot milk
salt and ground black pepper
Serves 6

4 Cover the Bolognese sauce in the
bottom of the dish with about a
quarter of the white sauce, followed by
four sheets of lasagne. Repeat the
layers twice more, then cover the top
layer of lasagne with the remaining
white sauce and sprinkle the grated
Parmesan evenly over the top.

5 Bake for 40–45 minutes or until
the pasta feels tender when
pierced with a skewer. Allow to stand
for about 10 minutes before serving.

COOK'S TIPS

• The Bolognese sauce can be made up
to 3 days in advance and kept in a
covered container in the refrigerator.
• The lasagne is best baked immediately
after layering or the pasta will begin to
absorb the sauces and dry out.
• To reheat leftover lasagne, prick it all
over with a skewer, then slowly pour a
little milk over to moisten. Cover with
foil and reheat in a 375°F oven for
20 minutes, or until bubbling.

1 Preheat the oven to 375°F. If the
Bolognese sauce is cold, reheat it.
Once it is hot, stir in enough stock to
make it quite runny.

2 Make the white sauce. Melt the
butter in a medium saucepan,
add the flour and cook, stirring, for
1–2 minutes. Add the milk a little at a
time, whisking vigorously after each
addition. Bring to a boil and cook,
stirring, until the sauce is smooth and
thick. Add salt and pepper to taste, whisk
well to mix, then remove from heat.

3 Spread about a third of the
Bolognese sauce over the bottom
of a baking pan.

Cannelloni alla Sorrentina

Cannelloni Sorrentina-style

THERE'S MORE THAN ONE way of making cannelloni. For this fresh-tasting dish, sheets of cooked lasagne are rolled around a tomato filling to make a delicious main course for a summer dinner party. The ingredients are similar to those used on a Neapolitan pizza.

INGREDIENTS

4 tablespoons olive oil
I small onion, finely chopped
2 pounds ripe Italian plum tomatoes,
  peeled and finely chopped
2 garlic cloves, crushed
I large handful fresh basil leaves, shredded,
  plus extra basil leaves, to garnish
I cup vegetable stock
I cup dry white wine
2 tablespoons sun-dried tomato paste
1/2 teaspoon sugar
16–18 fresh or dried lasagne sheets
generous I cup ricotta cheese
4 1/2 ounces fresh mozzarella cheese,
  drained and diced small
8 bottled anchovy fillets in olive oil, drained
  and halved lengthwise
2/3 cup freshly grated Parmesan cheese
salt and ground black pepper

Serves 4–6

| Heat the oil in a medium saucepan, add the onion and cook gently, stirring frequently, for about 5 minutes, until softened. Stir in the tomatoes, garlic and half the basil. Season with salt and pepper to taste and toss over medium to high heat for 5 minutes.

2 Scoop about half the tomato mixture out of the pan, place in a bowl and set it aside to cool.

3 Stir the vegetable stock, white wine, tomato paste and sugar into the tomato mixture remaining in the pan and simmer for about 20 minutes, stirring occasionally.

4 Meanwhile, cook the lasagne sheets in batches in a saucepan of salted boiling water, according to the instructions on the package. Drain and separate the sheets of lasagne and lay them out flat on a clean dish towel.

VARIATION

For vegetarians, use 8 pitted black olives instead of the anchovies. Chop them coarsely and sprinkle them in a line along the length of the cannelloni filling.

5 Preheat the oven to 375°F. Add the ricotta and mozzarella to the tomato mixture in the bowl. Stir in the remaining basil and season to taste with salt and pepper.

6 Spread a little of the mixture over each lasagne sheet. Place an anchovy fillet across the width of each sheet, close to one of the short ends. Starting from the end with the anchovy, roll each lasagne sheet up like a Swiss roll.

7 Purée the tomato sauce in a blender or food processor. Spread a little of the tomato sauce over the bottom of a large baking pan. Arrange the cannelloni seam-side down in a single layer in the dish and spoon the remaining sauce over them.

8 Sprinkle the Parmesan over the top and bake for 20 minutes or until the topping is golden brown and bubbling. Serve hot, garnished with basil leaves.

Lasagne ai Tre Formaggi

Lasagne with Three Cheeses

RICH AND FILLING, this is the type of lasagne that is popular here. It was invented by Italian immigrants who made full use of the abundant ingredients available to them.

INGREDIENTS

2 tablespoons butter

1 tablespoon olive oil

2–2¼ cups button mushrooms, quartered lengthwise

2 tablespoons chopped fresh Italian parsley

1 recipe Bolognese Sauce with Red Wine

1–1½ cups hot beef stock or water with stock cube

9–12 fresh lasagne sheets, precooked if necessary

2 cups ricotta cheese

1 large egg

13½ ounces fresh mozzarella cheese, drained and thinly sliced

1⅓ cups freshly grated Parmesan cheese

salt and ground black pepper

Serves 6–8

1 Preheat the oven to 375°F. Melt the butter in the oil in a frying pan. Add the mushrooms, with salt and pepper to taste, and toss over medium to high heat for 5–8 minutes, until the mushrooms are tender and quite dry. Remove the pan from heat and stir in the parsley.

2 Make the Bolognese sauce or, if it is cold, reheat it. Once it is hot, stir in enough hot beef stock to make the sauce quite runny.

3 Stir in the mushroom and parsley mixture, then spread about a quarter of this sauce over the bottom of a baking pan. Cover with three or four sheets of lasagne.

4 Beat together the ricotta and egg in a bowl, with salt and pepper to taste, then spread about a third of the mixture over the lasagne sheets. Cover with a third of the mozzarella slices, then sprinkle with about a quarter of the grated Parmesan.

5 Repeat these layers twice, using half the remaining Bolognese sauce each time, and finishing with the remaining Parmesan.

6 Bake the lasagne for 30–40 minutes or until the cheese topping is golden brown and bubbling. Allow to stand for about 10 minutes before serving.

VARIATIONS

• For a spicier alternative version of this recipe, replace the meat sauce with the sauce used for Spaghetti with Ground Beef Sauce.

• Grated aged cheddar cheese is very good in lasagne. Use it instead of some, or all, of the grated Parmesan. It is a good deal less expensive than Parmesan.

COOK'S TIP

If you have made the lasagne yourself, there is no need to precook it, but if you have bought fresh lasagne, check to see if it needs to be boiled briefly before being layered. Packages of fresh lasagne from the supermarket usually need to be boiled for 2 minutes before use.

Conchiglie Ripiene

Stuffed Shells

THIS MAKES AN EXCELLENT dinner party first course for six, or a vegetarian main course for four, in which case you should fill 20 shells, rather than 18; there will be plenty of filling.

INGREDIENTS

18 large pasta shells for stuffing
2 tablespoons butter
1 small onion, finely chopped
10 ounces fresh spinach leaves, trimmed,
   washed and shredded
1 garlic clove, crushed
1 envelope of saffron powder
nutmeg
generous 1 cup ricotta cheese
1 egg
1 recipe Winter Tomato Sauce
2/3 cup dry white wine, vegetable stock
   or water
scant 1/2 cup panna da cucina or
   heavy cream
2/3 cup freshly grated Parmesan cheese
salt and ground black pepper
Serves 6

1 Preheat the oven to 375°F. Bring a large pot of salted water to a boil. Add the pasta shells and cook for 10 minutes. Drain the shells, half fill the pot with cold water and place the shells in the water.

2 Melt the butter in a saucepan, add the onion and cook gently, stirring, for about 5 minutes, until softened. Add the spinach, garlic and saffron, then grate in plenty of nutmeg and add salt and pepper to taste. Stir well, increase the heat to medium and cook for 5–8 minutes, stirring frequently, until the spinach is wilted and tender.

3 Increase the heat to high and stir until the water boils off and the spinach is quite dry. Turn the spinach into a bowl, add the ricotta and beat well to mix. Taste for seasoning, then add the egg and beat well again.

4 Purée the tomato sauce in a blender or food processor; pour it into a measuring cup and fill it up to 3 cups with wine, stock or water. Add the cream, stir well to mix and taste for seasoning.

5 Spread about half the sauce over the bottom of six individual gratin dishes. Remove the pasta shells one at a time from the water, shake them well and fill them with the spinach and ricotta mixture, using a teaspoon. Arrange three shells in the center of each dish, spoon the remaining sauce over them, then cover with the grated Parmesan. Bake in the oven for 10–12 minutes or until hot. Allow to stand for about 5 minutes before serving.

Cannelloni di Carne Mista

Mixed Meat Cannelloni

A CREAMY, RICH FILLING and sauce make this an unusual cannelloni.

INGREDIENTS

4 tablespoons olive oil
1 onion, finely chopped
1 carrot, finely chopped
2 garlic cloves, crushed
2 ripe Italian plum tomatoes, peeled and
  finely chopped
4 1/2 ounces ground beef
4 1/2 ounces ground pork
9 ounces ground chicken
2 tablespoons brandy
2 tablespoons butter
6 tablespoons panna da cucina or
  heavy cream
16 cannelloni tubes
1 cup freshly grated Parmesan cheese
salt and ground black pepper
green salad, to serve

For the white sauce
1/4 cup butter
1/2 cup all-purpose flour
3 3/4 cups milk
nutmeg
Serves 4

1 Heat the oil in a medium skillet, add the onion, carrot, garlic and tomatoes and cook over low heat, stirring, for about 10 minutes or until very soft.

COOK'S TIP

Instead of pasta tubes you could roll fresh lasagne sheets around the filling.

2 Add all the ground meats to the pan and cook gently for about 10 minutes, stirring frequently to break up any lumps. Add the brandy, increase the heat and stir until it has reduced, then add the butter and cream and cook gently, stirring occasionally, for about 10 minutes. Allow to cool.

3 Preheat the oven to 375°F. Make the white sauce. Melt the butter in a medium saucepan, add the flour and cook, stirring, for 1–2 minutes. Add the milk a little at a time, whisking vigorously after each addition. Bring to a boil and cook, stirring, until the sauce is smooth and thick. Grate in fresh nutmeg to taste, then season with salt and pepper and whisk well. Remove the pan from heat.

4 Spoon a little of the white sauce into a baking pan. Fill the cannelloni tubes with the meat mixture and place in a single layer in the dish. Pour the remaining white sauce over them, then sprinkle with the Parmesan. Bake for 35–40 minutes or until the pasta feels tender when pierced with a skewer. Allow to stand for 10 minutes before serving with green salad.

Cannelloni con Ripieno di Carne

Cannelloni Stuffed with Meat

THIS IS A RICH AND SUBSTANTIAL dish, which takes quite a long time to prepare. Serve it for a party—it can be made a day ahead up to the baking stage. Your guests are bound to appreciate your efforts, because the cannelloni taste so good.

INGREDIENTS

1 tablespoon olive oil
1 small onion, finely chopped
1 pound ground beef
1 garlic clove, finely chopped
1 teaspoon dried mixed herbs
1/2 cup beef stock
1 egg
3 ounces cooked ham or mortadella
* sausage, finely chopped*
3 tablespoons fine fresh white
* bread crumbs*
1 2/3 cups freshly grated Parmesan cheese
18 precooked cannelloni tubes
salt and ground black pepper

For the tomato sauce

2 tablespoons olive oil
1 small onion, finely chopped
1/2 carrot, finely chopped
1 celery stalk, finely chopped
1 garlic clove, crushed
1 can (14 ounces) chopped Italian
* plum tomatoes*
a few sprigs of fresh basil
1/2 teaspoon dried oregano

For the white sauce

1/4 cup butter
1/2 cup all-purpose flour
3 3/4 cups milk
nutmeg

Serves 6

1 Heat the olive oil in a medium skillet or saucepan and cook the finely chopped onion over gentle heat, stirring occasionally, for about 5 minutes, until softened.

2 Add the ground beef and garlic and cook gently for 10 minutes, stirring and breaking up any lumps with a wooden spoon. Add the mixed herbs, and salt and pepper to taste, then moisten with half the stock. Cover the pan and simmer for 25 minutes, stirring from time to time and adding more stock as the mixture reduces. Spoon into a bowl and allow to cool.

3 Meanwhile, make the tomato sauce. Heat the olive oil in a medium saucepan, add the vegetables and garlic and cook over medium heat, stirring frequently, for about 10 minutes. Add the canned tomatoes. Fill the empty can with water, pour it into the pan, then stir in the herbs, with salt and pepper to taste. Bring to a boil, lower the heat, cover and simmer for 25–30 minutes, stirring occasionally. Purée the tomato sauce in a blender or food processor.

4 Add the egg, ham or mortadella, bread crumbs and 6 tablespoons of the grated Parmesan to the meat and stir well to mix. Taste for seasoning.

5 Spread a little of the tomato sauce over the bottom of a baking pan. Using a teaspoon, fill the cannelloni tubes with the meat mixture and place them in a single layer in the dish on top of the tomato sauce. Pour the remaining tomato sauce over the top.

6 Preheat the oven to 375°F. Make the white sauce. Melt the butter in a saucepan, add the flour and cook, stirring, for 1–2 minutes. Add the milk a little at a time, whisking vigorously after each addition.

7 Bring to a boil and cook, stirring, until the sauce is smooth and thick. Grate in fresh nutmeg to taste and season with a little salt and pepper. Whisk well, then remove from heat.

8 Pour the white sauce over the stuffed cannelloni, then sprinkle with the remaining Parmesan. Place in the oven and bake for 40–45 minutes or until the cannelloni tubes feel tender when pierced with a skewer. Allow the cannelloni to stand for about 10 minutes before serving.

Maccheroni ai Quattro Formaggi

Macaroni with Four Cheeses

RICH AND CREAMY, this is a deluxe macaroni and cheese casserole that can be served for an informal lunch or supper party. It goes well with both a tomato and basil salad or a leafy green salad.

INGREDIENTS

2¼ cups short-cut macaroni
¼ cup butter
½ cup all-purpose flour
2½ cups milk
scant ½ cup panna da cucina or
    heavy cream
scant ½ cup dry white wine
½ cup grated Gruyère or Emmental cheese
2 ounces fontina cheese, diced small
2 ounces Gorgonzola cheese, crumbled
1 cup freshly grated Parmesan cheese
salt and ground black pepper
Serves 4

3 Add the Gruyère or Emmental, fontina and Gorgonzola and about a third of the grated Parmesan to the sauce. Stir well to mix in the cheeses, then taste for seasoning and add salt and pepper if necessary.

4 Drain the pasta well and turn it into a baking pan. Pour the sauce over the pasta and mix well, then sprinkle the remaining Parmesan over the top. Bake for 25–30 minutes or until golden brown. Serve hot.

1 Preheat the oven to 350°F. Cook the pasta according to the instructions on the package.

2 Meanwhile, gently melt the butter in a medium saucepan, add the flour and cook, stirring, for 1–2 minutes. Add the milk a little at a time, whisking vigorously after each addition. Stir in the cream, followed by the dry white wine. Bring to a boil. Cook, stirring constantly until the sauce thickens, then remove the sauce from heat.

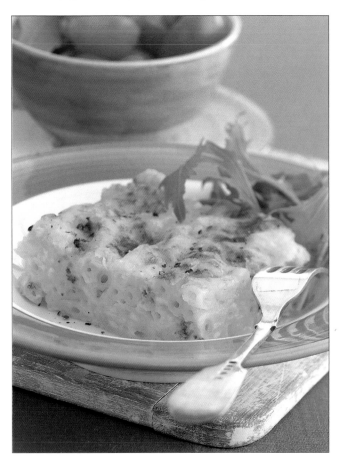

Lasagne alla Siciliana
Sicilian Lasagne

LASAGNE IS NOT TRADITIONAL in Sicily as it is in northern Italy, but the Sicilians have their own version.

INGREDIENTS

1 small onion

1/2 carrot

1/2 celery stalk

3 tablespoons olive oil

9 ounces diced boneless pork

4 tablespoons dry white wine

1 can (14 ounces) chopped Italian
    plum tomatoes or 1 2/3 cups tomato sauce

scant 1 cup chicken stock

1 tablespoon tomato paste

2 bay leaves

1 tablespoon chopped fresh Italian parsley

9 ounces fresh lasagne sheets, precooked
    if necessary

2 hard-boiled eggs, sliced

4 1/2-ounce package mozzarella cheese,
    drained and sliced

4 tablespoons freshly grated pecorino
    cheese

salt and ground black pepper

Serves 6

1 Chop the fresh vegetables finely, either in a food processor or by hand. Heat 2 tablespoons of the oil in a large skillet or saucepan, add the chopped vegetables and cook over medium heat, stirring frequently, for about 10 minutes.

2 Add the pork and fry for about 5 minutes, stirring occasionally, until well browned on all sides. Pour in the wine and let it bubble and reduce for a few minutes, then add the tomatoes or sauce, the stock and the tomato paste. Make a tear in each bay leaf to release the flavor, then add to the pan with the parsley and salt and pepper to taste, mixing well. Cover and cook for 30–40 minutes, until the pork is tender, stirring from time to time. Take the pan off the heat and remove and discard the bay leaves from the sauce.

3 Using a slotted spoon, lift the pieces of meat out of the sauce. Chop them coarsely, then return them to the sauce. Stir well.

4 Preheat the oven to 375°F. Bring a large pot of salted water to a boil. Cut the lasagne sheets into 1-inch strips and add them to a boiling water. Cook for 3–4 minutes, until just al dente. Drain well, then stir the strips into the sauce.

5 Spread out half the pasta and sauce mixture in a shallow baking pan and cover with half the egg and mozzarella slices and half the grated pecorino. Repeat the layers, then drizzle the remaining oil over the top. Bake for 30–35 minutes, until golden brown and bubbling. Allow to stand for about 10 minutes before serving.

Pasticcio di Fusilli

Fusilli with Ham and Cheese

WITH ITS CRISPY CRUST and moist and creamy center, this quick and easy pasta casserole is both filling and nutritious. Serve it for a winter supper, with a salad on the side.

INGREDIENTS

2³/₄ cups fusilli, eliche or other
   short pasta shapes
3 eggs
scant 1 cup milk
²/₃ cup light cream
5 ounces Gruyère cheese, grated
nutmeg
4 ounces cooked ham, cut into strips
2 tablespoons freshly grated
   Parmesan cheese
salt and ground black pepper
Serves 4

1 Preheat the oven to 375°F. Bring a large pot of salted water to a boil. Add the pasta and cook for 5 minutes.

2 Meanwhile, beat the eggs in a cup with the milk, cream and half the grated Gruyère. Grate in a little fresh nutmeg and season to taste.

3 Drain the pasta and turn half of it into a buttered baking pan. Arrange half the strips of ham on top, then follow with the remaining pasta and ham. Pour the egg and cream mixture into the pan, stir to mix a little, then sprinkle the remaining Gruyère and the Parmesan over the top. Bake for 30 minutes or until golden brown.

Lasagne al Ragù d'Agnello

Lasagne with Lamb

IT IS UNUSUAL TO MAKE lasagne with lamb, but the flavor is excellent.

INGREDIENTS

1 tablespoon olive oil
1 small onion, finely chopped
1 pound ground lamb
1 garlic clove, crushed
3 tablespoons dry white wine
1 teaspoon dried mixed herbs
1 teaspoon dried oregano
scant 2 cups tomato sauce
12–16 fresh lasagne sheets, precooked
   if necessary
2 tablespoons freshly grated Parmesan cheese
salt and ground black pepper

For the white sauce
¹/₂ cup butter
¹/₂ cup all-purpose flour
3³/₄ cups hot milk
2 tablespoons freshly grated Parmesan cheese
nutmeg
Serves 4–6

1 Heat the oil in a saucepan and cook the onion over gentle heat, stirring frequently, for about 5 minutes, until softened. Add the ground lamb and garlic and cook gently for 10 minutes, stirring frequently. Stir in salt and pepper to taste, then add the wine and cook rapidly for about 2 minutes, stirring constantly. Stir in the herbs and tomato sauce. Simmer gently for 45 minutes to 1 hour, stirring occasionally.

2 Preheat the oven to 375°F. Make the white sauce. Melt the butter in a saucepan, add the flour and cook, stirring, for 1–2 minutes. Add the milk a little at a time, whisking vigorously after each addition. Bring to a boil and cook, stirring, until the sauce is smooth and thick. Add the Parmesan, grate in fresh nutmeg to taste, season with a little salt and pepper and whisk well. Remove the pan from heat.

3 Spread a few spoonfuls of meat sauce over the bottom of a baking pan and cover with three or four sheets of lasagne. Spread a quarter of the remaining meat sauce over the lasagne, then quarter of the white sauce. Repeat the layers three times, finishing with white sauce.

4 Sprinkle the Parmesan over the surface and bake for 30–40 minutes or until the topping is golden brown and bubbling. Allow to stand for about 10 minutes before serving.

Pasticciata

Pasta Pie

THIS IS AN EXCELLENT SUPPER dish for vegetarians, and children absolutely love it. All the ingredients will probably already be in your pantry or refrigerator, so it makes a good "standby" meal if you have guests at short notice.

INGREDIENTS

2 tablespoons olive oil
1 small onion, finely chopped
1 can (14 ounces) chopped Italian
  plum tomatoes
1 tablespoon sun-dried tomato paste
1 teaspoon dried mixed herbs
1 teaspoon dried oregano or basil
1 teaspoon sugar
1¹/₂ cups conchiglie or rigatoni
2 tablespoons freshly grated
  Parmesan cheese
2 tablespoons dried bread crumbs
salt and ground black pepper

For the white sauce

2 tablespoons butter
¹/₄ cup all-purpose flour
2¹/₂ cups milk
1 egg
Serves 4

I Heat the olive oil in a large skillet or saucepan and cook the finely chopped onion over gentle heat, stirring frequently, for about 5 minutes, until softened. Stir in the tomatoes. Fill the empty can with water and add it to the tomato mixture, with the tomato paste, herbs and sugar.

2 Add salt and pepper to taste and bring to a boil, stirring. Cover the pan, lower the heat and simmer, stirring occasionally, for 10–15 minutes.

3 Meanwhile, preheat the oven to 375°F. Cook the pasta according to the instructions on the package.

4 Meanwhile, make the white sauce. Melt the butter in a pan, add the flour and cook, stirring, for 1 minute.

5 Add the milk a little at a time, whisking well after each addition. Bring to a boil and cook, stirring, until the sauce is smooth and thick. Season, then remove the pan from heat.

6 Drain the pasta and turn it into a baking dish. Taste the tomato sauce and add salt and pepper. Pour the sauce into the dish and stir well to mix with the pasta.

7 Beat the egg into the white sauce, then pour the sauce over the pasta mixture. Separate the pasta with a fork in several places so that the white sauce fills the gaps.

8 Smooth the surface, sprinkle it with grated Parmesan and bread crumbs and bake for 15–20 minutes or until the topping is golden brown and the cheese is bubbling. Allow to stand for about 10 minutes before serving.

VARIATIONS

• *If you don't have any dried bread crumbs, you can cheat by crushing a package of chips and sprinkling them over the pasticciata instead. Children love this crisp topping, especially if you use their favorite flavor.*
• *You could add chunks of roasted vegetables, such as zucchini, bell peppers or eggplant to the tomato sauce if you like. This will add extra flavor and make a more substantial meal.*
• *For meat lovers, Bolognese sauce can be used instead of the tomato sauce.*

Stuffed Pasta

Making your own pasta is easier than you think, especially if you have a pasta machine. You can make pasta by hand, but the machine will save you time and effort, and make the whole process much more interesting and fun.

The recipes in this chapter are for a variety of different shapes, but they all use the same basic pasta dough. For stuffing, the pasta is always made with eggs, which strengthens the dough. This helps to hold the filling in during cooking. Stuffed pasta originated in the north of Italy, but now every Italian town seems to have its own speciality, often associated with a particular day in the calendar, like a feast day or New Year. Homemade stuffed pasta is therefore a special-occasion dish, and it is usually served very simply, either drizzled with melted butter or oil, or floating in *brodo*.

If you are going to try your hand at making your own stuffed pasta, it is the ideal first course for a dinner party. Practice makes perfect when it comes to making anything by hand, but much of the charm of homemade pasta lies in its imperfections, so don't try too hard to make every shape precisely the same size. After all, you want your guests to know you have made it yourself.

Ravioli alla Romagnola

Ravioli with Pork and Turkey

THIS ROMAN-STYLE RAVIOLI stuffed with ground meat and cheese is scented with fresh herbs. It makes a substantial first course.

INGREDIENTS

1 recipe Pasta with Eggs
¹/4 cup butter
a large bunch of fresh sage, leaves removed and coarsely chopped
4 tablespoons freshly grated Parmesan cheese
extra sage leaves and freshly grated Parmesan cheese, to serve

For the filling
2 tablespoons butter
5 ounces ground pork
4 ounces ground turkey
4 fresh sage leaves, finely chopped
1 sprig of fresh rosemary, leaves removed and finely chopped
2 tablespoons dry white wine
generous ¹/4 cup ricotta cheese
3 tablespoons freshly grated Parmesan cheese
1 egg
nutmeg
salt and ground black pepper

Serves 8

1 Make the filling. Melt the butter in a medium saucepan, add the ground pork and turkey and the herbs and cook gently for 5–6 minutes, stirring frequently and breaking up any lumps in the meat with a wooden spoon. Add salt and pepper to taste and stir to mix.

2 Add the wine to the pan and stir again. Simmer for 1–2 minutes, until reduced slightly, then cover the pan and simmer gently for about 20 minutes, stirring occasionally. With a slotted spoon, transfer the meat to a bowl and set aside to cool.

3 Add the ricotta and Parmesan cheeses to the bowl with the egg and freshly grated nutmeg to taste. Stir well to mix the ingredients thoroughly.

4 Using a pasta machine, roll out one-quarter of the pasta into a 36-inch–40-inch strip. Cut the strip with a sharp knife into two 18–20-inch lengths (you can do this during rolling if the strip gets too long to manage).

5 Using a teaspoon, put 10–12 little mounds of the filling along one side of one of the pasta strips, spacing them evenly. Brush a little water onto the pasta strip around each mound, then fold the plain side of the pasta strip over the filling.

6 Starting from the folded edge, press down gently with your fingertips around each mound of filling, pushing the air out at the unfolded edge. Sprinkle lightly with flour.

7 With a fluted pasta wheel, cut along each long side, then in between each mound to make small square shapes. Dust lightly with flour.

8 Put the ravioli in a single layer on floured dish towels and set aside to dry while repeating the process with the remaining pasta, to make 80–96 ravioli altogether.

9 Drop the ravioli into a large pot of salted boiling water, bring back to a boil and boil for 4–5 minutes.

COOK'S TIP

Ground pork and turkey are widely available at supermarkets, but if you cannot get one or the other you can use just one type of meat, or substitute ground veal, beef or lamb to use in the ravioli filling.

10 While the ravioli are cooking, melt the butter in a small saucepan, add the fresh sage leaves and stir over medium to high heat until the sage leaves are sizzling in the butter.

11 Drain the ravioli and pour half into a warmed large bowl. Sprinkle with half the grated Parmesan, then half the sage butter. Repeat with the remaining ravioli, Parmesan and sage butter. Serve immediately, garnished with fresh sage leaves. Pass more grated Parmesan separately.

Meat-filled Agnolotti with Vodka Sauce

DAINTY HALF MOON SHAPES are filled with spiced ground meat and bacon and served with a cream and blue-cheese sauce spiked with vodka. This is a very special dish for a dinner party first course.

INGREDIENTS

1 recipe Pasta with Eggs
freshly grated Parmesan cheese, to serve

For the filling
1 tablespoon olive oil
3 ounces pancetta, lean bacon or ham, finely diced
9 ounces ground pork or veal
2 garlic cloves, crushed
good pinch of ground cinnamon
1/2 cup red wine
4 tablespoons chopped fresh Italian parsley
1 small egg
salt and ground black pepper

For the sauce
1/4 cup butter
1 cup panna da cucina or heavy cream
4 ounces Gorgonzola cheese, diced
3 tablespoons vodka
Serves 6–8

1 Make the filling. Heat the oil in a medium saucepan, add the pancetta, bacon or ham and stir-fry for a few minutes until lightly colored. Add the ground pork, the garlic, cinnamon and salt and pepper to taste and cook gently for 5–6 minutes, stirring frequently and breaking up any lumps.

2 Pour in the wine and stir well to mix, then simmer gently, stirring occasionally, for 15–20 minutes, until the meat is cooked and quite dry. Transfer the meat to a bowl with a slotted spoon and set aside to cool.

3 Add the parsley and egg to the meat mixture and stir well to mix.

4 Using a pasta machine, roll out one-quarter of the pasta into a 36-inch–40-inch strip. Cut the strip with a sharp knife into two 18–20-inch lengths (you can do this during rolling if the strip gets too long to manage).

5 Using a teaspoon, put 8–10 little mounds of the filling along one side of one of the pasta strips, spacing them evenly. Brush a little water around each mound, then fold the plain side of the pasta strip over the filling.

6 Starting from the folded edge, press down gently with your fingertips around each mound, pushing the air out at the unfolded edge.

7 Using only half of a 2-inch fluted round ravioli or biscuit cutter, cut around each mound of filling to make a half-moon shape. The folded edge should be the straight edge. If you like, press the cut edges of the agnolotti with the tines of a fork to give a decorative effect.

8 Put the agnolotti on floured dish towels, spreading them out in a single layer, so that they don't stick together. Sprinkle them lightly with flour and allow to dry while repeating the process with the remaining pasta, to get 64–80 agnolotti altogether.

9 Drop the agnolotti into a large pot of salted boiling water, bring back to a boil and boil for 4–5 minutes.

10 Meanwhile, make the sauce. Melt the butter in a medium saucepan, add the cream and cheese and heat through, stirring, until the cheese has melted. Add the vodka, season to taste with pepper and stir well to mix.

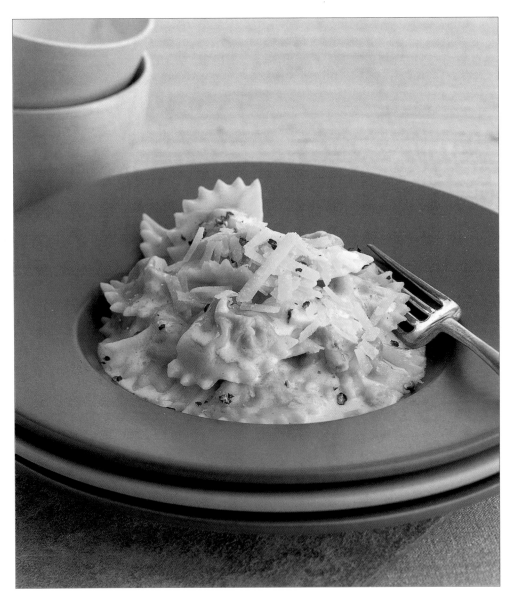

| | Drain the agnolotti and divide
| | them among six or eight
warmed bowls. Spoon the sauce over
them and sprinkle liberally with grated
Parmesan. Serve immediately.

VARIATIONS

• *Instead of the pancetta, bacon or ham,
you could use a spicy salami for the
agnolotti filling. Buy the salami in one
very thick piece, peel off the skin, then
chop the salami finely.*
• *Agnolotti are also often made with
prosciutto crudo, which gives them
a more delicate flavor than the
streaky pancetta.*

COOK'S TIP

*Gorgonzola is a sharp-tasting blue
Italian cheese with a soft and creamy
consistency. Gorgonzola piccante is a
particularly strong variety, while
gorgonzola dolce—better known as
dolcelatte—is creamier and less sharp in
flavor. Supermarkets, specialty cheese
stores and markets usually sell both
types of Gorgonzola.*

Ravioli con la Zucca

Ravioli with Pumpkin

THIS IS A VERY SIMPLE VERSION of a Christmas Eve specialty from Lombardy. In traditional recipes the pumpkin filling is flavored with *mostarda di frutta* (a kind of sweet fruit pickle), crushed amaretti biscuits and sugar. Here the pumpkin is seasoned with Parmesan and nutmeg. It is quite sweet enough for most tastes.

INGREDIENTS

1 recipe Pasta with Eggs
1/2 cup butter
freshly grated Parmesan cheese,
   to serve

For the filling
1 pound piece of pumpkin
1 tablespoon olive oil
scant 1/4 cup freshly grated
   Parmesan cheese
nutmeg
salt and ground black pepper
Serves 8

1 Make the filling. Preheat the oven to 425°F. Cut the piece of pumpkin into chunks and remove the seeds and fibers. Put the chunks, skin side down, in a roasting pan and drizzle the oil over the pumpkin flesh. Roast in the oven for 30 minutes, turning the pieces over once or twice.

2 Set aside the roasted pumpkin until it is cool enough to handle, then scrape the flesh out into a bowl and discard the pumpkin skin.

3 Mash the roasted pumpkin flesh with a fork, then add the grated Parmesan and freshly grated nutmeg and salt and pepper to taste. Stir well to mix, then set aside until cold.

4 Using a pasta machine, roll out one-quarter of the pasta into a 36-inch–40-inch strip. Cut the strip with a sharp knife into two 18–20-inch lengths (you can do this during rolling if the strip gets too long to manage).

5 Using a teaspoon, put 10–12 little mounds of the filling along one side of one of the pasta strips, spacing them evenly.

6 Brush a little water around each mound, then fold the plain side of the pasta strip over the mounds of filling. Starting from the folded edge, press down gently with your fingertips around each mound, pushing the air out at the unfolded edge. Sprinkle lightly with flour.

7 With a fluted pasta wheel, cut along each long side, then in between each mound to make small square shapes. Put the ravioli on floured dish towels, sprinkle lightly with flour and allow to dry, while repeating the process with the remaining pasta, to get 80–96 ravioli altogether.

8 Drop the ravioli into a large pot of salted boiling water, bring back to a boil and boil for 4–5 minutes. Meanwhile, melt the butter in a small saucepan until it is sizzling.

9 Drain the ravioli and divide them equally among eight warmed dinner plates or large bowls. Drizzle the sizzling butter over the ravioli and serve immediately, sprinkled with grated Parmesan. Pass more grated Parmesan separately.

VARIATION

You can buy mostarda di frutta *at Italian markets, especially at Christmas time. If you would like to try some in the filling, add about 3 tablespoons, together with a few crushed amaretti.*

Ravioli di Magro

Spinach and Ricotta Ravioli

THE LITERAL TRANSLATION OF *ravioli di magro* is lean ravioli. It is used to describe meatless ravioli, usually those with a spinach and ricotta filling. *Ravioli di magro* are served on Christmas Eve, a time when meat-filled pasta should not be eaten.

INGREDIENTS

1 recipe Pasta with Eggs
freshly grated Parmesan cheese, to serve

For the filling

3 tablespoons butter
6 ounces fresh spinach leaves, trimmed, washed and shredded
scant 1 cup ricotta cheese
1/3 cup freshly grated Parmesan cheese
nutmeg
1 small egg
salt and ground black pepper

For the sauce

1/4 cup butter
1 cup panna da cucina or heavy cream
2/3 cup freshly grated Parmesan cheese

Serves 8

1 Make the filling. Melt the butter in a medium saucepan, add the spinach and salt and pepper to taste and cook over medium heat for 5–8 minutes, stirring frequently, until the spinach is wilted and tender. Increase the heat to high and stir until the water boils off and the spinach is quite dry.

2 Tip the spinach into a bowl and set aside until cold, then add the ricotta, grated Parmesan and freshly grated nutmeg to taste. Beat well to mix, taste for seasoning, then add the egg and beat well again.

3 Using a pasta machine, roll out one-quarter of the pasta into a 36-inch–40-inch strip. Cut the strip with a sharp knife into two 18–20-inch lengths (you can do this during rolling if the strip gets too long to manage).

4 Using a teaspoon, put 10–12 little mounds of the filling along one side of one of the pasta strips, spacing them evenly. Brush a little water around each mound, then fold the plain side of the pasta strip over the filling.

5 Starting from the folded edge, press down gently with your fingertips around each mound of filling, pushing the air out at the unfolded edge. Sprinkle lightly with flour.

6 With a fluted pasta wheel, cut along each long side, then in between each mound to make small square shapes.

7 Put the ravioli on floured dish towels, sprinkle lightly with flour and allow to dry while repeating the process with the remaining pasta, to get 80–96 ravioli altogether.

8 Drop the ravioli into a large pot of salted boiling water, bring back to a boil and boil for 4–5 minutes.

9 Meanwhile, make the sauce. Gently heat the butter, cream and Parmesan in a medium saucepan until the butter and Parmesan have melted.

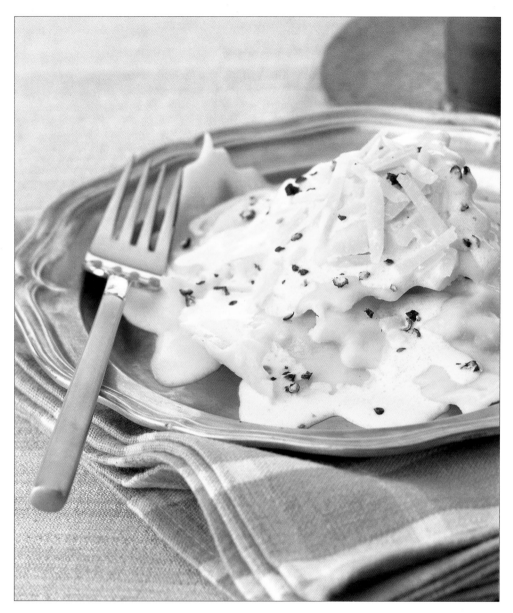

10 Increase the heat and simmer for a minute or two until the sauce is slightly reduced, then add salt and pepper to taste.

11 Drain the ravioli and divide them equally among 8 warmed large bowls. Drizzle the sauce over them and serve immediately, sprinkled with grated Parmesan.

VARIATION

If you prefer, serve the ravioli with sizzling sage butter. Melt 1/4 cup butter in a small pan, add a handful of fresh sage leaves and stir constantly over medium to high heat until sizzling. This will be slightly less rich than the cream sauce suggested here.

COOK'S TIP

To keep the pasta from sticking when working with it, lightly flour the work surface and your cutting tools and use more flour as necessary.

Ravioli al Granchio

Ravioli with Crab

THIS MODERN RECIPE for a dinner party first course uses chile-flavored pasta, which looks and tastes good with crab, but you can use plain pasta if you prefer.

INGREDIENTS

1 recipe Chile-flavored Pasta
    with Eggs
6 tablespoons butter
juice of 1 lemon

For the filling
3/4 cup mascarpone cheese
3/4 cup crabmeat
2 tablespoons finely chopped fresh
    Italian parsley
finely grated zest of 1 lemon
pinch of crushed dried chiles (optional)
salt and ground black pepper
Serves 4

COOK'S TIP

You can use all white crabmeat or a mixture of white and dark. If you use dark meat, the flavor will be stronger.

1 Make the filling. Put the mascarpone in a bowl and mash it with a fork. Add the crabmeat, parsley, lemon zest, crushed dried chiles (if using) and salt and pepper to taste. Stir well.

2 Using a pasta machine, roll out one-quarter of the pasta into a 36-inch–40-inch strip. Cut the strip with a sharp knife into two 18–20-inch lengths (you can do this during rolling if the strip gets too long to manage).

3 With a 2¹/₂-inch fluted biscuit cutter, cut out 8 squares from each pasta strip.

4 Using a teaspoon, put a mound of filling in the center of half the squares. Brush a little water around the edge of the filled squares, then top with the plain squares and press the edges to seal. For a decorative finish, press the edges with the tines of a fork.

5 Put the ravioli on floured dish towels, sprinkle lightly with flour and allow to dry while repeating the process with the remaining dough to make 32 ravioli altogether. If you have any stuffing left, you can re-roll the pasta trimmings and make more ravioli.

6 Cook the ravioli in a large pot of salted boiling water for 4–5 minutes. Meanwhile, melt the butter and lemon juice in a small saucepan until sizzling.

7 Drain the ravioli and divide them equally among four warmed bowls. Drizzle the lemon butter over the ravioli and serve immediately.

Sardinian Ravioli

THESE RAVIOLI, with their unusual mashed potato and mint filling, are from northern Sardinia. Here they are gratinéed in the oven with butter and cheese, but they are often served dressed with a tomato sauce.

INGREDIENTS

1 recipe Pasta with Eggs
1/4 cup butter
2/3 cup freshly grated pecorino cheese

For the filling

2 potatoes, each about 7 ounces, diced
generous 2/3 cup freshly grated hard salty pecorino cheese
3 ounces soft fresh pecorino cheese
1 egg yolk
1 generous handful fresh mint, leaves removed and chopped
good pinch of saffron powder
salt and ground black pepper

Serves 4–6

1 Make the filling. Cook the diced potatoes in salted boiling water for 15–20 minutes or until soft. Drain the potatoes and turn into a bowl, then mash until smooth. Set aside until cold. Add the cheeses, egg yolk, mint, saffron and salt and pepper to taste and stir well to mix.

2 Using a pasta machine, roll out one-quarter of the pasta into a 36-inch–40-inch strip. Cut the strip with a sharp knife into two 18–20-inch lengths.

3 With a fluted 4-inch biscuit cutter, cut out 4–5 circles from one of the pasta strips. Using a teaspoon, put a mound of filling on one side of each circle. Brush a little water around the edge of each circle, then fold the plain side of the circle over the filling to make a half-moon shape. Pleat the curved edge to seal.

4 Put the *culurgiones* on floured dish towels, sprinkle with flour and allow to dry. Repeat the process with the remaining dough to make 32–40 *culurgiones* altogether. If you have any stuffing left, re-roll the pasta trimmings and make more *culurgiones*.

5 Preheat the oven to 375°F. Cook the *culurgiones* in a large pot of salted boiling water for 4–5 minutes. Meanwhile, melt the butter in a small saucepan.

6 Drain the *culurgiones*, turn them into a large baking pan and pour the melted butter over them. Sprinkle with the grated pecorino and bake in the oven for 10–15 minutes, until golden and bubbly. Allow to stand for 5 minutes before serving.

COOK'S TIP

There is quite an art to pleating the curved edge of culurgiones, *but each cook has his or her own way of doing it, so don't worry about getting a precise finish. Do whatever you think looks best—some* culurgiones *look like miniature Cornish turnovers, others more like wontons. If you prefer, simply make square or round ravioli, or plain half-moons.*

Rotolo di Pasta Farcita

Stuffed Pasta Roll

THIS IS AN IMPRESSIVE **dinner party first course**. It takes quite a long time to make, but it can be made up to the baking stage the day before.

INGREDIENTS

6 tablespoons butter
I small onion, finely chopped
5 ounces fresh spinach leaves, washed
    and trimmed
generous I cup ricotta cheese
I egg
4 tablespoons freshly grated Parmesan cheese
4 tablespoons freshly grated pecorino cheese
nutmeg
$^2/_3$ recipe Pasta with Eggs
salt and ground black pepper

For the tomato sauce

4 tablespoons olive oil
I onion, finely chopped
I carrot, finely chopped
I celery stalk, finely chopped
I garlic clove, thinly sliced
a few leaves each fresh basil, thyme and
    oregano or marjoram, plus extra basil
    leaves, to garnish
2 cans (14-ounce) chopped Italian
    plum tomatoes
I tablespoon sun-dried tomato paste
I teaspoon sugar
5–7 tablespoons dry white wine

Serves 6

I Melt 2 tablespoons of the butter in a medium saucepan, add the finely chopped onion and cook gently, stirring frequently, for about 5 minutes, until softened.

2 Add the spinach and salt and pepper to taste and cook over medium heat for 5–8 minutes, stirring frequently, until the spinach is wilted and tender. Increase the heat to high and stir until the water boils off and the spinach is quite dry.

3 Finely chop the spinach mixture in a food processor or by hand. Transfer to a bowl and add the ricotta, egg and half the grated Parmesan and pecorino. Season to taste with freshly grated nutmeg and salt, and add plenty of pepper. Beat well to mix.

4 Roll out the pasta dough to a 20 × 16-inch rectangle. Place the rectangle on a large piece of cheese-cloth with one of the short sides nearest you.

5 Spread the spinach mixture thinly over the pasta, leaving a $^3/4$-inch margin along the two long sides and a 2-inch margin along the short side that is furthest away from you. Moisten the two long sides with water.

6 Starting from the short side that is nearest you, pick up the cloth and roll the pasta away from you as you would a jelly roll. Don't press it, just let it roll until you have a 16-inch long "sausage". Press the two open ends to seal the pasta, then roll the cloth around the *rotolo* a couple of times and tie the two ends tightly with string.

7 Half fill a fish steamer or large oval flameproof casserole with water and bring it to a boil. Add a large pinch of salt, then the *rotolo*. Half cover with a lid and simmer for 45 minutes, turning the *rotolo* over twice. Remove the *rotolo* from the water and place it on a board near the sink. Prop the board up at one end to allow the excess water to drain away from the *rotolo*, then set aside to cool.

8 Make the tomato sauce. Chop the onion, carrot and celery finely, either in a food processor or by hand. Heat the oil in a saucepan, add the garlic slices and stir over very low heat for 1–2 minutes. Add the chopped vegetables and the fresh herbs. Cook over low heat, stirring for 5–7 minutes, until the vegetables have softened and are lightly colored.

9 Add the tomatoes, tomato paste and sugar, then add salt and pepper to taste. Bring to a boil, stirring all the time, then lower the heat and simmer gently, uncovered, for about 45 minutes, stirring occasionally.

10 Preheat the oven to 400°F.
Unwrap the *rotolo* and cut it
into 12 thick slices. Melt the remaining
butter and brush a little of it over the
inside of six individual ovenproof dishes
or a large shallow baking dish.

11 Arrange the *rotolo* slices slightly
overlapping in the dishes or dish
and drizzle the remaining butter over
them. Sprinkle with the remaining
Parmesan and pecorino and bake in
the oven for 10–15 minutes or until
golden brown.

12 Meanwhile, blend the tomato
sauce in a food processor until
smooth. Transfer the sauce to a pan
and add enough wine to thin it down
to a pouring consistency, then heat
until bubbling. Serve the *rotolo* slices on
individual plates, on a pool of tomato
sauce, sprinkled with basil leaves.

COOK'S TIP

*If you have a pasta machine, roll out
half the dough into a 40-inch strip. Cut
the strip with a sharp knife into two
20-inch lengths (you can do this during
rolling if the strip gets too long to
manage). Brush the long edge of one of
the strips with water, then overlap the
other strip on top by about ¹/2 inch. Dust
lightly with flour and press together, then
seal the join by rolling over it with a rolling
pin. Repeat with the remaining dough,
then join the two pieces of pasta
together in the same way so that you
have a large rectangle.*

Cappellacci alla Bolognese

Cheese Cappellacci with Bolognese Sauce

IN EMILIA-ROMAGNA it is traditional to serve these *cappellacci* with a rich meat sauce, but if you prefer you can serve them with a tomato sauce, or just melted butter.

INGREDIENTS

1 recipe Pasta with Eggs
8 cups beef stock made with stock cubes and water or diluted canned consommé
freshly grated Parmesan cheese, to serve
basil leaves, to garnish

For the filling

generous 1 cup ricotta cheese
3 1/2 ounces taleggio cheese, rind removed, diced very small
4 tablespoons freshly grated Parmesan cheese
1 small egg
nutmeg
salt and ground black pepper

For the Bolognese meat sauce

2 tablespoons butter
1 tablespoon olive oil
1 onion
2 carrots
2 celery stalks
2 garlic cloves
4 1/2 ounces pancetta or lean bacon, diced
9 ounces lean ground beef
9 ounces lean ground pork
1/2 cup dry white wine
2 cans (14-ounce) crushed Italian plum tomatoes
2–3 cups beef stock
scant 1/2 cup panna da cucina or heavy cream

Serves 6

1 Make the filling. Put the ricotta, taleggio and grated Parmesan in a bowl and mash together with a fork.

2 Add the egg and freshly grated nutmeg and salt and pepper to taste and stir well to mix.

3 Using a pasta machine, roll out one-quarter of the pasta into a 36-inch–40-inch strip. Cut the strip with a sharp knife into two 18–20-inch lengths (you can do this during rolling if the strip gets too long to manage).

4 Using a 2 1/2–3-inch square ravioli cutter, cut 6–7 squares from one of the pasta strips. Using a teaspoon, put a mound of filling in the center of each square. Brush a little water around the edge of each square, then fold the square diagonally in half over the filling to make a triangular shape. Press to seal.

5 Wrap the triangle around one of your index fingers, bringing the bottom two corners together. Pinch the ends together to seal, then press with your fingertip around the top edge of the filling to make an indentation so that the "hat" looks like a bishop's miter.

6 Place the *cappellacci* on floured dish towels, sprinkle them lightly with flour and allow to dry while repeating the process with the remaining dough, to make 48–56 *cappellacci* altogether.

7 Make the meat sauce. Heat the butter and oil in a large skillet or saucepan until sizzling. Add the vegetables, garlic, and the pancetta or bacon and cook over medium heat, stirring frequently, for 10 minutes or until the vegetables have softened.

8 Add the ground beef and pork, lower the heat and cook gently for 10 minutes, stirring frequently and breaking up any lumps in the meat with a wooden spoon. Stir in salt and pepper to taste, then add the wine and stir again. Simmer for about 5 minutes, or until reduced.

9 Add the tomatoes and 1 cup of the stock and bring to a boil. Stir well, then lower the heat, half cover the pan with a lid and allow to simmer very gently for 2 hours. Stir occasionally during this time and add more stock as it becomes absorbed.

10 Add the *panna da cucina* or heavy cream to the meat sauce. Stir well to mix, then simmer the sauce, without a lid, for another 30 minutes, stirring frequently.

11 Bring the stock to a boil in a large saucepan.

12 Drop the *cappellacci* into the stock, bring back to a boil and boil for 4–5 minutes; drain the *cappellacci* and divide them equally among six warmed bowls. Spoon the hot Bolognese sauce over the *cappellacci* and sprinkle with grated Parmesan and basil leaves. Serve immediately.

COOK'S TIP

The exact shape of cappellacci *varies from one cook to another. Some are made from circles rather than squares of pasta, although these are more often called tortellini or tortelloni. It all depends on the region in which they are made. If you prefer a party-hat shape to a bishop's miter, don't make an indentation above the filling in Step 5, but instead turn up the bottom edge of each "hat" so that they have brims.* Cappelletti *are the same shape as* cappellacci *but are made from smaller squares of pasta (about 2-inches square). Not surprisingly, because of their size,* cappelletti *are trickier to make.*

Ravioli alla Napoletana

Cheese and Ham Ravioli with Tomato Sauce

TYPICAL OF SOUTHERN ITALIAN cuisine, these ravioli are very tasty. They are substantial enough for a main course, served with a green or mixed salad. If you prefer them as a first course, there are enough ravioli for 8 servings.

INGREDIENTS

1 recipe Pasta with Eggs
4 tablespoons freshly grated pecorino
    cheese, plus extra to serve

For the filling
3/4 cup ricotta cheese
2 tablespoons freshly grated Parmesan cheese
4 ounces prosciutto, finely chopped
5 ounces fresh mozzarella cheese, drained
    and finely chopped
1 small egg
1 tablespoon chopped fresh Italian parsley,
    plus extra to garnish

For the tomato sauce
2 tablespoons olive oil
1 onion, finely chopped
1 can (14 ounces) chopped Italian
    plum tomatoes
1 tablespoon sun-dried tomato paste
1–2 teaspoons dried oregano, to taste
salt and ground black pepper
Serves 4–6

1 Make the sauce. Heat the oil in a medium saucepan, add the onion and cook gently, stirring frequently, for about 5 minutes, until softened.

2 Add the tomatoes. Fill the empty can with water, pour it into the pan, then stir in the tomato paste, oregano and salt and pepper to taste. Bring to a boil and stir well, then cover the pan and simmer gently for 30 minutes, stirring occasionally and adding more water if the sauce becomes too thick.

3 Meanwhile, make the filling and the ravioli. Put all the filling ingredients in a bowl with salt and pepper to taste. Mix well with a fork, breaking up any lumps in the ricotta.

4 Using a pasta machine, roll out one-quarter of the pasta into a 36-inch–40-inch strip. Cut the strip with a sharp knife into two 18–20-inch lengths (you can do this during rolling if the strip gets too long to manage).

5 Using 2 teaspoons, put 10–12 little mounds of the filling along one side of one of the pasta strips, spacing them evenly. The filling will be quite moist. Brush a little water around each mound, then fold the plain side of the pasta strip over the filling.

6 Starting from the folded edge, press down gently with your fingertips around each mound, pushing the air out at the unfolded edge.

7 Sprinkle lightly with flour. With a fluted pasta wheel, cut along each long side, then in between each mound, to make small square shapes.

8 Put the ravioli on floured dish towels; sprinkle lightly with flour.

9 Allow the ravioli to dry while repeating the process with the remaining pasta, to get 80–96 ravioli altogether. Drop the ravioli into a large pot of salted boiling water, bring back to a boil and boil for 4–5 minutes.

10 Drain the ravioli well and pour about a third of them into a warmed bowl. Sprinkle 1 tablespoon freshly grated pecorino over the ravioli. Pour over a third of the tomato sauce.

11 Repeat the layers twice, then top with the remaining grated pecorino. Serve immediately, garnished with chopped parsley. Pass more grated pecorino separately.

VARIATION

If you like the flavor of garlic with tomatoes, gently cook 1–2 crushed garlic cloves with the onion when making the tomato sauce.

Agnolotti di Taleggio e Maggiorama

Agnolotti with Taleggio and Marjoram

THE FILLING FOR THESE LITTLE half-moons is very simple—only two ingredients—but the combination of flavors is absolutely delicious.

INGREDIENTS

1 recipe Pasta with Eggs
12–14 ounces taleggio cheese
2 tablespoons finely chopped
*   fresh marjoram, plus extra to garnish*
¹/₂ cup butter
salt and ground black pepper
freshly grated Parmesan cheese, to serve
Serves 6–8

1 Using a pasta machine, roll out a quarter of the pasta into a 36-inch–40-inch strip. Cut the strip with a sharp knife into two 18–20-inch lengths (you can do this during rolling if the strip gets too long to manage).

2 Cut 8–10 little cubes of taleggio and place them along one side of one of the pasta strips, spacing them evenly. Sprinkle each taleggio cube with a little chopped marjoram and pepper to taste.

3 Brush a little water around each cube of cheese, then fold the plain side of the pasta strip over them.

4 Starting from the folded edge, press down gently with your fingertips around each cube, pushing the air out at the unfolded edge. Sprinkle lightly with flour.

5 Using only half of a 2-inch fluted round ravioli or biscuit cutter, cut around each cube of cheese to make a half-moon shape. The folded edge should be the straight edge.

6 If you like, press the cut edges of the agnolotti with the tines of a fork to give a decorative effect.

7 Put the agnolotti on floured dish towels, sprinkle lightly with flour and allow to dry while repeating the process with the remaining pasta, cheese, marjoram and pepper, to get 64–80 agnolotti altogether.

8 Drop the agnolotti into a large pot of salted boiling water, bring back to a boil and boil for 4–5 minutes until *al dente*.

9 Meanwhile, melt the butter in a small saucepan until it is sizzling.

10 Drain the agnolotti and divide them equally among six or eight warmed large bowls. Drizzle the sizzling butter over them and serve immediately, sprinkled with freshly grated Parmesan and chopped fresh marjoram. Hand around more grated Parmesan separately.

COOK'S TIPS

• *Taleggio is a square-shaped, semi-soft cheese from Lombardy. It is quite easy to get in large supermarkets, or any Italian delicatessen. It has a mild, slightly nutty flavor and good melting qualities. For this recipe, make sure that you remove the rind, which tends to be quite tough and salty.*
• *If you are unable to get taleggio, use fontina cheese instead, or a strongly flavored blue cheese, such as Gorgonzola. If you use a blue cheese, substitute sage for the marjoram.*

VARIATION

Marjoram is traditional with the taleggio cheese in this recipe, both for the filling and the sizzling butter, but you can use other fresh herbs, such as sage, basil or Italian parsley.

Pansotti con Erbe e Formaggi

Pansotti with Herbs and Cheese

IN LIGURIA, THE DOUGH for *pansotti* is flavored with white wine, and the stuffing is made of cheese and *preboggion*, a mixture of many different types of fresh herbs and wild leaves. The dish is traditionally served with a kind of pesto made from walnuts, making it very rich and quite complex. The recipe given here is a simple version.

INGREDIENTS

1 recipe Herb-flavored Pasta
    with Eggs
1/4 cup butter
freshly grated Parmesan cheese,
    to serve

For the filling

generous 1 cup ricotta cheese
1 2/3 cups freshly grated Parmesan cheese
1 large handful fresh basil leaves,
    finely chopped
1 large handful fresh Italian parsley,
    finely chopped
a few sprigs fresh marjoram or oregano,
    leaves removed and finely chopped
1 garlic clove, crushed
1 small egg
salt and ground black pepper

For the sauce

3 1/2 ounces shelled walnuts
1 garlic clove
4 tablespoons extra virgin olive oil
1/2 cup panna da cucina or heavy cream
Serves 6–8

1 First make the filling and sauce. Put the ricotta, Parmesan, herbs, garlic and egg in a bowl with salt and pepper to taste and beat well to mix.

2 To make the sauce, put the walnuts, garlic clove and oil in a food processor and process to a paste, adding up to 1/2 cup warm water through the feeder tube to thin down the paste. Spoon the mixture into a large bowl and add the cream. Beat well to mix, then add salt and pepper to taste.

3 Using a pasta machine, roll out one-quarter of the pasta into a 36-inch –40-inch strip. Cut the strip with a sharp knife into two 18–20-inch lengths (you can do this during rolling if the strip gets too long to manage).

4 Using a 2-inch square ravioli cutter, cut 8–10 squares from one of the pasta strips. Using a teaspoon, put a mound of filling in the center of each square.

5 Brush a little water around the edge of each square, then fold the square diagonally in half over the filling to make a triangular shape. Press gently to seal.

6 Spread out the *pansotti* on clean floured dish towels, sprinkle lightly with flour and set aside to dry, while repeating the process with the remaining dough, to make 64–80 *pansotti* altogether.

7 Cook the *pansotti* in a large pot of salted boiling water for 4–5 minutes. Meanwhile, put the walnut sauce in a large warmed bowl and add a ladleful of the pasta cooking water to thin it down. Melt the butter in a small saucepan until sizzling.

8 Drain the *pansotti* and turn them into the bowl of walnut sauce. Drizzle the butter over them, toss well, then sprinkle with grated Parmesan. Alternatively, toss the pansotti in the melted butter, spoon into warmed individual bowls and drizzle over the sauce. Serve immediately, with more grated Parmesan passed separately.

COOK'S TIP

Take care not to overfill the pansotti, or they will burst open during cooking.

Tortellini Romagnoli

Tortellini from Emilia-Romagna

THESE ARE THE TORTELLINI that are
served on the day after Christmas in
Emilia-Romagna. Traditionally they
were made with ground leftover
capon from Christmas Day, but
nowadays turkey or chicken is
often used.

INGREDIENTS

1 recipe Pasta with Eggs
*8 cups beef stock made with stock cubes
and water or diluted canned consommé*
*freshly grated Parmesan cheese,
to serve*

For the filling
2 tablespoons butter
9 ounces ground turkey or chicken
1 teaspoon chopped fresh rosemary
1 teaspoon chopped fresh sage
nutmeg
1 cup chicken stock
*4 tablespoons freshly grated
Parmesan cheese*
*3 1/2 ounces mortadella sausage, very
finely chopped*
1 small egg
salt and ground black pepper
Serves 6–8

1 Make the filling. Melt the butter in a
medium skillet, then add the ground
turkey or chicken and chopped herbs.

2 Grate in a little nutmeg and add
salt and pepper to taste. Cook
gently for 5–6 minutes, stirring
frequently and breaking up any lumps
in the meat with a wooden spoon.

3 Add the stock and stir well to
mix, then simmer gently,
uncovered, for 15–20 minutes, until the
meat is cooked and quite dry. Transfer
the meat to a bowl with a slotted
spoon and allow to cool. Add the
grated Parmesan, mortadella and egg
to the meat and stir well to mix.

4 Using a pasta machine, roll out
one-quarter of the pasta into a
36-inch–40-inch strip. Cut the strip
with a sharp knife into two 18–20-inch
lengths (you can do this during rolling if
the strip gets too long to manage).

5 With a 2-inch fluted ravioli or
biscuit cutter, cut out 8–10 circles
from one of the pasta strips. Using a
teaspoon, put a little mound of filling in
the center of each circle. Brush a little
water around the edge of each circle.

6 Fold the circle in half over the filling
so that the edges do not quite
meet. Press to seal. Wrap the tortellini
shape around your index finger and pinch
the bottom corners together to seal.

7 Put the tortellini in a single layer
on floured dish towels, sprinkle
lightly with flour and allow to dry
while repeating the process with
the remaining dough, to make
64–80 tortellini altogether. If you
have any stuffing left, re-roll the pasta
trimmings and make more tortellini.

8 Bring the beef stock to a boil
in a large saucepan. Drop in
the tortellini, then bring back to a boil
and boil for 4–5 minutes. Taste the
stock and season with salt and pepper
if necessary.

9 Pour the tortellini and stock into
a warmed large soup tureen,
sprinkle with a little grated Parmesan
and serve immediately. Pass more
Parmesan separately.

COOK'S TIP

*In Emilia-Romagna, cooked leftover meat
is ground by hand for these tortellini, or
raw meat is cooked in the piece and
then ground. For speed and convenience
in this recipe, raw ground poultry is
cooked with herbs and seasonings
before being used in the filling.*

Fresh
and
Healthy

Roasted vegetables, mesclun and pesto made with arugula are just a few of the new ingredients being introduced to pasta by today's chefs. To call these sauces is stretching the point a little: many of them consist of little more than a handful of fresh ingredients tossed with hot pasta, but the results are simply sensational.

These are not traditional pasta dishes. Many of them originated in restaurants, in response to the current taste for lighter, healthier food, but they are so quick and easy to make at home that you will find there's no need to go out to eat them.

The recipes in this chapter are tried and tested, but there are no hard-and-fast rules. Half the fun is in inventing your own combinations, using fresh vegetables and herbs according to the season. The key to success lies in the quality of these ingredients, and only the best will do. This goes for the pasta as much as anything else. Buy Italian brands of pasta to be sure of good texture and taste or, if you have the inclination and time, make your own fresh egg pasta.

Pasta is a natural, additive-free food, packed with protein, vitamins and minerals—the perfect partner for other healthy ingredients to make a high-energy meal.

Penne con la Rucola e la Mozzarella

Penne with Arugula and Mozzarella

LIKE A WARM SALAD, this pasta dish is very quick and easy to make—perfect for an al fresco summer lunch. Its success depends on the very best Italian ingredients, so make sure they are as fresh as possible and in top condition.

INGREDIENTS

3 1/2 cups fresh or dried penne

6 ripe Italian plum tomatoes, peeled,
    seeded and diced

10 ounces mozzarella cheese,
    drained and diced

2 large handfuls of arugula, total weight
    about 5 ounces

5 tablespoons extra virgin olive oil

salt and freshly ground black pepper

Serves 4

1 Cook the pasta in a large pot of salted boiling water according to the package instructions.

2 Meanwhile, put the tomatoes, mozzarella, arugula and olive oil into a large bowl with a little salt and pepper to taste and toss well to mix.

3 Drain the cooked pasta and turn it into the bowl. Toss well to mix and serve immediately.

VARIATION

For a less peppery taste, use basil leaves instead of arugula, or a mixture of the two.

Eliche ai Peperoni Arrostiti

Eliche with Roasted Bell Peppers

ROASTED PEPPERS ARE GOOD with pasta because they have a soft juicy texture and a wonderful smoky flavor. This is a dish for high summer when peppers and tomatoes are plentiful and ripe. It is equally good cold as a salad.

INGREDIENTS

3 large bell peppers (red, yellow
    and orange)

3 cups fresh or dried eliche or fusilli

1–2 garlic cloves, to taste,
    finely chopped

4 tablespoons extra virgin olive oil

4 ripe Italian plum tomatoes, peeled,
    seeded and diced

1/2 cup pitted black olives, halved or
    quartered lengthwise

1 handful of fresh basil leaves

salt and ground black pepper

Serves 4

1 Put the whole peppers under a hot broiler and broil them for about 10 minutes, turning them frequently until they are charred on all sides. Put the hot peppers in a paper bag, seal the bag and set aside until the peppers are cold.

2 Remove the peppers from the bag and hold them one at a time under cold running water. Peel off the charred skins with your fingers, split the peppers open and pull out the cores. Rub off all the seeds under the running water, then pat the peppers dry on paper towels.

3 Cook the pasta in a large pot of salted boiling water according to the instructions on the package until *al dente*.

4 Meanwhile, thinly slice the peppers and place them in a large bowl with the remaining ingredients and salt and pepper to taste.

5 Drain the cooked pasta and turn it into the bowl. Toss well to mix and serve immediately.

VARIATION

Add a few slivers of bottled or canned anchovy fillets in Step 4.

Tagliatelle Verdissime

Tagliatelle with Broccoli and Spinach

THIS IS AN EXCELLENT vegetarian supper dish. It is nutritious and filling, and needs no accompaniment. If you like, you can use tagliatelle flecked with herbs.

INGREDIENTS

2 heads of broccoli
1 pound fresh spinach, stalks removed
nutmeg
1 pound fresh or dried egg tagliatelle
about 3 tablespoons extra virgin olive oil
juice of 1/2 lemon, or to taste
salt and ground black pepper
freshly grated Parmesan cheese,
    to serve
Serves 4

1 Put the broccoli in the basket of a steamer, cover and steam over boiling water for 10 minutes. Add the spinach to the broccoli, cover and steam for 4–5 minutes or until both are tender. Towards the end of the cooking time, sprinkle the vegetables with freshly grated nutmeg and salt and pepper to taste. Transfer the vegetables to a colander.

2 Add salt to the water in the steamer and fill the steamer pot with boiling water, then add the pasta and cook according to the instructions on the package. Meanwhile, chop the broccoli and spinach in the colander.

3 Drain the pasta. Heat 3 tablespoons oil in the pasta pan, add the pasta and chopped vegetables and toss over medium heat until evenly mixed. Sprinkle in the lemon juice and plenty of black pepper, then taste and add more lemon juice, oil, salt and nutmeg if you like. Serve immediately, sprinkled liberally with freshly grated Parmesan and black pepper.

VARIATIONS

• *If you like, add a sprinkling of crushed dried chiles with the black pepper in Step 3.*
• *To add both texture and protein, garnish the finished dish with one or two handfuls of toasted pine nuts. They are often served with broccoli and spinach in Italy.*

Conchiglie from Pisa

NOTHING COULD BE SIMPLER than hot pasta tossed with fresh ripe tomatoes, ricotta and sweet basil. Serve it on hot summer days—it is surprisingly cool and refreshing.

INGREDIENTS

3 cups conchiglie

generous $^1/_2$ cup ricotta cheese

6 ripe Italian plum tomatoes, diced

2 garlic cloves, crushed

1 handful fresh basil leaves, shredded, plus
   extra basil leaves to garnish

4 tablespoons extra virgin olive oil

salt and ground black pepper

Serves 4–6

1 Cook the pasta in salted boiling water according to the instructions on the package.

COOK'S TIP

If you like, peel the tomatoes before you dice them. It won't take long if the tomatoes are ripe.

2 Meanwhile, put the ricotta in a large bowl and mash with a fork.

3 Add the tomatoes, garlic and basil, with salt and pepper to taste, and mix well. Add the olive oil and whisk thoroughly. Taste for seasoning.

4 Drain the cooked pasta, turn it into the ricotta mixture and toss well to mix. Garnish with basil leaves and serve immediately.

VARIATIONS

• *You can use diced fresh mozzarella instead of ricotta cheese and call the dish* Conchiglie Caprese, *after the salad of tomatoes, mozzarella and basil known as* Caprese.

• *An avocado is the ideal ingredient for adding extra color and flavor to this pasta dish. Halve, pit and peel, then dice the flesh. Toss it with the hot pasta at the last minute.*

Tagliatelle alle Erbe

Tagliatelle with Herbs

THIS IS A LOVELY dish for summer when fresh herbs are plentiful. It is quick and ideal for vegetarians.

INGREDIENTS

3 rosemary sprigs
1 small handful fresh Italian parsley
5–6 fresh mint leaves
5–6 fresh sage leaves
8–10 large fresh basil leaves
2 tablespoons extra virgin olive oil
1/4 cup butter
1 shallot, finely chopped
2 garlic cloves, finely chopped
pinch of cayenne pepper, to taste
14 ounces fresh egg tagliatelle
1 bay leaf
1/2 cup dry white wine
6–8 tablespoons vegetable stock
salt and ground black pepper
Serves 4

1 Strip the rosemary and parsley leaves from their stalks and chop them together with the fresh mint, sage and basil.

2 Heat the olive oil and half the butter in a large skillet or saucepan. Add the shallot and garlic and the cayenne pepper, and cook over very low heat, stirring frequently, for 2–3 minutes.

3 Cook the pasta in salted boiling water according to the package instructions.

4 Add the chopped herbs and the bay leaf to the shallot mixture and stir for 2–3 minutes, then add the wine and increase the heat. Boil rapidly for 1–2 minutes, until the wine reduces. Lower the heat, add the stock and simmer gently for 1–2 minutes.

5 Drain the pasta and add it to the herb mixture. Toss well to mix and remove and discard the bay leaf.

6 Put the remaining butter in a warmed large bowl, turn the dressed pasta into it and toss well to mix. Serve immediately.

Garganelli Primavera

Garganelli with Spring Vegetables

YOUNG FRESH VEGETABLES both look and taste good with pasta. Butter is used to marry the two, but you can use extra virgin olive oil if you prefer.

INGREDIENTS

1 bunch asparagus, about 12 ounces
4 young carrots
1 bunch scallions
1 cup shelled fresh peas
3 cups garganelli
4 tablespoons dry white wine
6 tablespoons unsalted butter, diced
*a few sprigs each fresh Italian parsley, mint
    and basil, leaves stripped and chopped*
salt and ground black pepper
freshly grated Parmesan cheese, to serve
Serves 4

1 Trim off and discard the woody part of each asparagus stem, then cut off the tips on the diagonal. Cut the stems on the diagonal into 1 1/2-inch pieces. Cut the carrots and scallions on the diagonal into similar pieces.

2 Plunge the asparagus stems, carrots and peas into a pot of salted boiling water. Bring back to a boil and simmer for 5–8 minutes, adding the asparagus tips for the last 3 minutes.

3 Meanwhile, cook the pasta in salted boiling water according to the instructions on the package.

4 Drain the vegetables and return them to the pot. Add the wine, butter and salt and pepper to taste, then toss over medium to high heat until the wine has reduced and the vegetables glisten with melted butter.

5 Drain the pasta and turn it into a warmed large bowl. Add the vegetables, scallions and herbs and toss well. Serve immediately, with freshly grated Parmesan.

COOK'S TIP

Garganelli are rolled short pasta shapes made with egg. If you can't get garganelli, use another short shape made with egg.

Fresh and Healthy

Spaghetti with Arugula Pesto

THIS IS THE PESTO for real arugula lovers. It is sharp and peppery, and delicious for a summer pasta meal with a glass of chilled dry white wine.

INGREDIENTS

4 garlic cloves

6 tablespoons pine nuts

2 large handfuls arugula, total weight about
    5 ounces, stalks removed

2/3 cup Parmesan cheese, freshly grated

2/3 cup pecorino cheese, freshly grated

6 tablespoons extra virgin olive oil

14 ounces fresh or dried spaghetti

salt and ground black pepper

freshly grated Parmesan and pecorino
    cheese, to serve

Serves 4

1 Put the garlic and pine nuts in a blender or food processor and process until finely chopped.

2 Add the arugula, Parmesan and pecorino, oil and salt and pepper to taste and process for 5 seconds. Stop and scrape down the side of the bowl. Process for 5–10 seconds more until a smooth paste is formed.

3 Cook the spaghetti in a large pot of salted boiling water according to the package instructions.

4 Turn the pesto into a large bowl. Just before the pasta is ready, add 1–2 ladlefuls of the cooking water to the pesto and stir well to mix.

5 Drain the pasta, turn it into the bowl of pesto and toss well to mix. Serve immediately, with the grated cheeses handed separately.

VARIATION

To temper the flavor of the arugula and make the pesto milder, add 1/2 cup ricotta or mascarpone cheese to the pesto in Step 4 and mix well before adding the water.

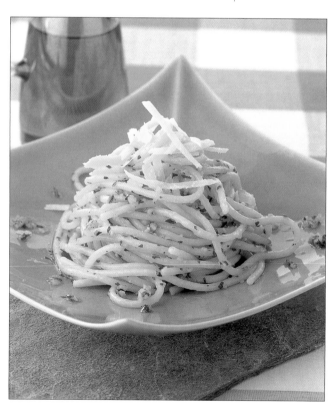

Spaghetti al Limone

Spaghetti with Lemon

THIS IS THE DISH TO MAKE when you get home and find there's nothing to eat. If you keep spaghetti and olive oil in the pantry and garlic and lemons in the vegetable rack, you can prepare the most delicious meal in minutes.

INGREDIENTS

12 ounces spaghetti
6 tablespoons extra virgin olive oil
juice of 1 large lemon
2 garlic cloves, cut into very thin slivers
salt and ground black pepper
freshly grated Parmesan cheese, to serve

Serves 4

1 Cook the pasta in a large pot of salted boiling water according to the instructions on the package, then drain well and return to the pan.

2 Pour the olive oil and lemon juice over the cooked pasta, sprinkle in the slivers of garlic and add salt and pepper to taste.

3 Toss the pasta over medium to high heat for 1–2 minutes. Serve immediately in four warmed bowls, with freshly grated Parmesan.

COOK'S TIP

Spaghetti is the best type of pasta for this recipe, because the olive oil and lemon juice cling to its long thin strands—even more so if you serve it with freshly grated Parmesan. If you are out of spaghetti, use another long pasta shape instead, such as spaghettini, linguine or tagliatelle.

Pipe con Ricotta e Spinaci

Pipe with Ricotta, Saffron and Spinach

TOSSING PASTA IN RICOTTA is popular in Sicily and Sardinia, where this cheese is widely used in cooking. For best results, use fresh white ricotta, which is sold by weight in Italian markets. Serve this fairly rich dish in small quantities. Omit the saffron, with its quite strong flavor, if liked.

INGREDIENTS

1 small pinch of saffron threads
2³/4 cups pipe
11–12 ounces fresh spinach,
stalks removed
nutmeg
generous 1 cup ricotta cheese
salt and ground black pepper
freshly grated pecorino cheese, to serve
Serves 4–6

1 Soak the saffron threads in 4 table-spoons warm water. Cook the pasta according to the package instructions.

2 Meanwhile, wash the spinach and put the leaves in a saucepan with only the water clinging to the leaves. Season with freshly grated nutmeg, salt and pepper to taste,

3 Cover the pan and cook over medium to high heat for about 5 minutes, shaking the pan occasionally, until the spinach is wilted and tender. Turn into a colander, press it to extract as much liquid as possible, then coarsely chop it, letting the water drain through.

4 Put the ricotta in a large bowl. Strain in the saffron water. Add the spinach, beat well to mix, then add a ladleful or two of the pasta cooking water to loosen the mixture. Season.

5 Drain the pasta, reserving some of the cooking water. Add the pasta to the ricotta mixture and toss well, adding a little of the water if necessary. Serve at once, sprinkled with pecorino.

Tagliarini al Tartufo Bianco

Tagliarini with White Truffle

THERE IS NOTHING QUITE like the fragrance and flavor of the Italian white truffle. It is one of the rarest and therefore most expensive of truffles, which comes from around the towns of Alba and Asti in Piedmont. This simple style of serving it is one of the best ways to enjoy it.

INGREDIENTS

12 ounces fresh tagliarini
6 tablespoons unsalted butter, diced
4 tablespoons freshly grated
Parmesan cheese
nutmeg
1 small white truffle, about 1–1¹/2 ounces
salt and ground black pepper
Serves 4

1 Cook the pasta in salted boiling water according to the instructions on the package.

2 Drain the cooked pasta thoroughly and turn it into a warmed large bowl. Add the diced butter, grated Parmesan, freshly grated nutmeg and a little salt and pepper to taste. Toss well until the pasta is coated in melted butter.

3 Divide the pasta equally among four warmed bowls and shave paper-thin slivers of the white truffle on top. Serve immediately.

COOK'S TIPS

• *White Italian truffles can be bought during the months of September and October from specialty food stores and markets. They are very expensive, however, and there are some alternative ways of getting the flavor of truffles without the expense. Some Italian markets sell "truffle cheese", which is a mountain cheese with shavings of truffle in it, and this can be used instead of the Parmesan and truffle in this recipe. Another alternative is to toss hot pasta in truffle oil and serve it with freshly grated Parmesan.*
• *In Piedmont a very thin home-made egg pasta called* tagliarin *or* tajarin *is used for this dish. Tagliarini are the nearest equivalent, or you could use tagliatellini or tagliolini instead, or even fettuccine if you like.*

Linguine con la Rucola

Linguine with Arugula

THIS IS A FIRST COURSE THAT you will find in many fashionable restaurants in Italy. It is very quick and easy to make at home and is worth trying for yourself.

INGREDIENTS

12 ounces fresh or dried linguine
1/2 cup extra virgin olive oil
1 large bunch arugula, about 5 ounces,
*   stalks removed, shredded or torn*
1 cup freshly grated Parmesan cheese
salt and ground black pepper

Serves 4

1 Cook the pasta in a large pot of salted boiling water according to the instructions on the package, then drain thoroughly.

2 Heat about 4 tablespoons of the olive oil in the pasta pot, then add the drained pasta, followed by the arugula. Toss over medium to high heat for 1–2 minutes or until the arugula is just wilted, then remove the pan from heat.

3 Turn the pasta and arugula into a warmed large bowl. Add half the freshly grated Parmesan and the remaining olive oil. Add a little salt and black pepper to taste.

4 Toss the mixture quickly to mix. Serve immediately, sprinkled with the remaining Parmesan.

COOK'S TIP

Buy arugula by the bunch from the greengrocer. The type sold in small cellophane packages in supermarkets is very expensive for this kind of dish. Always check when buying arugula that all the leaves are bright green. In hot weather, arugula leaves quickly turn yellow.

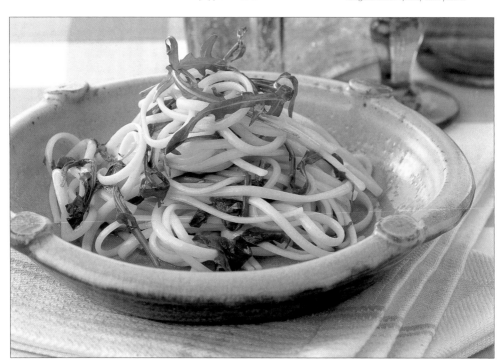

Strozzapreti ai Fiori di Zucca

Strozzapreti with Zucchini Flowers

THIS PRETTY, SUMMERY DISH is strewn with zucchini flowers, but you can make it even if you don't have the flowers. In Italy, bunches of fresh zucchini flowers are a common sight on vegetable stalls in summer, and are frequently used for stuffing and cooking.

INGREDIENTS

1/4 cup butter
2 tablespoons extra virgin olive oil
1 small onion, thinly sliced
7 ounces small zucchini, cut into
    thin julienne
1 garlic clove, crushed
2 teaspoons finely chopped fresh marjoram
3 cups strozzapreti
1 large handful zucchini flowers,
    thoroughly washed and dried
salt and ground black pepper
thin shavings of Parmesan cheese, to serve

Serves 4

1 Heat the butter and half the olive oil in a medium skillet or saucepan, add the sliced onion and cook gently, stirring frequently, for about 5 minutes until softened. Add the zucchini to the pan and sprinkle with the crushed garlic, chopped marjoram and salt and pepper to taste. Cook for 5–8 minutes until the zucchini have softened but are not colored, turning them over from time to time.

2 Meanwhile, cook the pasta in a large pot of salted boiling water according to the package instructions.

3 Set aside a few whole zucchini flowers for the garnish, then coarsely shred the rest and add them to the zucchini mixture. Stir to mix and taste for seasoning.

4 Drain the pasta, turn it into a warmed large bowl and add the remaining oil. Toss, add the zucchini mixture and toss again. Top with Parmesan and the reserved flowers.

COOK'S TIP

Strozzapreti or "priest stranglers" are a special kind of short pasta shape from Modena. You can buy packages of them in Italian markets, or use gemelli, a similar kind of twisted pasta.

Tagliatelle Tricolore

Three-color Tagliatelle

ZUCCHINI AND CARROTS are cut into delicate ribbons so that when they are cooked and tossed with tagliatelle they look like colored pasta. Serve as a side dish, or sprinkle with freshly grated Parmesan cheese for a light first course or vegetarian main course.

INGREDIENTS

2 large zucchini

2 large carrots

9 ounces fresh egg tagliatelle

4 tablespoons extra virgin olive oil

flesh of 2 roasted garlic cloves, plus extra roasted garlic cloves, to serve (optional)

salt and ground black pepper

Serves 4

1 With a vegetable peeler, cut the zucchini and carrots into long thin ribbons. Bring a large pot of salted water to a boil, then add the zucchini and carrot ribbons. Bring the water back to a boil and boil for 30 seconds, then drain and set aside.

2 Cook the pasta according to the instructions on the package.

3 Drain the pasta and return it to the pot. Add the vegetable ribbons, oil, garlic and salt and pepper and toss over medium to high heat until the pasta and vegetables are glistening with oil. Serve immediately, with extra roasted garlic, if you like.

COOK'S TIP

To roast garlic, put a whole head of garlic on a lightly oiled baking sheet. Place in a 350°F oven and roast for about 30 minutes. Remove the garlic from the oven and set aside. When cool enough to handle, dig out the flesh from the cloves with the point of a knife. If you don't want to go to the trouble of roasting garlic, you can use crushed raw garlic but the flavor will be stronger.

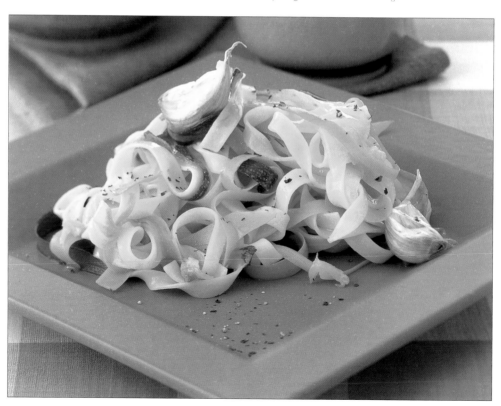

Maccheroni con i Broccoli in Tegame

Macaroni with Broccoli and Cauliflower

THIS IS A SOUTHERN ITALIAN DISH, full of flavor. Without the anchovies, it can be served to vegetarians.

INGREDIENTS

6 ounces cauliflower florets, cut into
    small sprigs
6 ounces broccoli florets, cut into
    small sprigs
3 cups short-cut macaroni
3 tablespoons extra virgin olive oil
1 onion, finely chopped
3 tablespoons pine nuts
1 envelope of saffron powder, dissolved in
    1 tablespoon warm water
1–2 tablespoons raisins, to taste
2 tablespoons sun-dried tomato paste
4 bottled or canned anchovies in olive oil,
    drained and chopped, plus extra
    anchovies to serve (optional)
salt and ground black pepper
freshly grated pecorino cheese,
    to serve
Serves 4

1 Cook the cauliflower sprigs in a large pot of salted boiling water for 3 minutes. Add the broccoli and boil for another 2 minutes. Remove the vegetables from the pan with a large slotted spoon and set aside.

2 Add the pasta to the vegetable cooking water and bring the water back to a boil. Cook the pasta according to the instructions on the package until it is *al dente*.

3 Meanwhile, heat the olive oil in a large skillet or saucepan, add the finely chopped onion and cook over low to medium heat, stirring frequently, for 2–3 minutes or until golden. Add the pine nuts, the cooked broccoli and cauliflower, and the saffron water. Add the raisins, sun-dried tomato paste and a couple of ladlefuls of the pasta cooking water until the vegetable mixture has the consistency of a sauce. Finally, add plenty of pepper.

4 Stir well, cook for 1–2 minutes, then add the chopped anchovies. Drain the pasta and turn it into the vegetable mixture. Toss well, then taste for seasoning and add salt if necessary. Serve the pasta immediately in four warmed bowls, sprinkled with freshly grated pecorino. If you like the flavor of anchovies, add 1–2 whole anchovies to each serving.

Pasta Salads

Although not traditionally Italian, pasta salads have earned their place in the Italian cook's repertoire. They are extremely versatile in that they can be served as part of an antipasto, as a first course or a main course. Salads can be prepared well in advance, so make marvelous party food, and are popular for picnics, because they are so easy to transport.

Freshly cooked pasta soaks up oil, lemon juice, vinegar and seasonings so that when the pasta cools down, the shapes are separate, moist and full of flavor. Never soak pasta in cold water after cooking; this makes the pasta waterlogged and soggy, especially with shapes like shells and tubes that trap liquid. Simply cook the pasta until it is *al dente*, then drain it thoroughly and toss it in extra virgin olive oil or dressing until it glistens. This method works well for any vinaigrette-type dressing, but if you are using mayonnaise it is best to wait until the pasta has cooled down before tossing, or the mayonnaise may spoil.

Any pasta shape can be used in a salad, although shells and tubes are particularly good, because they trap the dressing so well. Many Italians prefer egg pasta to plain durum wheat pasta, because it has a good color, holds its shape well and does not stick.

Insalata Nizzarda

Pasta Salade Niçoise

ALONG THE MEDITERRANEAN coast, where Italy meets France, the cuisines of both countries have many similarities. In this salad the ingredients of a classic French *salade niçoise* are given a modern Italian twist.

INGREDIENTS

4 ounces green beans, ends trimmed and cut into 2-inch lengths
2¹/4 cups penne rigate
7 tablespoons extra virgin olive oil
2 fresh tuna steaks, total weight 12 ounces–1 pound
6 baby Italian plum tomatoes, quartered lengthwise
¹/2 cup pitted black olives, halved lengthwise
6 bottled or canned anchovies in olive oil, drained and chopped
2–3 tablespoons chopped fresh Italian parsley, to taste
juice of ¹/2–1 lemon, to taste
2 heads of Belgian endive, leaves separated
salt and ground black pepper
lemon wedges, to serve
Serves 4

1 Cook the beans in a large pot of salted boiling water for 5–6 minutes. Remove the beans with a large slotted spoon and refresh under the cold tap.

2 Add the pasta to the pan of bean cooking water; bring back to a boil and cook according to the instructions on the package.

3 Meanwhile, heat a ridged grill pan over low heat. Dip a piece of paper towel in the oil, wipe it over the surface of the pan and heat gently. Brush the tuna steaks on both sides with oil and sprinkle liberally with pepper; add to the pan and cook over medium to high heat for 1–2 minutes on each side. Remove and set aside.

4 Drain the cooked pasta well and turn into a large bowl. Add the remaining oil, the beans, tomato quarters, black olives, anchovies, parsley, lemon juice and salt and pepper to taste. Toss well to mix, then set aside to cool.

5 Flake or slice the tuna into large pieces, discarding the skin, then fold it into the salad. Taste the salad for seasoning. Arrange the Belgian endive leaves around the insides of a large shallow bowl. Spoon the pasta salad into the center and serve with lemon wedges.

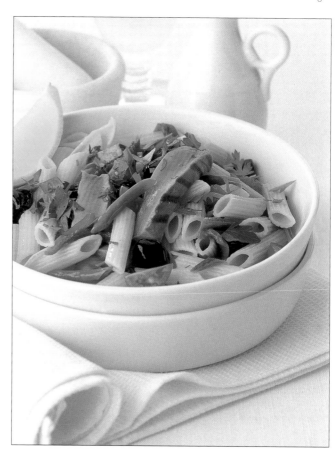

Insalata ai Peperoni Arrostiti

Roasted Bell Pepper Salad

THIS IS A GOOD SALAD to serve on the side with plain broiled or barbecued chicken or fish. The ingredients are simple and few, but the overall flavor is quite intense.

INGREDIENTS

2 large bell peppers (red and green)
2¹/₄ cups fusilli tricolore
1 handful fresh basil leaves
1 handful fresh cilantro leaves
1 garlic clove
salt and ground black pepper

For the dressing

2 tablespoons bottled pesto
juice of ¹/₂ lemon
4 tablespoons extra virgin olive oil

Serves 4

1 Put the peppers under a hot broiler and broil them for about 10 minutes, turning them frequently until they are charred on all sides. Put the hot peppers in a paper bag, seal the bag and set aside until the peppers are cool. Meanwhile, cook the pasta according to the instructions on the package.

2 Whisk all the dressing ingredients together in a large bowl. Drain the cooked pasta well and turn it into the bowl of dressing. Toss well to mix and set aside to cool.

COOK'S TIP

Serve the salad at room temperature or chilled, whichever you prefer.

3 Remove the peppers from the bag and hold them one at a time under cold running water. Peel off the charred skins with your fingers, split the peppers open and pull out the cores. Rub off all the seeds under the running water, then pat the peppers dry on paper towels.

4 Chop the peppers and add them to the pasta. Put the basil, cilantro and garlic on a board and chop them all together. Add to the pasta and toss to mix, then taste for seasoning and serve.

Insalata con Tonno e Mais

Tuna and Corn Salad

THIS IS AN EXCELLENT main course
salad for a summer lunch outside.
It travels very well, so it is good for
picnics, too.

INGREDIENTS

1 1/2 cups conchiglie
6-ounce can tuna in olive oil,
   drained and flaked
1 can (6 ounces) corn, drained
3 ounces bottled roasted red bell pepper,
   rinsed, dried and finely chopped
1 handful of fresh basil leaves, chopped
salt and ground black pepper

For the dressing
4 tablespoons extra virgin olive oil
1 tablespoon balsamic vinegar
1 teaspoon red wine vinegar
1 teaspoon Dijon mustard
1–2 teaspoons honey, to taste
Serves 4

1 Cook the pasta according to package
  instructions. Drain it into a colander,
and rinse under cold running water.
Allow to drain until cold and dry,
shaking the colander occasionally.

2 Make the dressing. Put the oil in a
  large bowl, add the two kinds of
vinegar and whisk well together until
emulsified. Add the mustard, honey and
salt and pepper to taste and whisk
again until thick.

3 Add the pasta to the dressing and
  toss well to mix, then add the
tuna, corn and roasted pepper and toss
again. Mix in about half the basil and
taste for seasoning. Serve at room
temperature or chilled, with the
remaining basil sprinkled on top.

VARIATION

*To save time, you could use canned corn
with peppers.*

Insalata Rosa e Verde

Pink and Green Salad

SPIKED WITH A LITTLE fresh chile, this
pretty salad makes a delicious light
lunch served with hot crusty rolls
and a bottle of sparkling dry Italian
white wine. Shrimp and avocado are
a winning combination, so it's also a
good choice for a buffet party.

INGREDIENTS

2 cups farfalle
juice of 1/2 lemon
1 small fresh red chile, seeded and very
   finely chopped
4 tablespoons chopped fresh basil
2 tablespoons chopped cilantro
4 tablespoons extra virgin olive oil
1 tablespoon mayonnaise
1 1/2 cups peeled cooked shrimp
1 avocado
salt and ground black pepper
Serves 4

1 Cook the pasta in a large pot of
  salted boiling water according to the
package instructions.

2 Meanwhile, put the lemon juice
  and chile in a bowl with half the
basil and cilantro and salt and pepper
to taste. Whisk well to mix, then whisk
in the oil and mayonnaise until thick.
Add the shrimp and gently stir to coat
in the dressing.

3 Drain the pasta into a colander,
  and rinse under cold running
water until cold. Allow to drain and dry,
shaking the colander occasionally.

4 Halve, pit and peel the avocado,
  then cut the flesh into neat dice.
Add to the shrimp and dressing with
the pasta, toss well to mix and taste for
seasoning. Serve immediately, sprinkled
with the remaining basil and cilantro.

COOK'S TIP

*This pasta salad can be made several
hours ahead of time, without the
avocado. Cover the bowl with plastic
wrap and chill in the refrigerator. Prepare
the avocado and add it to the salad just
before serving or it will discolor.*

Insalata di Mare

Seafood Salad

THIS IS A VERY SPECIAL SALAD which can be served as a first course or main meal. The choice of pasta shape is up to you, but one of the unusual "designer" shapes would suit it well.

INGREDIENTS

1 pound mussels
1 cup dry white wine
2 garlic cloves, coarsely chopped
1 handful of fresh Italian parsley
1 cup prepared squid rings
1 1/2 cups small pasta shapes
1 cup peeled cooked shrimp

For the dressing
6 tablespoons extra virgin olive oil
juice of 1 lemon
1–2 teaspoons capers, to taste,
   coarsely chopped
1 garlic clove, crushed
1 small handful fresh Italian parsley,
   finely chopped
salt and ground black pepper
Serves 4–6

1 Scrub the mussels under cold running water to remove the beards. Discard any that are open or that do not close when sharply tapped against the work surface.

2 Pour half the wine into a large pot, add the garlic, parsley and mussels. Cover the pan tightly and bring to a boil over a high heat. Cook for about 5 minutes, shaking the pot frequently, until the mussels are open.

3 Turn the mussels into a colander set over a bowl. Set the mussels aside until cool enough to handle. Reserve a few mussels for garnishing, then remove the rest from their shells, pouring the liquid from the mussels into the bowl of cooking liquid. Discard any closed mussels.

4 Return the mussel cooking liquid to the pan and add the remaining wine and the squid rings. Bring to a boil, cover and simmer gently, stirring occasionally, for 30 minutes or until the squid is tender. Let the squid cool in the cooking liquid.

5 Meanwhile, cook the pasta according to package instructions and whisk all the dressing ingredients in a large bowl, adding a little salt and pepper to taste.

6 Drain the cooked pasta well, add it to the bowl of dressing and toss well to mix. Allow to cool.

7 Turn the cooled squid into a sieve and drain well, then rinse it lightly under the cold tap. Add the squid, mussels and shrimp to the dressed pasta and toss well to mix. Cover the bowl tightly with plastic wrap and chill in the refrigerator for about 4 hours. Toss well and adjust the seasoning to taste before serving.

COOK'S TIP

For a quick and easy short cut, buy prepared seafood salad from an Italian delicatessen or supermarket and toss it with the pasta and dressing.

Insalata con Pomodori Arrostiti e Rucola

Roasted Cherry Tomato and Arugula

THIS IS A GOOD SALAD to accompany barbecued chicken, steaks or chops. Roasted tomatoes are very juicy, with an intense, smoky-sweet flavor.

INGREDIENTS

2 cups chifferini or pipe

1 pound ripe baby Italian plum tomatoes, halved lengthwise

5 tablespoons extra virgin olive oil

2 garlic cloves, cut into thin slivers

2 tablespoons balsamic vinegar

2 pieces sun-dried tomato in olive oil, drained and chopped

large pinch of sugar, to taste

1 handful arugula, about 2^1/2 ounces

salt and ground black pepper

Serves 4

1 Preheat the oven to 375°F. Meanwhile, cook the pasta in salted boiling water according to the instructions on the package.

2 Arrange the halved tomatoes cut side up in a roasting pan, drizzle 2 tablespoons of the oil over them and sprinkle with the slivers of garlic and salt and pepper to taste. Roast in the oven for 20 minutes, turning once.

3 Put the remaining oil in a large bowl with the vinegar, sun-dried tomatoes, sugar and a little salt and pepper to taste. Stir well to mix. Drain the pasta, add it to the bowl of dressing and toss to mix. Add the roasted tomatoes and mix gently.

4 Before serving, add the chopped arugula, toss lightly and taste for seasoning. Serve either at room temperature or chilled.

VARIATIONS

• *If you are in a hurry and don't have time to roast the tomatoes, you can make the salad with halved raw tomatoes instead.*

• *If you like, add 5 ounces fresh mozzarella cheese, drained and diced, with the arugula in Step 4.*

Summer Salad

RIPE RED TOMATOES, mozzarella and olives make a good base for a fresh and tangy salad that is perfect for a light summer lunch.

INGREDIENTS

3 cups penne
3 ripe tomatoes, diced
5 ounces mozzarella di bufala,
*   drained and diced*
10 pitted black olives, sliced
10 pitted green olives, sliced
1 scallion, thinly sliced on the diagonal
2 tablespoons chopped fresh Italian parsley
a few fresh basil leaves

For the dressing

6 tablespoons extra virgin olive oil
1 tablespoon balsamic vinegar or lemon juice
salt and ground black pepper
Serves 4

1 Cook the pasta in salted boiling water according to the instructions on the package. Turn it into a colander and rinse under cold running water until cold, then shake the colander to remove as much water as possible.

2 Make the dressing. Whisk the olive oil and balsamic vinegar or lemon juice into a large bowl with a little salt and pepper to taste.

3 Add the pasta, mozzarella, tomatoes, olives and scallions to the dressing and toss together well. Taste for seasoning before serving.

COOK'S TIP

Mozzarella made from buffalo milk has more flavor than the kind made with cow's milk. It is sold in some delicatessens and supermarkets.

VARIATION

Make the salad more substantial by adding other ingredients, such as sliced peppers, flaked tuna, bottled or canned anchovy fillets or diced ham.

Country Pasta Salad

COLORFUL, TASTY and nutritious, this is the ideal pasta salad for a summer picnic.

INGREDIENTS

2³/4 cups fusilli
5 ounces green beans, ends trimmed
*   and cut into 2-inch lengths*
1 potato, about 5 ounces, diced
7 ounces cherry tomatoes, hulled and halved
2 scallions, finely chopped
1¹/4 cups Parmesan cheese, diced or
*   coarsely shaved*
6–8 pitted black olives, cut into rings
1–2 tablespoons capers, to taste

For the dressing

6 tablespoons extra virgin olive oil
1 tablespoon balsamic vinegar
1 tablespoon chopped fresh Italian parsley
salt and ground black pepper
Serves 6

1 Cook the pasta according to the instructions on the package. Drain it into a colander, rinse under cold running water until cold, then shake the colander to remove as much water as possible. Allow to drain and dry, shaking the colander occasionally.

2 Cook the beans and diced potato in a saucepan of salted boiling water for 5–6 minutes or until tender. Drain and allow to cool.

3 Make the dressing. Put all the ingredients in a large bowl with salt and pepper to taste and whisk well to mix.

4 Add the cherry tomatoes, scallions, Parmesan, olive rings and capers to the dressing, then the cold pasta, beans and potato. Toss well to mix. Cover and set aside for about 30 minutes. Taste for seasoning before serving.

COOK'S TIP

Buy a piece of fresh Parmesan from the delicatessen. This is the less mature, softer type, which is sold as a table cheese, rather than the hard, mature Parmesan used for grating.

Insalata di Pollo e Broccoli

Chicken and Broccoli Salad

GORGONZOLA MAKES A tangy dressing that goes well with both chicken and broccoli. Serve for a lunch or supper dish, with crusty Italian bread.

INGREDIENTS

6 ounces broccoli florets, divided into
*   small sprigs*
2 cups farfalle
2 large cooked chicken breasts

For the dressing
3 1/2 ounces Gorgonzola cheese
1 tablespoon white wine vinegar
4 tablespoons extra virgin olive oil
1/2–1 teaspoon finely chopped fresh sage,
*   plus extra sage sprigs to garnish*
salt and ground black pepper

Serves 4

1 Cook the broccoli florets in a large saucepan of salted boiling water for 3 minutes. Remove with a slotted spoon and rinse under cold running water, then spread out on paper towels to drain and dry.

2 Add the pasta to the broccoli cooking water, then bring back to a boil and cook according to the package instructions. When cooked, drain the pasta into a colander, rinse under cold running water until cold, then allow to drain and dry, shaking the colander occasionally.

3 Remove the skin from the cooked chicken breasts and cut the meat into bite-size pieces.

4 Make the dressing. Put the cheese in a large bowl and mash with a fork, then whisk in the wine vinegar followed by the oil and sage and salt and pepper to taste.

5 Add the pasta, chicken and broccoli. Toss well, then season to taste and serve, garnished with sage.

Insalata Saporita

Pasta Salad with Salami and Olives

GARLIC AND HERB DRESSING gives a Mediterranean flavor to a handful of ingredients from the pantry and refrigerator, making this an excellent salad for winter. There are many different types of Italian salami that can be used. *Salame napoletano* is coarse cut and peppery, while *salame milanese* is fine cut and mild in flavor.

INGREDIENTS

2 cups gnocchi or conchiglie

¹/2 cup pitted black olives,
    quartered lengthwise

3 ounces thinly sliced salami, any skin
    removed, diced

¹/2 small red onion, finely chopped

1 large handful fresh basil leaves

For the dressing

4 tablespoons extra virgin olive oil

good pinch of sugar, to taste

juice of ¹/2 lemon

1 teaspoon Dijon mustard

2 teaspoons dried oregano

1 garlic clove, crushed

salt and ground black pepper

Serves 4

1 Cook the pasta in a large pot of salted boiling water according to the package instructions.

2 Meanwhile, make the dressing for the pasta. Put all the ingredients for the dressing in a large bowl with a little salt and pepper to taste, and whisk well to mix.

3 Drain the pasta thoroughly, add it to the bowl of dressing and toss well to mix. Let the dressed pasta cool, stirring occasionally.

4 When the pasta is cold, add the remaining ingredients and toss well to mix again. Taste for seasoning, then serve immediately.

Index

Author's Acknowledgments

I am indebted most of all to Elisa Surini, for her invaluable assis-
tance with this book, and also to Roberta Mitchell in Rome, for her
up-to-the-minute knowledge and advice. I would also like to thank
my daughter Sophie and the following friends, each of whom has
given me some of her favorite recipes: Alessia Ferretti, Silvana
Hobcraft-Caparo, Isabella Medri, Stefania Spiga and Karin Trczka.
Last, but by no means least, I would like to thank Liz Mizon, for her
unstinting administrative and technological support.

Publisher's Acknowledgments

The publishers would like to thank Jenni Fleetwood for her
skilful editing, Annabel Ford for tracking down the pasta
shapes for photography, photographers William Lingwood
(recipes) and Janine Hosegood (cut-outs), props stylist
Helen Trent, Lucy McKelvie and Kate Jay, who prepared the
food for photography, Elisa Surini for checking the Italian
terms, and Giuseppe Tranchina of Italbrokers Foodservice,
who supplied egg pasta for recipe testing and photography.

NOTES

NOTES

NOTES

NOTES

NOTES

NOTES

NOTES

NOTES